FRANK STITT'S
SOUTHERN TABLE

RECIPES AND GRACIOUS TRADITIONS
FROM HIGHLANDS BAR AND GRILL

FRANK STITT

PHOTOGRAPHS BY CHRISTOPHER HIRSHEIMER

ARTISAN

NEW YORK

To Pardis, Marie, and Weston

CONTENTS

There are austere rules in the writing of novels that vex the young writer every bit as much as the master chef imposing the finesse and discipline and the art of cuisine on a headstrong apprentice. Young masochists are drawn to melodrama and coincidence the way the brand-spanking-new apple-cheeked hotshot cooking school graduate grows enamored of the magic of rémoulade, gribiche, and aïoli, saucing everything with a heavy hand until restrained by a patient seasoned chef. Young writers and young cooks have much in common; so do older writers and master chefs.

I speak now of coincidence and the detached collision of fates. In the early 1980s, I had spent an extraordinary week in New York City, where I attended plays that seemed necessary and life changing, thrilled to an opera with my agent, Julian Bach, and had dinner at the Four Seasons. Like a bird-watcher, I keep a list of great restaurants that I would like to eat my way through during my passage on this earth. I had also checked off Lutèce and La Côte Basque on this particular journey, where I presented the full outline of *The Prince of Tides* to my elegant editor, Nan Talese. Julian Bach and Nan Talese were not coincidences, though, but part of the natural architecture of my life.

On the flight back to Atlanta, my fate cleared its throat as I heard a handsome young man in the aisle seat across from me whistling softly. I am not the kind of person who starts up conversations with strangers on airplanes and then pulls out pictures of his children to show to any passenger within earshot. When I travel, I prize my anonymity and solitude and have no desire to be seated next to a compulsive chatterbox. While the whistling from the right drew my attention, it was the stack of cookbooks that I found riveting. In a neatly stacked pile, the young man was looking up recipes from the very best cookbooks published that year, both cutting edge and outer rim. It was long before the dawning of the era of celebrity chefs and the Food Network, but a revolution was in the air. Already extra virgin olive oil had started to appear in southern supermarkets, bringing sex, at last, to southern kitchens. Arugula, watercress, and daikon radishes were making shy appearances in produce departments in my part of the world, and Paul Prudhomme had already made his mark in New Orleans, initiating the era where you could not meet a redfish that someone had not blackened. In my hometown of Atlanta, the glittering era of Primordial Paul's had begun, Buckhead began to strut with restaurants pushing for four stars, and I heard a Frenchman say you could get a better Russian meal at Nicolai's Roof than you could in Moscow. Cuisine was breaking out all over the South, as luxuriant and uncontrollable as kudzu. And the man across the aisle from me was about to change the history of his home state of Alabama forever.

"Sir," I said as he scribbled down recipes and ideas in a notebook, "those cookbooks you're reading, they're wonderful."

"I think I just spent the best year of my life working in the kitchens of these four chefs," he said. "It's amazing what you can learn in even just a few weeks. My name is Frank Stitt, sir."

"Mine is Pat Conroy," I said. "Are you a chef?"

"Yes, I am, though I've never run my own place," Frank said. "I'm about to open a restaurant."

"Can I ask where?"

"Birmingham, Alabama."

"It's a wasteland for good food," I said. "I was there a month ago."

"It won't be a wasteland anymore," Frank replied with a confidence that both surprised and delighted me.

"If you're any good at all," I remember saying, "you're going to be a very rich man."

Frank appraised me with care, as though he were making a decision about the freshness of a mahimahi fillet, and then said, "I'm good. I'm very good."

He said it with a measure of conviction and authority that carried much weight. He declared it like a man with keenly earned self-knowledge, an awesome respect for the art of cooking, and a firm knowledge of the great gift he was about to bestow on his home state. Already, he carried himself with the lordly confidence all the great chefs possessed as their birthright. He spoke with uncontainable enthusiasm about French food, cooking, the passionate pursuit of quality and excellence, and French chefs' fanatic insistence on fresh ingredients. He was already comfortable speaking in the vocabulary and techniques of Escoffier, Robuchon, and Ducasse. His curiosity about his world was insatiable, and I could not mention a restaurant whose breadth of accomplishment he did not have the deepest knowledge about. His long apprenticeship now over, Frank was coming home to deliver the goods to Alabama.

Highlands Bar and Grill changed the way the people of Alabama thought about food. It was a revolution in the center of a neighborhood that was going slightly to seed. The coming of Highlands changed the fate of that part of Birmingham and began its renaissance. The quality of its restaurants is one of the strictest gauges for a city to measure its call to greatness. Frank Stitt put Birmingham on the culinary map the day he opened his restaurant. I heard about it from a white-shoe lawyer from one of those Atlanta law firms with enough WASP names to start a hive that Highlands was better than any restaurant in Atlanta. That's long before the kinks were worked out and long before Frank hit his amazing stride. I made it to the restaurant in the first six months of its existence and discovered that Frank was a far, far better chef than anyone who had ever crossed the Chattahoochee River from Georgia or entered the Birmingham city limits under the cover of darkness after a lost weekend in New Orleans. He was much more than the real thing; Frank Stitt was a chef for the ages.

Here is what you get in a Frank Stitt meal and what you will get with every recipe in this magnificent cookbook: the full measure and passion of a man on fire with devotion to his chosen work. He gives you all the artistry at his command every single time you sit down for a meal and he does not tolerate lapses in the kitchen or produce that is not the freshest possible. I have eaten at the Highlands Bar and Grill more than twenty times and have never had a single dish that was not superb—the restaurant still remains the best reason to move to Birmingham that I can think of. I would call Frank the best chef in America, but that would cause undo jealousy in the ranks of other chefs whose powers of cruelty are exceeded only by genocidal despots or serial killers with bad tattoos. So let me simply state that I think that Frank is the best chef in America and that America itself is starting to come around to my position.

I have watched with great interest the growing reputation of Frank and his restaurant on the national scene. Whenever I return to Birmingham, I return to Highlands or its sister restaurants, Chez Fonfon and Bottega Café. I look forward to the changes and evolution of the menu and I am

never disappointed. When I ordered a pork tenderloin with a bourbon and molasses sauce, I thought it was the best thing I ever put in my mouth. But I had said the same thing about the soft-shell crab with brown butter and bacon vinaigrette. That night I also had the chilled crabmeat in a basmati rice salad with roasted peppers, slivers of olive, and mushrooms folded into a lemon mayonnaise that was both delicate and fragrant. I could write poems about the seared duck breast and his Louisiana rabbit simmered in red wine. Even about the lowly southern dish of grits Frank uses as a palette that he tops with strips of country ham and wild mushrooms and finishes with a buttery Parmesan sauce.

At Highlands, there is a genius and a sensibility at work in the smallest of details. Once Frank offered me a watermelon margarita, and I could think of no more nauseating a combination of tastes than a sweet fruit and tequila. Naturally, I was wrong, and watermelon has seemed a noble fruit, kingly as pineapple, ever since that encounter. Frank's bar makes a better gin martini than they do at New York's Plaza Hotel, and his Chilton County peach bellini is far superior to the one served in Harry's Bar in Venice, where the Bellini was invented. You can enjoy all of these drinks at the best raw oyster bar outside New Orleans, where the Apalachicola oysters are often harvested from the Gulf of Mexico the same day you consume them. They are cold and salty and Gulf-born and wonderful. Just when you think that an oyster on the half-shell is the most perfect food on earth, Frank will present you with baked oysters with wilted greens and a bread crumb crust, or his oyster pan roast with crawfish and buttery croutons, or the spicy baked oysters with caramelized onions, pan juices, and chiles.

But then there are the lamb shanks with favas and the cobia with the beet relish, and how can I leave out the magic he works with South Carolina quail or his ravioli with sweet potatoes, mustard greens, and country ham. I cannot do justice to Frank if I fail to praise his crab cakes or his roast leg of lamb with spring vegetable ragout—or the wine list that grows and mellows and deepens in complexity with each passing year. I have failed to mention the desserts, which is often the weak spot of restaurants with the raw ambition displayed by Highlands. But the desserts are otherworldly—the stuff of both dreams and paradise, and I have heard grown men say aloud in front of their wives that they would marry the pastry chef, as they scooped up clouds of cinnamon crème anglaise or moaned over the bourbon panna cotta. There are no weaknesses in Frank Stitt's restaurant, ladies and gentlemen—none at all. Frank's beautiful wife, Pardis, runs the front with elegance and panache. The waiters are courteous and well trained. His chef de cuisine is masterful, and the cooks know what they are doing. The knife work is deft and Zen-like, and every single night the men and women of Highlands Bar and Grill know that they are in the process of making both history and art.

The food world has been showing signs of coming around to my opinion formed so many years ago. I was on another airplane heading to Atlanta when I read that *Gourmet* magazine had named Highlands Bar and Grill the fifth best restaurant in the nation. In the same year, Frank won a James Beard award as Best Chef of the Southeast. The inimitable R. W. "Johnny" Apple Jr. of *The New York Times* made one of his baptismal visits to the restaurant and left shouting kudos and benedictions like all the rest of us.

The only thing Frank lacked in his sprint toward greatness was a cookbook, which is now in your hands. It will be a seminal cookbook, one that every chef in the world will own and steal from. I love the sheer ambitiousness of the man, and he gets better every single year because he is out to be the best chef on earth. He has not told me that, but I have eaten my way into that secret knowledge.

Over a year ago, my wife, the novelist Cassandra King, and I joined Frank and Pardis for a spectacular meal at Alain Ducasse's restaurant in New York. It was a meal for the ages, and it was one of the great joys of my life to watch Frank smell each dish as it arrived steaming from the kitchen and his eyes light up with pleasure as he tasted each bite with discernment and lapidary pleasure. The restaurant was as formal and plush and forbidding as Highlands is welcoming and all-inclusive. The meal was Proustian and fabulous and indescribable, as all great meals are.

When Cassandra and I bid farewell to Frank and Pardis that night and walked toward our hotel with all the clamor and splendor and mystery of the great city swarming about us, we both agreed that Alain Ducasse was a splendid chef, but that he was no Frank Stitt.

—Pat Conroy

Monday morning, 9:00 A.M.: The day begins. I walk in the kitchen door at Highlands Bar and Grill, and Verba Ford greets me. "Hello, Mr. Stitt." "Hello, Ms. Verba." The banter begins just as it has every other Monday morning, for countless years.

We talk about what dishes were hits last week, which ones were not. Whose fish we sent back and whose was most beautiful. Once again, there is trouble with our veal purveyor—they try to slip us frozen meats. We make arrangements for a pickup/return and gamble on how far we can trust them the next time. The arugula from a neighbor was spectacular, and the watercress from Huntsville beautiful and mighty peppery, fresh from the Limestone Springs.

The seasons define us. If it's springtime, we talk asparagus, favas, baby artichokes, sweet baby Vidalias, little sweet peas, spring lettuces. The cobia season is winding down, the Apalachicola flounder have been fat and iridescent, the occasional speckled trout shiny and firm. The soft-shells from Apalach and the Carolinas are expensive but "live & kickin'." The crawfish were late in arriving this year, but the last thirty-pound sacks are the biggest we've ever seen. We found a little box turtle in the last bag, and one of the cooks, John Washington, has adopted a new pet.

If it is autumn, the farmers' market is full of pumpkins, gourds, and cornstalks. Pickup trucks are piled high with just-dug Cullman sweet potatoes and all kinds of greens—collard, turnip, and mustard. Since the first frost probably will not come until mid-November, the Chandler Mountain tomatoes are still surprisingly good, as are the pink-eyed peas from south Alabama. Our fish purveyor has oysters and a boatful of black grouper, which will be shipped up tonight. Shrimp boats off Mobile Bay are bringing in loads of white shrimp, and the crabmeat is plentiful, though still steeply priced. Hearty fare and long-simmered braises will soon make their welcome return.

10:00 A.M.: Michael Dean, a former waiter at Bottega Café and now an organic farmer, calls and lets us know about the mizuna, arugula, baby beets, and tiny carrots he has for tomorrow. Our usual provider of mint came in empty-handed, so I make a note to run by my house and gather some to bring back before service.

11:00 A.M.: Greg Abrams, our number one fish purveyor on the Gulf Coast, says the tuna boat came in and he has sushi-grade. His best fisherman for day-boat black grouper has just unloaded, and they're only hours out of the water. His buddy gigged about sixty pounds of "stiff as a board" (so called because of its impeccable

freshness) Apalachicola flounder. And his uncle has three dozen whale-sized soft-shell crabs. The oysters, he swears, are salty (he had some for breakfast and assures us they are a surefire cure for hangovers). He wants our recipe for the crab cake sauce—he says the sauce we serve is what makes 'em great. Though what you order isn't necessarily what you get, Greg is an intuitive soul and comes up with some of the most pristine fish you'll ever see. He is a country boy, a "fishhead" from the panhandle of Florida who now adds Silver Oak (and other high-profile overpriced Napa Cabernets) to his Budweiser diet.

11:30 A.M.: We order pork bellies, shanks, and shoulders—all naturally raised—from Niman Ranch. The beef for carpaccio is from the grasslands of Montana. The free-range chicken is coming on Wednesday. For now, the Amish in Pennsylvania have the best chicken, but soon, I hope, we will have farmers nearby who will provide us with naturally raised birds.

We are on a daily quest for the most wonderful ingredients, those raised with care that allow us to cook simply and confidently. This search is not unlike the search for the Holy Grail—we have to pursue it continually, and sometimes we get close, and we celebrate in the unique seasonality, yet there are many setbacks that force us to try ever harder. This search for wonderful food is one of the most important aspects of my job.

By around 12 o'clock, the ordering is complete and the game plan for the week is in motion. *Highlands is ready to begin again.*

This cookbook is about cooking from the heart and soul with knowledge, dedication, and harmony. Balance, complexity, and simplicity are what we're after. And sharing food at table is ultimately about sharing one's love for life.

My mother was the most talked about cook in our small north-Alabama town of Cullman. She was beautiful, prone to drive convertible sports cars too fast, her long blond hair flying wildly behind her. During my parents' time living in New York during the late 1940s (he was in medical school, she studied dietetics), our food veered away from the traditional southern country table. *The New York Times Cookbook* was an early reference point for my mother as she wove her traditional southern cooking into the cosmopolitan qualities of Craig Claiborne's recipes. Back in Alabama, most of her days were spent in the kitchen or in the garden. And her children and their friends were the beneficiaries of her generous sharing.

My interest in the kitchen at that time was primarily with licking clean mixing bowls thick with cake batter. Football, basketball, and girls were far too important for me to realize what a phenomenal kitchen we had. And my father's involvement with the national board of surgeons and his love of grand restaurants had taken us to Miami, New Orleans, and New York, where we would enjoy the fanciest places. Walking up the steps to The Four Seasons as an eight-year-old boy, I felt that I had entered another world. Back in the sixties, Brennan's and Antoine's in New Orleans were magical. They held an excitement and a sense of adventure that intrigued me. In New York, the St. Regis trembled with power. Chicago's Pump Room exuded extravagance. And in Birmingham our personal waiters at the Club (overlooking the Magic City)—Rufus and then Lovejoy— were like uncles who loved us and always took care of the little ones with a twinkle in their eyes. My birthday meal, usually lamb chops, became a ritual. These grand outings were trips that my brother, sister, and I treasured. The magic of great restaurants fascinated me: The energized excitement, the anticipation, the drama, the graciousness, the smells and sounds captured my attention like nothing else. Even now, whether it's a rustic oyster bar, a glistening brasserie, or the hallowed rooms of a three-star restaurant in France, I am still completely enthralled. Most of my life has been spent trying to figure out the secrets behind this magic.

After high school, I ran away from the South as fast as I could. Tufts University in Boston was my first stopping point after the summer of 1972 in Europe. Then San Francisco and Berkeley were my home while I studied philosophy. That's where the lure of working with food and wine really began.

Instead of poring over the texts of Kierkegaard and Nietzsche, I began to find myself more and more drawn to the poetry of food writers such as Richard Olney and Elizabeth David. They became my new teachers of philosophy. I was eager to try my hand and learn to create the wonders I had read about, but one after another, the classic French kitchen doors were slammed in my face. René Verdon (former chef to the Kennedys) of San Francisco's Le Trianon tossed an artichoke at me and, when he saw that I did not know how to trim it properly, immediately whisked me out the door. The only thing I knew for sure was that I had a lot to learn. I persisted, and finally a Swiss chef, Fritz Luenberger of Casablanca restaurant, took me in and showed me how to chop onions. After several weeks, I graduated to more aristocratic vegetables and finally to meats. Fritz cultivated in me an enthusiasm for cooking and a pure joy in eating. I remember his sheer exaltation in unmolding his pâté. He would squeal with delight at the shimmering meat jelly slipping down its sides, so aromatic with quatre épices, slurping up every little bit. I still have that same feeling every time I unmold one of my own.

While working for Fritz and then at other French restaurants in the area, I kept hearing of Alice Waters and her restaurant with its revolutionary ideas. Chez Panisse represented the truest pursuit of beauty; here was a passion that embodied my drive toward authenticity. A place that was a reflection of Richard Olney's and Elizabeth David's writings and the glories of French provincial food. A business that had integrity and that was driven by an intellectual zeal for knowledge and sensual delight. Every day I would stop by to read the menus, sometimes splurging on a café au lait. After many, many requests, Alice kindly allowed me to work—for free—in the kitchen. So close to the ideals I had come to love, I knew I was ready to make the next step: to Provence, where I could immerse myself completely in the source of this great cooking, the source of these incomparable foods. Alice obliged me once more and wrote our mentor, Richard Olney, a letter of introduction, helping to pave my way to France.

Richard agreed to meet me in London the following month. With anxiety and a little fear, I walked up to the Time-Life offices on Conduit Street, and there working on the twenty-volume *Good Cook* series with Richard was Jeremiah Tower, the famous chef from Chez Panisse who had also recently arrived from California. After a little chopping, listening, and helping out, I listened as Elizabeth David was phoned and asked to recommend her favorite food shops in London. The next morning Jeremiah and I were on our way visiting the Queen's *poultier* (just across from the Connaught), and the best markets for cheese, coffee, tea, seafood, and so on. Soon afterward, as luck would have it, I was able to take on the role of Richard's personal assistant at his home in Solliès-Toucas.

When I arrived in France, walking up that dirt road to Richard's house was like going to the mountain to sit with Buddha. Each morning, we would begin the day with a bowl of café au lait and lightly toasted leftover country bread, pure butter, some preserves, and maybe a glass of freshly squeezed orange juice. Afterward, I would help tend the arugula bed, weed the rose garden, and take care of many little household tasks.

Lunch often consisted of composed salads, artfully incorporating leftovers and sometimes experimenting with ideas for the Time-Life series: tomatoes scattered with marjoram, farm eggs boiled until their deep yellow yolks had just passed from their liquid form, cuttlefish with garlic and olive oil. One dinner was a brochette of lamb parts, the kidney being a new sensation for me (and still not my favorite). We would roll up lamb chops and skewer them with arrows made of rosemary. Earthenware dishes cradled gratins made with love and those incredible Provençal vegetables. Asparagus was served just out of the pot, resting on a clean kitchen towel. Guests would swirl sea salt and pepper into homemade red wine vinegar and local olive oil right on their plates, then reach for a stalk to roll in the dressing and eat with their fingers. Heaven!

Later in the afternoon, I would go to the markets to shop with the master. Richard refused to learn how to drive, leaving me to learn to navigate the little streets of the South of France.

The elderly Moutton sisters ran the tiny, tile-lined butcher shop of Solliès-Toucas. As this was the only butcher shop in the area, these women had a special relationship with each of the customers. Well aware of Richard's sometimes peculiar tastes, they would giggle when we'd come to the shop, and they made such fun of him for his recipe of boning and stuffing an oxtail—to them an obsessive process and much too difficult. Yet they respected this eccentric American artist who was absolutely passionate about his ingredients. The trip to the Toulon market, with its unbelievable displays of olives, vegetables, fruit, and seafood, was always a highlight. As usual, Richard would be attracted to the most bizarre items, such as sea dates or oursins—the essence of the sea. But we would buy anchovies, sardines, or mackerel for a feast, not so expensive, but luxurious in flavors and textures. Richard exhibited a wisdom shared by my forefathers—a sense of frugality and stewardship, using all that the Good Lord has blessed us with and a sincere desire to honor these ingredients with respect and care. In our kitchen today, we still focus on blending humble ingredients with a little extravagance.

The daily ritual of taking the fifty or so paces up to Richard's hand-hewn *cave*, or wine cellar, always filled me with a sense of wonderment and awe. In the cool, dark, humid space that he himself had dug lay some of the truly great French wines. With lunch, we usually had simple wines made by a local monastery or perhaps his favorite Corbières blanc, but at dinner, treasures from the cellar would be most graciously shared: Figeac, Batailley, Pape Clément, Vieux Château Certan, and countless other ambrosial wines. Richard bought directly from the châteaus, and these wines slept peacefully in his cellar, though minus their labels—the humidity in his cave quickly dissolved the glue that attached them.

Richard's sense of balance in composing a menu to harmonize with wine is still, I think, unsurpassed. His vast knowledge of food and wine and the depth of that knowledge continue to inspire me. I thank him for allowing me to share his table and for his guidance.

Later that same year, Steven Spurrier at L'Académie du Vin in Paris allowed me to spend time tasting wines with him. His knowledge was amazing and his style of tasting was profound. He landed me a job back in Provence for the *vendange*, the harvesting of the grapes. I hitchhiked down the first week of September and slept between the vines for the first couple of nights. Just at sunrise, out there in the vineyards near Vidauban, I experienced an epiphany: This rural land with country people working hard to transform the vineyards into soul-satisfying wine seemed such a noble quest to me—and strangely similar to the small farmers of Alabama whose hard work filled kitchen tables with the finest of country vegetables. The thought of picking grapes, making wine, and cooking food was transcendent. I knew I had an opportunity to transform a daily task into a glorious event.

And so I returned to Alabama to begin the process of opening my own restaurant. I had briefly considered Savannah, Charleston, and Atlanta, but my home, family, and friends were in Alabama. Birmingham was a bit down-and-out then. The 1960s and 1970s were a rough time for the Magic City—the steel mill had closed—but there was a glimmer of hope with the university and medical center making their way to the forefront. So, after teaching cooking classes and working in a wine shop and at the rooftop Hyatt restaurant, I was determined that I could make a difference; I was convinced that the people of Alabama would support a restaurant with southern soul and Provençal flavors.

Searching for the location, I came upon a building built in the mid-1920s, with a red tile roof and cream-colored stucco. In its most recent incarnation, it had housed the Colonial Dining Club, a business that sold discount coupons to restaurants. The façade was vaguely Mediterranean. Inside, a drop-in acoustic tile ceiling and other modern additions hid the magnificent architectural bones lurking behind. We uncovered a stunning coffered ceiling with great detailing and a grand fireplace opposite beautiful columns with masonry capitals that formed an arcade. An adjoining room was the perfect size for a bar—too good to be true. And all of this located at the great historical intersection known as Five Points South. A trolley had once rolled up from downtown and turned down Highland Avenue through what was Birmingham's first fine residential community away from downtown. With the university complex nearby and the affluent suburbs just over the mountain from us, this was a choice location.

I raised a little money from a few devout cooking class attendees and my mother mortgaged her home, so that on November 21, 1982, with high hopes, we opened on a shoestring. The first night was wild, the food stunning, our guests astounded. And the reviews read as if a savior had come to town.

We are very fortunate that our community needed us. Highlands has been a grand success, with an eclectic mix of people we call our regulars—powerful people rub elbows with eccentric hippies and local guys who live for Alabama football. This microcosm of Highlands Bar and Grill is a pure example of the vitality of life in the South.

This cookbook is our attempt to share our love for cooking and for being at table. It is about the passion we have for flavorful, healthy, and impeccable ingredients. Here we share our philosophy and the best dishes we have prepared these past twenty years. I encourage you to use these recipes as a springboard for cooking with your own sense of balance and aesthetic to create something magical.

By the way, around 11:00 P.M. each night, Pardis, my wife, and I usually taste a few interesting wines, cook a simple meal, and toast to being together at table.

SOUTHERN TRADITIONS

Summertime midday

meals at my grandparents' farmhouse table were feasts. My brother and sister, and I, along with our cousins, would sit down to a lunch made almost entirely from my maternal Grandmother Eullalha White's garden: sliced Atkinson tomatoes, cucumbers, and sweet onions soaked in vinegar with fresh dill, crisp pickles and relishes, fried or maybe boiled okra, green beans cooked in a pot with new potatoes and sliced onions (boiled to smithereens, but still delicious). Yellow squash with a few chopped onions stewed in their own juices, butter beans or pink-eyed peas cooked with a bit of streak o' lean (cured pork belly), and turnip greens with little cubes of potato always doused with hot pepper vinegar at the table. There was the creamed corn—always made from field corn, not sweet corn—picked that morning, cut and scraped, then cooked in a little homemade butter. Grandmother churned her own butter from the milk produced by her Jersey cow. I remember the startling sensation when sneaking a big slug of milk from the jug in the fridge, of realizing that the milk that filled my mouth was so fresh it had not had time to cool down.

There were jams, jellies, and preserves, and pickles, relishes, chutneys, conserves, and amber honey straight from the hive with the comb. There was Concord grape marmalade thick with grapey nuggets and always plenty of corn bread.

If it happened to be the Fourth of July, a blackberry cobbler made in a washtub would appear, the galvanized tub being the only dish big enough to feed all the mouths present. In late summer, there would be Grandmother's heavenly fried apple pies made from apples grown on the farm, then dried in the sun and turned into a cinnamon-and-clove-flavored essence. What a finale!

{ **Corn bread, page 26**

FRIED GREEN TOMATO AND ARUGULA SALAD

SERVES 4 AS AN APPETIZER

Fried green tomatoes add unexpected flavor and texture when they are served right alongside ripe yellow and red cherry tomatoes, tossed with peppery arugula. We prefer *selvetica* arugula, an heirloom of sorts, which grows slowly but yields intensely flavorful small, firm, vibrant leaves. For a sandwich to remember, combine crunchy slices of fried green tomato with a few thin, crisp strips of bacon, a spicy Aïoli (page 337), and some romaine or arugula.

1 large egg

1 cup buttermilk

3 very firm green tomatoes, cut into 1/3-inch-thick slices

3/4 cup cornmeal

1/4 cup all-purpose flour

Kosher salt and freshly ground black pepper

Dash of cayenne pepper

2 cups peanut, corn, or canola oil for frying

1/2 cup Buttermilk Vinaigrette (page 331)

12 cherry and/or grape tomatoes of different colors and shapes, halved or quartered, depending on size

1 large bunch arugula

1 tablespoon extra virgin olive oil

Preheat the oven to 200°F.

Lightly beat the egg in a shallow bowl and stir in the buttermilk. Place the tomato slices in the buttermilk mixture, turning to coat them. In a shallow pan, combine the cornmeal and flour and season with 1 teaspoon salt, the pepper, and the cayenne, stirring well.

In a large cast-iron or other heavy skillet, heat the peanut oil over high heat to 360°F.

Meanwhile, dredge one tomato slice at a time in the cornmeal, turning to coat and gently pressing into the cornmeal so it adheres. Transfer each prepared slice to a rack set over a baking sheet.

Using tongs, carefully ease the breaded tomatoes into the hot oil in batches of about 4 at a time so that the oil does not cool down. Cook for about 2 minutes, then turn and cook on the other side until the coating is a nice even golden brown, about 2 minutes more. Transfer the fried tomatoes to a baking sheet lined with paper towels and put them in the oven to keep warm while you fry the remaining slices.

Ladle or spoon 2 tablespoons vinaigrette onto each plate and stack the fried tomatoes on top. Toss the cherry tomatoes and arugula with the olive oil and salt and pepper to taste. Arrange the arugula and tomatoes alongside.

TO DRINK: Soave Classico Superiore, Pieropan
Soave, Anselmi

HOPPIN' JOHN

SERVES 6 TO 8 AS A LIGHT LUNCH

Hoppin' John, one of the South's great traditions, is basically flavorful rice cooked and served with the "pot liquor" from long-simmered shell peas—cow peas, black-eyed peas, or, as we do, pink-eyed peas. The broth from the cooked shell peas is naturally rich in flavor and the ham hock (or slab bacon) provides that cured pork goodness. There are all sorts of wonderful ways to embellish this classic, in addition to the chutney used here. Try topping it with a dollop of pesto and some chopped ripe tomato. Or include a handful of fresh crabmeat sprinkled with chopped basil, lemon juice, and olive oil.

1 cup small fresh or frozen peas, such as pink-eyes,
  black-eyes, or crowders (see page 15)
7 cups water, preferably spring water
1 medium onion, cut into quarters
1 carrot, peeled and cut into quarters
1 celery stalk, cut into quarters
1 smoked ham hock (see page 218) or ¼ pound slab bacon
1 dried hot chile pepper
1 bay leaf
1 thyme sprig
Large pinch of Kosher salt
2 cups basmati rice
3 scallions, chopped
2 tomatoes, halved, seeded, and chopped
Several basil leaves, chopped or torn
Extra virgin olive oil
¼ cup Alecia's tomato chutney (see Sources, page 352) or
  Pickapeppa or other Jamaican-style sweet-hot sauce

Wash and pick over the peas, removing any misshapen ones or pebbles. Place the peas in a medium saucepan, add the water, and bring to a simmer. Add the onion, carrot, celery, ham hock, chile pepper, bay leaf, thyme sprig, and salt and simmer until the vegetables are tender, about 25 minutes.

Drain the peas, reserving the broth, and return them to the pan, along with a little broth to keep them moist.

Transfer 3½ cups of the reserved broth to a saucepan and bring to a simmer. Add the rice and cook until it is fluffy and tender and has absorbed almost all the liquid, 16 to 18 minutes. Remove from the heat and let the rice continue to steam, covered, for 5 to 10 minutes while you reheat the peas. Add the remaining broth to the peas and reheat gently.

Transfer the rice to a serving bowl and spoon the warm peas and broth on top. Scatter the chopped scallions, tomatoes, and basil over the peas. Drizzle everything with a little extra virgin olive oil and finish with a large dollop of the chutney.

VARIATION: Serve the peas with just the chopped tomatoes, scallions, basil, and olive oil, or substitute Pecan Pesto (page 103) for the chutney or hot sauce.

LOWCOUNTRY RED RICE

SERVES 6 AS A SIDE DISH

From the North Carolina border all the way down to the Florida state line, almost every old-time southern family along the coast serves red rice—red because of the tomato broth in which the rice is cooked. This flavorful rice is packed with tomatoes, bacon, onions, and peppers. (We use basmati rice for its distinctive nutty flavor.) Toss in a few shrimp, hot off the grill, and you've got a delicious meal.

2 cups peeled, seeded, and chopped tomatoes, with their juices
    (or substitute canned, reserving the liquid)
1/4 pound bacon, cut into 1/2-inch-wide strips
1 large onion, cut into 1/4-inch dice
1 large red bell pepper, cored, seeded, and cut into
    1/4-inch dice
2 celery stalks, finely diced
Extra virgin olive oil if needed
2 jalapeños, seeded and diced
1 poblano or yellow bell pepper, cored, seeded, and diced
2 bay leaves
4 thyme sprigs
Kosher salt and freshly ground black pepper to taste
1 3/4 cups Chicken Broth (page 339) or canned low-sodium
    broth, or a combination of half chicken and half shrimp
    broth or bottled clam juice
1 cup basmati rice
4 scallions, thinly sliced
1 small bunch basil or cilantro, leaves removed
1/2 lemon

If using fresh tomatoes, drain them in a sieve or colander set over a bowl to catch their juices; set the juices aside.

In a large Dutch oven, cook the bacon over medium heat until it is beginning to crisp. With a slotted spoon, transfer the bacon to paper towels to drain. Return the Dutch oven of drippings to the stove, add the onion, bell pepper, and celery and sauté until softened, about 10 minutes. (Add a little olive oil if the bacon fat seems insufficient.) Add the chile peppers, tomatoes, bay leaves, and thyme to the pot, season with salt and pepper, and simmer for about 10 minutes, until the chile peppers have softened.

Meanwhile, in a medium saucepan, combine the broth with a scant 1/4 cup of the reserved tomato juices (discard any remaining juice) and add salt to taste. Bring to a simmer. Add the rice, return to a simmer, and stir a few times. Lower the heat to the lowest setting, cover, and cook until the rice is tender, about 16 minutes.

Add the rice to the vegetable mixture, along with the bacon, and taste for seasonings. Stir in the scallions, basil, and a big squeeze of lemon. Serve immediately.

In June and July, when lady peas, pink-eyes, zipper peas, butter beans, and crowders, our beloved "shell peas," hit their prime, you can find the pea-shelling machine at the farmers' market simply by looking for the biggest crowd of people. Folks buy their peas in the pod from nearby stands and then take them to the sheller, who tosses them into the machine to let it do its thing. The machine can shell two bushels of peas or beans in under ten minutes. It's easy to become hypnotized by the spinning barrel that tumbles around and around as pressure is applied to the pea pods inside. The pressure splits the pods open, while the tumbling action releases the green peas from their cocoons so that they can filter through the mass of pods, down a shoot, and into a bucket for the waiting customer. This same process done by hand would take hours. It is common to see old-timers standing by the machine with a vigilant eye, making quite sure that every last precious pea that can be claimed as theirs is deposited into the bucket and bagged before heading for home. The season for these peas and beans is fleeting. It seems as if no sooner than they've come to market and we've cooked up the first delectable batches and returned for more they have already begun to disappear. And, like everything else good that is fleeting, we mourn their passing.

Mike Arnold, the pea sheller at Sun Up Produce at the Alabama Farmers' Market, is busy from the time the market opens at dawn until it closes at dusk during the six- to eight-week pea season. Pallets of shell peas arriving from farms line the warehouse floor. Once picked, shell peas must be cooled before shipping or, like green hay, they will heat up and steam on the truck—and occasionally ignite—ruining the crop. This cooling is done with thirty-four-degree high-velocity air—a fast way to cool down the crop and get it quickly and safely to market. Mike loads the large

{ **Butter Beans, page 15**

sacks of pods into the sheller and runs the machine, then picks over the shelled peas and bags them for the customer. It is a nonstop, backbreaking job, one that proves just what a commodity shell peas are in the South. Mike's refrigerators are brimming with ten-pound bags of shelled peas awaiting pickup.

Local peas and shell beans are ingredients in which southerners take special pride—something that is worth savoring and learning about. In Italy, native beans like favas are treasured. Here, we cherish our lady peas, crowders, zippers, pink-eyes, and butter beans.

BUTTER BEANS

SERVES 8 TO 10 AS A SIDE DISH • PHOTOGRAPH PAGE 12

Fresh summer baby green limas, known locally as "butter beans," are highly prized in the South—they command a higher price than other peas or beans because of their fine texture and flavor. The speckled butter beans may look prettier at the farmers' market with their attractive multi-colored skin, but when cooked, their novel coloring is lost and their flavor not nearly as fine as that of the green ones. When picked young and cooked soon afterward, butter beans have a delicacy to be treasured. We like to flavor spring water with an onion and a few sprigs of thyme and savory for cooking the beans. (We prefer spring water for these simple dishes for its purity of flavor.) For an Old South note, drizzle a bit of sizzling bacon fat over the top just before serving—or add a splash of good fruity Italian olive oil and chopped fresh herbs, such as tarragon, basil, dill, or parsley.

Peas of all kinds (black-eyes, pink-eyes, crowders, butter peas, lady peas, etc.—see page 251) may be prepared in a similar fashion. If fresh peas are not available, use frozen. You might also consider finishing the beans with a few chopped scallions and tomatoes, and a sprinkling of cilantro.

6 cups water, preferably spring water
1 onion, quartered
1 bay leaf
4 thyme sprigs, plus a scattering of leaves for garnish
4 savory sprigs, plus a scattering of leaves for garnish
Kosher salt
1 pound small green butter beans, picked over and rinsed
2 tablespoons fruity extra virgin olive oil, bacon fat,
    or unsalted butter, melted
Freshly cracked black pepper

Combine the water, onion, herbs, and salt in a medium saucepan and bring to a boil. Reduce the heat to a simmer and cook gently for 15 minutes. Add the beans, adjust the heat to maintain a simmer, and cook until the beans are just tender, 15 to 20 minutes. Taste for seasoning, and add salt if necessary. Remove the pan from the heat and let the beans rest in their liquid for 10 minutes.

Serve sprinkled with the herbs and drizzled with olive oil. Finish with cracked black pepper.

FRIED OKRA

SERVES 6 TO 8 AS A SIDE DISH

Prepared well, fried okra embodies the flavors of a primal southern garden. The problem is that most commercial establishments go too heavy on the breading and cook way too much at a time, which keeps the okra from getting crisp on the outside and tender inside. But at home, with a big cast-iron skillet, and no more than six to eight hungry mouths to feed, you'll be able to cook up a perfect batch. Although larger okra is sold "for frying," I prefer the flavor and texture of the smaller pods.

2 pounds small okra, stem ends trimmed, sliced into
    ¼-inch-thick slices
1 cup cornmeal
½ cup all-purpose flour
1 teaspoon Kosher salt, or to taste
½ teaspoon freshly ground black pepper, or to taste
1 cup buttermilk
1½ cups vegetable oil or lard, or as needed

Place the okra in a bowl of ice water for 15 minutes to crisp; drain and pat dry.

Combine the cornmeal, flour, salt, and pepper in a shallow pan. Transfer the okra to a large bowl and toss with the buttermilk. Lift the okra out with a slotted spoon and place in the pan of cornmeal, tossing it around to lightly coat. Transfer the okra to a rack set over a baking sheet.

In a large deep cast-iron or other heavy skillet, heat ¾ cup of the oil over high heat until almost smoking. Add just enough okra to cover the bottom of the skillet in a single layer, without crowding, lower the heat to medium, and cook until golden and crusty on the bottom, about 6 minutes. Turn and cook, tossing the okra once or twice, until well colored and crisp on all sides. With a slotted spoon, transfer to a paper towel–lined sheet pan and season with salt and pepper. Keep warm in a low oven while you continue to cook the okra in batches, adding the remaining oil as needed. Dig in while the okra is warm!

POLE BEANS WITH ONIONS AND POTATOES

SERVES 6 TO 8 AS A SIDE DISH

Typically pole beans are bigger and thicker than bush beans such as Kentucky Wonder or Blue Lake. The beans are broader and usually take longer to cook. In the old days, you would start with a pot of water and maybe some pork neck bones, a ham hock, or a little salt pork or fatback, then add the beans, along with some halved new potatoes and sliced onions, and let it cook "until tender"—which meant at least two hours. Or tender enough for those without teeth! This version needs only 15 to 20 minutes' cooking time.

2 onions, quartered
Several thyme sprigs
Several savory sprigs
1 teaspoon Kosher salt
2 garlic cloves, crushed
2 quarts water, preferably spring water
1 pound small new red or white potatoes, scrubbed and halved
2 pounds pole beans, strings and stem ends removed
1 tablespoon extra virgin olive oil

Combine the onions, herbs, salt, and garlic in a medium pot, add the water, and bring to a boil. Add the potatoes and cook for 5 minutes. Add the beans and cook until tender, 10 to 15 minutes, depending on how fresh and young the beans are. Drain and reserve the broth for another use.

Serve the beans, potatoes, and onions in a bowl, drizzled with the olive oil.

To harvest corn by hand in the middle of summer is to get lost in a sea of green. The six- and seven-foot-high stalks sway with the weight of the plump, tasseled cobs. When the husks and the silks are pulled back and you take a bite of fresh corn, raw and milky, the experience is beyond compare. My grandfather White won awards for corn crops, and I can still remember eating the most outstanding creamed corn at my grandparents' table. The "field corn," as opposed to "sweet corn" (see page 22), would be picked in the morning, then scraped and cooked with some home-churned butter or a little bacon fat, resulting in an almost risottolike, creamy dish. That, served with some okra (both boiled and fried) and sliced tomatoes, made for a perfect southern lunch.

Historically, corn has had a major impact on our regional diet. When people could not afford wheat flour to make bread, cornmeal was the available cheaper substitute, and thus corn bread became daily sustenance by default. I've heard of families who would eat corn bread at each and every meal—in the morning with syrup, the breakfast leftovers as part of a snack or lunch, and a helping at dinner with a vegetable soup. Eventually, in more prosperous times, corn bread became a mainstay of our culinary lexicon, made less out of necessity than out of a deep craving. An old-time, country way to enjoy it is to dunk a wedge of hot corn bread into a glass of ice-cold buttermilk—the embodiment of southern flavor, something many of us recall our parents and grandparents doing. To taste the tang of the buttermilk and the crumbly goodness of warm corn bread is to partake in a communion of sorts.

SPOONBREAD

SERVES 8 AS A SIDE DISH

Spoonbread is what country folk in the South would make for company or special occasions when corn bread was just too plain. The texture is similar to a dense polenta pudding and is enriched with eggs, cream, and Parmesan. I can hardly resist swiping a spoonful whenever a batch is cooking in our kitchens. Undeniably beautiful when pulled from the oven, it remains delicious for several hours afterward. To reheat, cover tightly with foil and heat in a 300°F oven for 15 minutes. It is wonderful with Red Wine–Braised Rabbit (page 228) or Roast Venison with Cabbage, Spoonbread, and Bourbon (page 214).

3 cups water
Kosher salt
½ cup heavy cream
½ cup buttermilk
8 tablespoons (1 stick) unsalted butter
1 cup self-rising yellow cornmeal (or substitute 1 cup regular
    cornmeal plus ½ teaspoon baking powder, ½ teaspoon
    baking soda, and ½ teaspoon salt)
¼ cup finely grated Parmigiano-Reggiano
Hot sauce, such as Tabasco or Cholula
3 large eggs, beaten
Freshly ground white pepper

Preheat the oven to 375°F. Butter a 9-inch gratin dish.

Bring the water to a boil in a medium heavy saucepan and add a good pinch of salt. Meanwhile, in a small pan, combine the cream, buttermilk, and butter and bring to a gentle simmer.

When the water is boiling, add the cornmeal, whisking constantly, and return to a simmer. Simmer for 2 to 3 minutes, stirring occasionally with a wooden spoon, until just thickened, then add the Parmigiano and hot sauce. Stir in the cream mixture and simmer for 2 minutes more. Remove from the heat and let cool slightly.

Stir in the eggs vigorously, mixing well. Add white pepper to taste. Pour into the prepared gratin dish and bake until golden and set, 20 to 25 minutes.

HIGHLANDS BAKED GRITS

SERVES 8 TO 10 AS AN APPETIZER

This signature appetizer is simple southern with a little finesse. The grits are baked in individual ramekins, then served with a buttery Parmesan sauce, garnished with wild mushrooms and strips of country ham. This is pure comfort, warm and homey with a soothing contrast in textures. Organic stone-ground corn grits are essential—don't even think about trying this with "quick" grits!

FOR THE GRITS
4 cups water, preferably spring water
1 teaspoon Kosher salt
1 cup yellow stone-ground grits, preferably organic
2 tablespoons unsalted butter, at room temperature
¼ cup finely grated Parmigiano-Reggiano
Freshly ground white pepper to taste
1 large egg, beaten

FOR THE SAUCE
½ cup white wine
¼ cup sherry vinegar, or to taste
2 shallots, minced
1 bay leaf
1 dried red chile pepper
1 to 2 ounces country ham (trimmings, end pieces,
    and scraps from the shank are fine)
1 tablespoon heavy cream
8 tablespoons (1 stick) unsalted butter, cut into cubes
2 tablespoons finely grated Parmigiano-Reggiano
Kosher salt and freshly ground white pepper
Juice of ½ lemon, or to taste
Hot sauce, such as Tabasco or Cholula

1 tablespoon olive oil
2 thin slices country ham or prosciutto, cut into julienne strips
½ cup chanterelle, morel, shiitake, or oyster mushrooms
    cut into 1- to 2-inch pieces
1 shallot, minced
Thyme leaves for garnish

In a large heavy saucepan, bring the water and salt to a boil. Stirring with a wooden spoon, add the grits in a slow, steady stream and cook, stirring frequently, until thickened and tender, 45 minutes to 1 hour. Remove from the heat and add the butter, Parmigiano, and white pepper, stirring until combined. Add the egg and stir to incorporate.

Meanwhile, preheat the oven to 375°F. Butter eight to ten 4- to 6-ounce ramekins.

Divide the grits among the buttered ramekins, place in a baking pan, and add enough hot water to the pan to come halfway up the sides of the ramekins. Cover with foil and bake for 15 minutes. Remove the foil and bake for about 20 minutes longer, or until the tops are crusty and beginning to brown.

Meanwhile, in a medium sauté pan, combine the wine, vinegar, shallots, bay leaf, chile pepper, and ham and bring to a boil. Cook until only 1 tablespoon of liquid remains. Reduce the heat to low and stir in the cream. Whisk in the butter bit by bit, adding each new piece as the previous one is incorporated.

Strain the sauce into a saucepan. Add the Parmigiano and season with salt and pepper, lemon juice, and hot sauce to taste. Keep warm.

Heat the oil in a small sauté pan over medium-high heat. Add the julienned ham, mushrooms, and shallot and cook until the mushrooms are barely tender, 3 to 4 minutes.

Unmold the grits onto serving plates and turn browned side up. Ladle a little sauce around the grits and top with the mushrooms and ham. Garnish with thyme leaves.

NOTE: The grits can be baked up to 1 hour ahead and set aside at room temperature. Reheat on a baking sheet in a 400°F oven until warmed through.

TO DRINK: Châteauneuf-du-Pape blanc, Domaine du
    Vieux Télégraphe

CREAMY GRITS

SERVES 10 AS A SIDE DISH

Stone-ground grits from old-fashioned mills that use locally grown, organic corn has significant texture and vivid corn flavor. It bears no relation to the "quick" grits served in greasy spoons throughout the country. If your local grocer doesn't carry stone-ground grits, check your local health food store. For years we have bought Arrowhead Mills organic yellow grits from Birmingham's health food store. We cook our grits in water, not milk, for a pure corn flavor. Some cooks finish the grits with cream, which makes the dish too rich—but we enrich them with plenty of butter and grated Parmesan cheese.

4 cups water, preferably spring water
1½ teaspoons Kosher salt
1 cup yellow stone-ground grits
2 tablespoons unsalted butter, or a little more if desired,
    at room temperature
¼ cup finely grated Parmigiano-Reggiano or Grana Padano,
    or a little more if desired
Kosher salt and freshly ground white pepper
Hot sauce, such as Tabasco or Cholula

In a medium saucepan, bring the water to a boil. Add the salt, then whisk in the grits in a slow, steady stream, whisking constantly to prevent clumps and thoroughly mix in the grits. Bring to a boil whisking, then turn the heat down to low and simmer for 45 minutes to 1 hour, stirring occasionally with a wooden spoon until the grits are thickened and tender.

Add the butter and Parmigiano, stirring to combine, then add the salt, white pepper, and hot sauce to taste. Taste and add more butter, cheese, and/or salt if desired.

VARIATION: Use part cheddar or Comté cheese with the Parmigiano.

CREAMED CORN

SERVES 4 AS A SIDE DISH

Creamed corn is at its best right in the middle of the summer. Sweet corn is by far the most widely available corn, but true creamed corn is made from "field corn," which is much starchier and less sweet. It is the old-fashioned variety southerners would grow for their livestock feed as well as for their table. The problem with field corn is that it deteriorates and dries up very quickly once picked, so, unless you live in a corn-farming area, you may not have much access to it. When you make this dish with field corn, no added thickener is needed, but I've included flour here since you are likely to be using sweet corn. Whichever type you use, the key is not to cut off the kernels too close to the cobs; you want to slice off just the tips of the kernels, leaving a good bit on the cob. Then you can scrape what remains on the cob with the back side of a knife to extract its milky essence, filled with corn juices and pulp.

6 ears corn, shucked
2 tablespoons bacon fat (or additional butter)
1 tablespoon unsalted butter
1 heaping tablespoon all-purpose flour
¾ cup water
Kosher salt and freshly ground white pepper to taste

Cut the ears of corn in half, then cut just the tips of the kernels off the cob as described above, and place them in a bowl. (Cutting the ears of corn in half before removing the kernels makes the task less messy, as the kernels are less likely to fly all over the kitchen.) With the back of your knife, scrape the cobs thoroughly to release their juices and pulp into the bowl.

Heat the bacon fat and butter in a large cast-iron skillet over medium heat. Add the corn mixture, then stir in the flour, and cook for 5 minutes, stirring from time to time, until thickened. Add the water and salt and pepper and continue cooking, stirring occasionally, until the bottom gets a little crusty. Continue to cook, scraping up the crusty bottom from time to time, until creamy, 30 to 40 minutes total. Serve in a warm bowl (and just try to resist eating all the little bits left in the pan).

Dol Miles, our kitchen manager, and Verba Ford, our earliest employee, are first cousins who have worked side by side with me for more than twenty years. They have been with me from the beginning. Dol made the curtains that once graced our front window, and I continue to rely upon her artistic eye and her aesthetic when pondering how best to plate an entrée. Verba helped me to appreciate my own upbringing by talking me into putting corn bread in our breadbaskets and serving wilted young collards mixed with chard and escarole.

When my mother passed away, these women stepped into their roles as the restaurant's maternal standard-bearers. They have looked after me in a manner that borders upon protective. They have been willing and able to rein me in when I need it, to keep our food from veering too far toward French and fancy. They keep me grounded in my native groceries. They have been sources of strength and security for me, and they have exhibited the patience of Job, putting up with my mistakes and my personal problems.

My respect for Dol and Verba is not some holdover from the Old South. The restaurant we have built together is a beacon of the New South, where what matters is the pursuit of quality, the pursuit of perfection. Those imperatives give everyone who works at Highlands a common frame of reference.

It is my hope that Highlands has had a positive impact upon our community, that we have built a restaurant that southerners, both white and black, can claim as a kind of home away from home—as a space where, over good food and drink, they can learn to be honest with one another. Highlands has become just that sort of place for me. And I know the catalyst for that success has been my relationship with Dol Miles and Verba Ford.

{ **Verba Ford and Dolester Miles**

CORN BREAD

SERVES 6 TO 8 AS A SIDE DISH • PHOTOGRAPH PAGE 6

Corn bread sweetened with sugar must be a Yankee invention, because corn bread in the South is always a savory staple. We like to keep it simple, but don't stint on the fat, whether butter or bacon fat (or oil, if you must). Corn bread, corn muffins, and corn sticks should all be cooked to a dark shade of golden brown and turned out while hot, the steam rising fragrant with the aromas of corn and bacon, as you break into them.

2 cups self-rising yellow cornmeal (or substitute 2 cups regular cornmeal plus 1 teaspoon baking powder, 1 teaspoon baking soda, and 3/4 teaspoon salt)
1/2 cup all-purpose flour
3/4 cup whole milk
3/4 cup buttermilk
Scant 1/2 cup rendered bacon fat, 7 tablespoons unsalted butter melted, or scant 1/2 cup vegetable oil (or a mixture)
1 extra-large egg, lightly beaten

Preheat the oven to 450°F.

Preheat an 8- to 9-inch cast-iron skillet in the hot oven.

Place the cornmeal and flour in a large bowl and stir in the milks a little at a time, mixing with a large wooden spoon. The batter will be quite loose.

Meanwhile, add the bacon fat to the preheated skillet, return it to the oven, and heat until the fat is very hot, about 5 minutes.

Remove the skillet from the oven. Pour all but 1 tablespoon of the hot fat into the cornmeal mixture and stir to combine. Add the egg and stir to combine. Pour the cornmeal mixture into the hot skillet and immediately place it in the oven. Bake for 20 to 25 minutes, until golden brown. Remove from the oven and unmold. Serve hot.

CRACKLIN'S

Little crispy bits of bacon or duck skin cooked until dark and golden, cracklin's are a delicious addition to corn bread or salads. Free-range chicken or guinea hen skin is also an option.

Slab bacon or duck skin, cut into 1/2-inch pieces

Place the bacon or duck skin and water to cover in a heavy skillet or saucepan and cook over medium-low heat until the fat is rendered, the water has evaporated, and the cracklin's are crisp and golden brown, 30 to 40 minutes. With a slotted spoon transfer the cracklin's to a plate lined with paper towels to drain. Reserve the remaining fat to make corn bread (left).

CORN PUDDING

SERVES 8 AS A SIDE DISH

This savory pudding goes with practically everything—fish, pork, beef, and poultry. The little individual servings add a bit of elegance to even a simple meal.

3 cups corn kernels (from about 8 ears)
1 cup heavy cream
2 large eggs, beaten
Tiny pinch of grated nutmeg
Pinch of Kosher salt
Pinch of freshly ground white pepper

Preheat the oven to 325°F. Butter eight 6-ounce ramekins.

Puree half of the corn kernels in a food processor. Transfer to a large bowl and add the remaining corn kernels, the cream, beaten eggs, nutmeg, salt, and white pepper. Stir to combine.

Ladle the mixture into the prepared ramekins. Set the ramekins in a baking pan and pour in enough hot water to reach halfway up the sides of the ramekins. Place the pan in the oven and bake until the puddings are set, about 45 minutes. Remove the puddings from the oven and let stand for 5 to 10 minutes.

To serve, run a paring knife around the edge of each ramekin to loosen the pudding from the sides, then carefully invert the puddings onto serving plates.

CHARRED CORN RELISH

MAKES 3 CUPS

Like our Artichoke–Charred Onion Relish (page 155), which we pair with grilled black grouper, this adds a superbly bright and fresh nuance to simple grilled fish, especially salmon, tuna, or grouper. It is also delicious with chicken, pork, or beef. Make the relish with one predominant herb—if you have really fresh basil, let parsley and chives sing backup. If you choose cilantro as the headliner, then certainly add a little parsley or chives, but, again, let the cilantro dominate. Varieties of sweet onion to seek out include Vidalia, Texas Sweet, Maui, or Wadamalaw. You want a vinegar with a bright aroma and lively acidity here, such as L'Estornell's garnacha.

4 ears corn, shucked
1 sweet onion, such as Vidalia, cut into ½-inch-thick slices
½ cup quartered cherry tomatoes
1 shallot, finely minced
2 tablespoons red wine vinegar
¼ cup extra virgin olive oil
Kosher salt and freshly ground black pepper to taste
½ cup loosely packed basil leaves, coarsely chopped
Several flat-leaf parsley sprigs, leaves removed and coarsely chopped
A few chives, chopped

Prepare a hot grill or preheat the broiler.

Char the corn and onion on the grill or under the broiler, turning occasionally, until slightly blackened on all sides. Let cool slightly.

Cut the corn kernels off the cobs and place them in a medium bowl. Cut the onion slices into ¼-inch dice and combine with the corn. Add the cherry tomatoes, shallot, vinegar, olive oil, salt, and pepper and toss to combine. (The relish can be made to this point up to 2 hours ahead. Set aside, covered, at room temperature.)

Just before serving, add the herbs and toss again. Taste and adjust the seasoning before serving.

CUCUMBER SALAD

SERVES 6

Whether added to a tomato or lettuce salad, combined with herbs and maybe some yogurt or buttermilk dressing, or just tossed with oil and vinegar, small, firm cucumbers have a cool, refreshing crunch few other vegetables can claim. Fresh dill is always delicious with cucumbers. Parsley, chives, tarragon, cilantro, and basil, picked fresh from the garden, are similarly welcome—though not all together.

6 small Kirby cucumbers (or other unwaxed pickling types,
    such as Persian)
Kosher salt
1 small sweet onion, such as Vidalia, cut into quarters
    and thinly sliced
2 tablespoons champagne vinegar or white wine, sherry,
    or cider vinegar
4 large tomatoes, sliced 1/3 inch thick
1/4 pound French or Greek feta, crumbled
1 large bunch dill, feathery leaves coarsely chopped
1 small bunch chives, finely sliced
1/4 cup extra virgin olive oil
Freshly ground black pepper

Peel the cucumbers in "zebra stripes" by peeling away alternating strips of skin with a vegetable peeler. If seeds have developed, halve the cucumbers lengthwise and scrape out the seeds with a little spoon. Slice into 1/4-inch rounds or half-moons. Toss the cucumber slices with a little salt in a bowl and put in the refrigerator to chill for 30 minutes.

Meanwhile, toss the onion with the vinegar in another bowl and refrigerate for 20 minutes.

Arrange the tomato slices on a platter and place the feta in the center. Drain the cucumbers and pat them dry. Toss with the macerated onions and scatter over the tomatoes. Sprinkle with the dill and chives, drizzle with the olive oil, and finish with some freshly ground pepper.

SPICY COLESLAW

SERVES 8 TO 10 AS A SIDE DISH

The refreshing crunch of coleslaw is a staple at any southern picnic or barbecue. I like to allow the flavors of the shredded vegetables and tangy dressing to come together for a couple of hours in the refrigerator before serving.

1 pound green cabbage, cored and finely sliced
1/4 pound red cabbage, cored and finely sliced
3/4 cup Homemade Mayonnaise (page 336)
1/4 cup white wine vinegar or 1/4 cup cider vinegar
    plus 1 teaspoon honey
1 tablespoon sugar
1 teaspoon fennel seeds
1/2 teaspoon mustard seeds
1/2 bunch scallions, thinly sliced
Kosher salt and freshly ground black pepper to taste
2 large carrots, peeled and cut into julienne strips
1 jalapeño, seeded and cut into julienne strips
1 poblano, seeded and cut into julienne strips
Hot sauce, such as Tabasco or Cholula

Soak the cabbages in a large bowl of ice water for 10 minutes to crisp and refresh them.

Meanwhile, in a medium bowl, combine the mayonnaise, vinegar, sugar, fennel seeds, mustard seeds, scallions, and salt and pepper and mix well. Drain the cabbage and add to the bowl, along with the carrots and chiles. Toss to distribute the dressing evenly. Add hot sauce to taste, then taste and adjust the seasoning.

Cover and refrigerate for 1 to 2 hours before serving to allow the flavors to meld.

GREEN TOMATO
AND PEACH RELISH

MAKES 2 CUPS

We make this relish in July when our local Chilton or Blount County peaches are in peak form. Substitute whatever variety you can get your hands on, making sure that the fruit is still firm and not overly ripe. We use this surprising combination of a relish on grilled fish, with shrimp or scallops, soft-shell crabs, or with roast pork; it also makes a refreshing dip. If peaches are not in season, you can substitute one large not-too-ripe mango for the peaches, for an equally versatile relish.

½ large Vidalia or other sweet onion, cut into thick slices
2 large firm green tomatoes
1 lime
1 firm not-too-ripe peach, peeled, pitted, and cut into
     ¼-inch dice
1 jalapeño, roasted (see page 345), peeled, seeded, and diced
2 scallions, cut into ¼-inch-thick slices
A 2-inch piece fresh ginger, peeled and grated
2 tablespoons extra virgin olive oil
Kosher salt and freshly ground black pepper to taste
1 small bunch chives, finely chopped, or 1 small bunch parsley,
     basil, or cilantro, leaves removed and chopped (optional)

Prepare a hot grill or preheat the broiler. Grill or broil the onion slices for 3 to 4 minutes per side, or until blackened and charred.

Cut the tomatoes into wedges and remove the pulp and seeds, leaving the tomato flesh. Cut the flesh into ½-inch dice and place in a small bowl.

Grate the zest from ½ the lime, then halve the lime.

Add the peaches to the tomatoes, along with the lime zest and juice of ½ lime. Add the jalapeño, grilled onion, scallions, and ginger and toss to mix. Add the olive oil and salt and pepper. Adjust the seasonings as necessary—more lime juice may be needed. Add the fresh herb if desired.

WATERMELON
AND RED ONION RELISH

SERVES 4 TO 6

Summertime heat is cooled by this refreshing, chilled watermelon relish. Crunchy and a little spicy, it is a wonderful embellishment for grilled steak, particularly flank steak or our skirt steak (page 209).

1 medium red onion, thickly sliced
1 cup cubed watermelon (about ½-inch cubes), chilled
2 tablespoons extra virgin olive oil
1 tablespoon champagne vinegar
1 tablespoon chopped mint or chives
1 tablespoon chopped flat-leaf parsley
1 teaspoon finely minced jalapeño
Kosher salt and freshly ground black pepper to taste

Prepare a hot grill or preheat the broiler. Grill or broil the onion slices for 3 to 4 minutes per side, or until evenly charred. Chop the onion slices into ¼-inch pieces.

In a large bowl, combine the watermelon, onion, olive oil, vinegar, herbs, jalapeño, and salt and pepper. Toss, taste, and adjust the seasoning as needed. Cover and refrigerate until chilled.

Serve cold, straight from the refrigerator, for a wonderful crunchy contrast to tender meat hot off the grill.

After twenty years of working with me, Verba Ford has a tremendous sense of ownership, not only in terms of the restaurant and its vision, but also the family of staff she's overseen throughout the years. She has literally watched young chefs grow up before her, training them from prep cooks to sending them off to open their own establishments. I don't know if she thinks of herself as an adoptive parent of sorts, but for some of the staff passing through our doors, she's often been the only solid, loving support they've ever known. She's quick with an opinion, even quicker with corrections, and lightning fast when there's a gap to fill—especially if it involves whipping up some food. Long before news circulates about an unfortunate accident or death, Verba will be in the kitchen putting together some platter or box to offer comfort and a message of concern in the way that only a batch of her potato salad—now known to some of us as "dead people's potato salad"—and pimiento cheese can.

Her pimiento cheese is a powerful thing—so much so that she can use it as currency to purchase lawn mower repair, massages from one of our employees, and virtually anything else she might need from anyone who has ever tasted her simple but magical recipe. It's your lucky day indeed if you can convince her that you "just gotta have" some for your party or wedding shower, or can flatter her into making some for you with an "I've been tellin' my Aunt Maddie about your pimiento cheese and she's just dyin' to try it.... Did I tell you my family reunion is next weekend?" It's like gold.

Just a few times a year, she'll get the urge and for no readily apparent reason make a batch for a staff meal, creating a buzz among everyone—cooks, waiters, managers, and administration alike, who forsake their lunch plans and diets, sneaking peeks to check her progress as they (we!)

gather their saltine crackers and wait for the announcement over the intercom. "Come and get it!" The line forms and the sounds of happy eaters begin: "Mmmmm," "Uh-huh," and even a few lip smacks accompany the rustling of the saltine wrappers and then the snaps of the crackers slathered with the red-flecked, deep orange–colored cheese. She always makes a big stainless steel bowl full, but heaping spoonful by heaping spoonful, it quickly disappears, much to the disappointment of those who were out on errands or didn't drop everything to run to the kitchen for a taste.

MISS VERBA'S PIMIENTO CHEESE

MAKES ABOUT 2 CUPS • PHOTOGRAPH PAGE 31

Whenever Verba has the urge, she will make a huge bowl of the best pimiento cheese you have ever tasted. Little drugstore lunch counters throughout the South inevitably include pimiento cheese sandwiches on their menus as an economical option. But the cheese is usually the commercially prepared variety, of indifferent quality. Making your own, as Verba does, with lots of charred roasted peppers, gives the spread a whole new life. It is perfect for a light sandwich or as a down-home dip for crudités and crackers.

1 pound sharp yellow cheddar
¼ pound cream cheese, softened
1 teaspoon freshly ground white pepper
3 large red bell peppers, roasted (see page 345), peeled, seeded, and chopped
½ cup Homemade Mayonnaise (page 336) or best-quality commercial mayonnaise
1 teaspoon sugar
Splash of hot sauce, such as Tabasco or Cholula
⅛ teaspoon cayenne pepper (optional)

Grind the cheddar in a food processor fitted with the grating disk, or grate it on the small-holed side of a hand grater. Transfer the grated cheese to a bowl, add the cream cheese, white pepper, bell peppers, mayonnaise, sugar, hot sauce, and cayenne, if using, and blend all together thoroughly. Refrigerate and serve chilled. (The spread will keep for several days in the refrigerator, but it usually disappears long before that.)

LEMONADE FOR A CROWD

MAKES ABOUT 1½ GALLONS

Our twist on this old-fashioned staple is the addition of a vanilla bean, which makes the lemonade complex, exotic, and a bit more sophisticated. For an extra kick, add a shot of rum or vodka and a splash of soda.

10 lemons, washed under warm water and halved
1½ gallons water, preferably spring water
2 cups sugar
⅓ cup honey
½ vanilla bean, split
Thin lemon slices for garnish
Mint sprigs for garnish

Combine all of the ingredients in a nonreactive pot and bring to a simmer over medium heat. Cook, stirring occasionally, until the sugar and honey are dissolved, about 10 minutes. Remove from the heat, cover, and let steep for 30 minutes to 1 hour.

Squeeze the juice from each lemon half into the lemonade, then discard. Strain the lemonade into a pitcher and chill. (The lemonade will keep for several days or more.)

Serve in ice-filled glasses garnished with lemon slices and mint sprigs.

HIGHLANDS MINT TEA

MAKES ALMOST 2 QUARTS

At simple restaurants and barbeque joints throughout the South, you will be asked, "Sweet or unsweet?" That you'll want iced tea is a given. Most order sweet, but the question is always posed. At our restaurants, we serve a mint-infused simple syrup to sweeten tea. Unlike granulated sugar, it is immediately incorporated into iced tea. It's hard to dissolve sugar in an iced liquid, despite the fact that my buddies John Egerton and John T. Edge have written beautiful prose about the symphonic sounds produced when spoon and glass meet, when one stirs and stirs, striving to whisk the sugar into that favorite southern elixir—chilled sweet tea.

7 cups water, preferably spring water, chilled
3 tablespoons orange pekoe tea leaves
1 recipe Mint Simple Syrup (page 343)
Mint sprigs for garnish
Lemon slices for garnish

Bring 3 cups of the water to a boil in a medium nonreactive saucepan. Add the tea, remove from the heat, cover, and let steep for 5 to 10 minutes.

Strain the tea into a large pitcher and add the remaining 4 cups cold water. Serve in tall ice-filled glasses, along with a small pitcher with the simple syrup for adding to taste. Garnish with mint sprigs and slices of lemon.

A LITTLE SOMETHING TO START...

GOOD SPIRITS

LITTLE BITES

Chilton County Peach Bellini, page 47

When I was growing

up in Cullman in the 1960s, cocktail hour was a nightly tradition. While my mother was putting the finishing touches on dinner, my father would be at the bar in the basement, where, with great flourish, he would prepare cocktails. My job was that of cocktail server. I would invariably be sent to take "dear mother Marie" her drink—a gimlet perhaps, or a martini, or maybe a scotch and soda—with the instructions to "take this to your mother and give her a kiss from me."

Daddy's golfing buddies or a few of my parents' friends would often gather at our house, "the" party house, and Mother would send down hors d'oeuvres—marinated avocado, broiled chicken livers wrapped with bacon, or one of our standards, cottage cheese and crudités. (The recipe for it, provided in the pages ahead, is still good after all these years.) These early experiences with my family and their friends laid the groundwork for what I would later, as a young adult, discover about mixing drinks and entertaining.

No doubt, a lively and attractive bar that serves up cocktails made with care along with superb wines by the glass is a rare and valuable institution. In the 1970s, coming of age in San Francisco, I experienced a city that appreciated a good bar—juices squeezed fresh to order and shaken with a flourish, freshly whipped cream to top Irish coffee, unusual spirits and aperitifs. Bars were meeting places where politics, sports, philosophy, and sex were talked about with enthusiasm. Those bars, too many to mention all by name except Stars, Jeremiah Tower's paradigm of the sexy urban bar, influenced me in shaping our bar at Highlands.

A salty nibble, a glass that feels good in the hand, a bartender, crisp and starched, who remembers your name, delicious wines—some familiar and some new—and the possibility of staying for dinner, all create a sense of intrigue and wonder of what could come next. And to participate in the ritual of the cocktail hour after a hard-worked day, to be showered and fresh for dinner, and to sit at a handsome bar in anticipation of a perfect cocktail is certainly a great pleasure. That is what we try to accommodate at our little bar in Birmingham, and what you can certainly bring into your own home. So get out your cocktail shaker and whip up one of these thirst quenchers. Then relax, sip, and enjoy.

THE HIGHLANDS MARTINI

SERVES 1

Long before the 1990s martini craze, we set the standard for the finest martini—not bragging, just fact. Not long after we opened in 1982, our head bartender came up with this unique technique. True martinis, by the way, are made with gin. As a member of a very small minority of gin, as opposed to vodka, drinkers, I always try to educate others on the ingredients in a proper martini.

3½ ounces Bombay gin (not Sapphire—the alcohol
    percentage is too high), chilled
3 juicy drops of dry white vermouth, such as Cinzano
    or Martini & Rossi, chilled
A strip of lemon zest
2 green olives, preferably Picholine

Fill a cocktail shaker half full with ice cubes. Add the gin and vermouth and, with a wooden pestle or spoon, muddle vigorously for about 10 seconds, giving it at least 10 strokes. Strain into a chilled martini glass.

Twist a lemon zest strip over the glass before dropping it in. Toss in the olives. There should be the slightest suggestion of a glacier of ice forming on the surface. Inhale deeply and take a big sip.

ORANGE THING

SERVES 1

This drink was created by accident by our longtime bartender and friend Wayne Russell. One evening, Wayne mistakenly poured Triple Sec instead of vermouth into a vodka martini. When he saw me approaching, he quickly added some fresh-squeezed orange juice and talked a few young ladies sitting at the bar into giving it a try. When asked, "What is it called?" Wayne replied, "It's just an orange thing." Now this is one of our most requested drinks.

2 ounces Absolut vodka
1 ounce Triple Sec or Cointreau
2 ounces fresh orange juice
An orange slice for garnish

Fill a cocktail shaker half full with ice cubes. Add the vodka, Triple Sec, and orange juice, cover, and shake vigorously for about 10 seconds. Strain into a martini glass and garnish with the slice of orange.

{ *Clockwise from top:* Alabama Sunset (page 46), Orange Thing (above), Manhattan, Sazerac

Buddy "the Watermelon King" Payton can read a watermelon the way a palm reader reads the lines of your palm. As he wanders through the pallets loaded with melons at the Alabama Farmers' Market in Birmingham, he stops to sweep his hand across these impressive fruits to see what's in store. He can tell by the thickness and fullness of the lighter bands on the striped Jubilees or Crimson Sweets how close they are to ripe perfection. In the case of a watermelon, this is crucial knowledge, because he must get the melons to market seventy-two hours before they are perfectly ripe to be at their peak when they reach the consumer. Watermelons, like tomatoes, continue to develop and ripen after harvest. Buddy points out that the skin of yellow doll watermelons, for example, a sweet variety with a dedicated following in Alabama, should be a clear yellowish-green when they arrive at a wholesaler like himself so that when they land in produce aisles a few days later, they will have had time to develop the hazy, almost milky, shade of yellow that indicates full maturation and sweet flesh. Another telltale sign of watermelon ripeness is a slightly sunken stem end. If a melon bows outward toward the stem, it needs a few more days before carving.

Alabama produce, unlike that from California, is of variable quality. This is not to say it is of lesser quality: California has the luxury of a mild climate and relies mostly on irrigation for controlled consistent watering; Alabama is a slave to the weather. There is nothing a farmer can do to turn off the rain, and when the rains come, there is often a deluge. Some summers are so wet that the soil doesn't ever have a chance to dry out. Watermelons need sunshine to concentrate their sugars to yield the intensity of flavor that has made an ice-cold slice of watermelon a summertime standby for generations. Certainly rains will give you a bigger watermelon, but it will be an anemic, tasteless one. Many a farmer has held out for that extra cent per pound by keeping his crop on the vine just a little longer, only to be hit by Mother Nature's wrath and end up with a crop of large diluted melons that no one wants at market. It is also not uncommon for a farmer to lose some of his crop during rainy times due to explosion. Watermelons first ripen on top, where they have faced the sun during the growing season, leaving the skin there weak and thin. Rain causes the melons to expand and they can, in turn, explode at their weakest point. So, it's a delicate dance. While the farmer needs the sunshine along with a decent rainy season for a respectable yield, he curses rains that are relentless because he may, quite literally, watch his cash crop go bust.

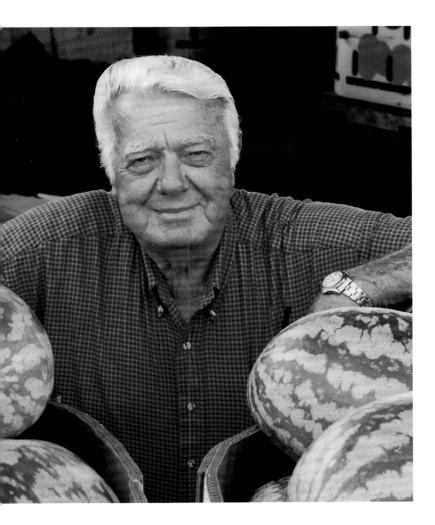

WATERMELON MARGARITA

MAKES 4 POWERFUL DRINKS • PHOTOGRAPH PAGE 45

This drink's full watermelon flavor comes from squeezing chunks of fruit to capture its essence. The result is an elixir that is so perfumed and fresh tasting it's irresistible. Mixed with some good tequila and lime, it may become your new favorite summer cocktail.

A 2-pound chunk of watermelon (about ⅛ watermelon),
 rind removed and flesh cut into chunks
1 lime
Coarse salt
9 ounces high-quality tequila, such as Herradura or
 Patron Silver
2 ounces Cointreau
4 ounces fresh lime juice
1 ounce Simple Syrup (page 343)

Reserve 4 small cubes of watermelon for garnish. Or, instead, remove 4 strips of zest from the lime for garnish; reserve. Cut the lime into quarters and set aside.

Set a strainer or colander over a bowl and, with clean hands, squeeze the remaining chunks of watermelon over the strainer to extract the juice. You need ¾ cup juice.

Rub the outside rims of four martini glasses with the lime, then invert each glass into a container of coarse salt (or onto a layer of salt on a small plate) to coat the rim.

Add the watermelon juice, tequila, Cointreau, lime juice, and simple syrup to a large cocktail shaker filled with ice cubes. Cover and shake vigorously for about 20 seconds. Strain into cocktail glasses and garnish with the chunks of watermelon or lime zest.

PARDIS'S MARGARITA

SERVES 1

My wife, Pardis, prefers this version of the classic margarita. The addition of fresh orange juice makes this deceptively harmless drink all too gulpable.

2 ounces high-quality tequila,
 such as Patron Silver or Don Julio
Juice of 1 lime
¾ ounce fresh orange juice
½ ounce Cointreau
1 lime, cut into 6 to 8 wedges
Coarse salt

Pour the tequila, fruit juices, and Cointreau over ice into a cocktail shaker. Add all but one lime wedge and muddle well with a wooden pestle or spoon, mashing and bruising the lime wedges to release their juice and fragrant oil. Then cover and shake vigorously.

Rub the outside rim of a margarita glass with the reserved lime wedge and invert the glass into a container of coarse salt (or onto a layer of salt on a small plate) to coat the rim. Strain the margarita into the glass and garnish with the lime wedge.

MINT JULEP

SERVES 2 • PHOTOGRAPH PAGE 35

Synonymous with southern hospitality, horse racing, and hot summer evenings on a big front porch, the mint julep is a Kentucky-born cocktail traditionally served in a silver cup. With its refreshing mint muddled with sugar over ice and, of course, that delightful kick of bourbon thrown in, it is a perfect drink for summertime.

4 ounces bourbon, such as Maker's Mark
Scant 2 ounces Simple Syrup (page 343)
6 to 10 mint leaves
2 cups crushed ice
2 big mint sprigs for garnish (big enough to brush
    the drinker's face)

Combine the bourbon, simple syrup, mint leaves, and ice in a cocktail shaker and vigorously muddle with a wooden pestle or spoon, bruising the mint leaves to release their fragrant oils. Pour into a chilled julep cup or tall glass. Garnish with mint sprigs.

VARIATION: Substitute Mint Simple Syrup (page 343) for the regular simple syrup.

ALABAMA SUNSET

SERVES 2 • PHOTOGRAPH PAGE 40

Blackberries are wonderful prepared many ways, including our Lattice-Topped Blackberry Cobbler (page 282), but this apéritif came about years ago, in the middle of July, when a friend brought in a huge basket of local blackberries he'd just gathered. Throughout north Alabama—in fact, throughout the Appalachian hills and mountains—we berry pick. The labor that goes into gathering "free fruit" somehow makes them seem all the sweeter. The name of the cocktail comes from the lovely sunset tones created when blackberries are muddled with sugar and brandy and then strained into a glass of Champagne.

½ cup ripe blackberries
1 tablespoon sugar
1 ounce brandy
8 ounces Champagne or sparkling wine, such as prosecco

With a wooden pestle or spoon, crush the blackberries with the sugar in a cocktail shaker. Let macerate for a few minutes.

Add the brandy and strain into two champagne flutes. Top each with 4 ounces of the Champagne.

CHILTON COUNTY
PEACH BELLINI

SERVES 4 • PHOTOGRAPH PAGE 36

Thirty miles south of Birmingham is one of the nation's great peach-growing regions—Chilton County. Orchards there provide us with just-picked, never-refrigerated fruit from late May to early September. A different variety comes in about every two weeks and in mid-July the most aromatic of all, the "Georgia Belle" white peach, makes its all-too-brief appearance. It is the ultimate peach for Bellinis.

This is one drink that really gets your hands dirty making it, but the resulting cocktail is well worth it. We prefer Nino Franco Rustico prosecco.

8 very ripe peaches, preferably white-fleshed
1 ounce Simple Syrup (page 343), or to taste
Fresh lemon juice to taste
1 bottle (750 ml) prosecco, well chilled

Wash the peaches. Set a conical strainer or colander over a large bowl and, with clean hands, squeeze the whole peaches one at a time over the strainer to extract every bit of juice possible. You will need ¾ cup juice. Add to the bowl the simple syrup and lemon juice to taste—depending on the ripeness of the peaches, you may need a little more syrup—and whisk to combine. Refrigerate the peach juice until well chilled.

In a large cocktail shaker or pitcher, combine the peach juice mixture with half of the prosecco. Let the foam settle and add the remaining prosecco. Give a quick stir, and divide among four chilled champagne flutes or pretty juice glasses.

VARIATION: For a nonalcoholic alternative, replace the prosecco with ginger ale.

TOMATO AND LIME 'TINI

SERVES 1

We like to use higher-acid red tomatoes for this cocktail: Atkinson, Early Girl, or Better Boy. Some of the current darlings of the tomato world include the yellow, golden, orange, and pink varieties which, although beautiful, are to me often a little soft and low in acid. But sometimes when making a salad, I will combine these colorful ones with higher-acid red tomatoes for a more dramatic and complex offering.

6 tablespoons tomato juice, preferably freshly squeezed
    (quarter ripe tomatoes and run them through a food mill
    fitted with the fine disk)
Juice of ½ lime, used lime reserved
Dash of Worcestershire sauce
Dash of hot sauce, such as Tabasco or Cholula
Pinch of sugar
Pinch of Kosher salt
Freshly ground black pepper to taste

Combine all the ingredients in a cocktail shaker half filled with ice and shake vigorously.

Rub the outside rim of a martini glass with the used lime and invert the glass into a container of coarse salt (or onto a layer of salt on a small plate) to coat the rim. Strain the drink into the martini glass.

My love affair with wine began in the mid-seventies while I was living in San Francisco. This was the advent of the modern wine boom, and the Bay Area was an exciting place to learn. Both my culinary and oenophilic passions were ignited as I devoured the works of Richard Olney and Elizabeth David. By developing working friendships with a few of the better wine shops around the Bay, I was able to compare tasting impressions with the clerks and owners, which enabled me to develop an understanding of my own palate and the intricate complexities of wine.

Many people are intimidated when it comes to talking about wine. Part of this comes from a fear of being judged "wrong" and part stems from a reluctance to talk about what our senses are experiencing. So, here's how it works for me: I look at the wine in the glass. I swirl it. I tip the glass to my nose and really breathe it in. Then I taste it. I close my eyes, get lost in the moment, and use my food memories. I swirl, chew, and inhale, all in an effort to better analyze the wine at hand. I love blind tastings, where unknown wines are sampled and participants attempt to identify each one. One of my first steps is to try to determine what the wine is *not*. Often this helps me focus on what the wine *is*. I almost always learn from a fellow taster about some aspect of the wine that I have overlooked but, upon suggestion, see it clear as day. This is why the discussion is so important. At these blind tastings, the thrill of victory is great when you pick the correct wine and the agony of defeat is not too bad when your choice is from halfway around the world. The more you attempt to articulate your impressions, the faster your tasting abilities will improve, making the world of wine all the more interesting.

By tasting and talking with professionals in the wine trade, I was able to quickly learn my likes and dislikes. For me, the enjoyment of wine is the pursuit of balance and harmony; delicacy is often preferred to power. I will always remember tasting a flight of grand cru Bordeaux from the very light 1973 vintage—the stylistic differences were so wonderfully apparent between the Latour, Margaux, Lafite, and Haut-Brion. As it turned out, the Haut-Brion, with its autumnal aromas of leafy tobacco and minerallike complexity, remains my favorite. Typically I would taste through a particular wine shop's preferred arrivals: One week it might be Zinfandels, and another week would bring California Chardonnays and their French counterparts. These times of examining and discussing the merits of wines helped me to develop a greater sense of tasting in regard to food and cooking. Working at Chez Panisse also began to influence me. Wine was such an important part of the Chez Panisse gestalt: The menus were based on French provincial dishes, and the appropriate regional wines were always served, tasted, and talked about. The incredible menus with unusual foods and mysterious wines with beautiful names like Romanée-Saint-Vivant, Ducru-Beaucaillou, Climens, and Charmes-Chambertin were like a siren's call, exotic and alluring. All of this led me to Chez Panisse's unofficial mentor, Richard Olney.

Through a series of introductions, I was able to work for a short time at Richard's residence in Solliès-Toucas. My time cooking at his home and pulling wines from his cellar was one of the greatest highlights of my life. His wines were always shipped directly from the châteaus and then allowed to rest in his very humid, hand-dug hillside cellar. Few labels remained (casualties of the cellar's moist air), but Richard always had a profound story about every one. His menus still inspire my cooking and love of wine.

Later in 1978, while spending a couple of months in Paris, I was fortunate to spend time with Steven Spurrier at L'Académie du Vin. Steven's wine shop and school, located on a charming alley off the place Madeleine, was a center for wine lovers from all over the world. Steven was gracious enough to invite me to taste with him when he reviewed wines for the shop or class. His intellectual intensity and historical knowledge made me feel as though I was in the presence of one of the great wine minds of our time. The tasting of each appellation of the Domaine Leflaive white Burgundies was the paradigm of sensing the uniqueness of each village or vineyard's personality. The Chevalier-Montrachet's stony, racy elegance was of such stunning beauty we were mesmerized.

Steven also helped me arrange a job working the *vendange* (grape harvest) at one of his friend's properties in Provence. So, after hitchhiking to the tiny town of Vidauban, I began one of the most wonderful jobs of my life—picking grapes and working in the cellar. I am still very much a student of wine, and, fortunately, my work sends me back into the world's great vineyards to taste, to learn, and to buy.

As a chef, my cooking begins with a conscious (or subconscious) thought of how wine will be enhanced by each preparation. The next page offers some basic guidelines for the enjoyment of wine. I also offer wine recommendations for many dishes throughout the book. I have tried to suggest wines that will be delicious with my food, and while these are merely suggestions and an insight into what types of wine I enjoy, the selections are based upon what I believe to be one of our greatest strengths at Highlands: the ability to match food and wine so they will complement rather than compete. I hope these serve as a starting point for lively conversation and an enjoyable meal. Cheers!

I love planning menus and pairing each course with a wine. In our "hurry-up-and-do-something-else" society, people do not often plan a first course with one wine and a main course with another (and maybe a third with some cheese or fruit to finish), but I encourage you to extend your time and pleasure at table. There is a subtle rhythm to orchestrating a meal that has progressively complex courses. On these occasions, plan accordingly, and indulge in a selection of wines. But remember, wines do not have to be expensive. Develop a good relationship with a wine merchant and rely on him or her for suggestions to suit your budget.

When serving more than one wine, keep in mind these guidelines: light before heavy—more delicate wines seem a little out of balance after a "big" wine. Dry before sweet—drier wines taste too acidic and shrill after a sweeter wine. Young before old (usually)—for a progression of complexities. Simple before more profound—both will seem all the more "right." And cool before less cool—serve chilled whites or rosés before a red.

A word about temperature: White wines are often served too cold, and red wines are definitely served too warm. Keep an ice bucket filled with ice water to bring that Pinot Noir down to around sixty to sixty-five degrees, the Cabernet to around sixty-five degrees. Champagnes and sparkling wines should be well chilled.

When food and wine are paired, there are some logical general considerations: delicate foods with delicate wines (sole with Sancerre), and big-flavored foods with big-flavored wines (steak with Cabernet). Oaky wines with high alcohol and a bit of residual sugar (many California and Australian Chardonnays) do not in fact pair well with most foods. But wines with good acidity and low tannin (Barbera, Beaujolais, Chianti, Pinot Noir, Côtes-du-Rhône) are very versatile and enhance a variety of foods.

Great wines have a tremendous length of flavor: Their "finish" continues for a minute or two after swallowing. When describing the aromas you detect, think of the familiar aromas of fruits—apple, green apple, pear, apricot, quince, pineapple, blackberry, cherry, blueberry, raspberry, cranberry—or the distinctive aromas of jams, olives, truffle, chocolate, bacon fat, pepper, vanilla, toast, and rose blossom. All can be used to describe wine.

And, finally, remember that a small percentage of wines may be "corked"—they will smell like cardboard or a musty basement because of a chemical reaction within the cork. These should be returned for another bottle.

One joy of entertaining

is that you have the power to orchestrate pleasure. In planning a menu, you get to consider an enormous range of possibilities. Through your preferences—bound by seasonal availability, time, and financial constraints—you choose a menu that builds like a symphony with subtlety and surprises. Organize your day, and remember that although many things are at their best when just prepared or sliced, others lose nothing when prepared in advance. Plan your menu so you aren't doing it all just before serving.

For starters, I have a great weakness for little bites that don't leave me stuffed before the main event. The idea is to serve something provocative, to coax the appetite, to develop a tantalizing unrequited hunger, not to satiate it. While I'm certainly a fan of foie gras, usually I prefer a lighter beginning: fresh favas or baby turnips with maybe a sliver of country ham. I cannot refuse a raw scallop, a shimmering slice of tuna, or an oyster with a splash of acidity—or a surprising crostini of green mango and crabmeat (page 62). These are all wonderful examples of appetizers that can be eaten in one or two bites, each bite leaving you eager for the next. Another is our Grilled Figs with Country Ham, Walnuts, and Lemon-Mint Cream (page 56). The salty ham is quickly charred, and the fig begins to soften. The nuts crunch against the fruit's unctuous sweetness, and the lemon cream offers acidity and an herbal perfume. With a glass of Champagne, it is utter perfection.

GRILLED FIGS WITH COUNTRY HAM, WALNUTS, AND LEMON-MINT CREAM

SERVES 4

Richard Olney was the inspiration for this dish. He loved figs more than any other fruit and was especially fond of their affinity with cured ham. The lightly charred and salty flavor of grilled prosciutto is in perfect contrast with the sweetness of the warm and tender fig. When making this simple recipe, use only the freshest ingredients: perfectly ripe figs, the finest prosciutto, and new-crop walnuts. The smoky ham combined with the just-beginning-to-warm, plump fig is one of the sexiest bites ever.

A handful of mint leaves, plus sprigs for garnish
Juice of 1½ lemons
½ cup heavy cream
Kosher salt and freshly ground black pepper to taste
8 ripe Black Mission figs
16 walnut halves
16 very thin slices prosciutto (see Note)
4 fig leaves for serving (optional)

Prepare a hot grill.

Finely chop the mint leaves and place in a mortar. Add the lemon juice and pound to a paste with the pestle. (Or mash and pound to a paste with a wooden spoon in a small bowl.) Strain into a medium bowl, add the cream, salt, and pepper and stir to incorporate. (The acidity of the lemon juice will thicken the cream.)

Halve the figs and place a walnut half on the cut side of each. Wrap a slice of prosciutto around each fig half, only slightly overlapping the ends.

Char the figs on the hot grill for about 30 to 45 seconds per side. The figs should be just warmed through and the prosciutto crisp in parts. Place the figs on small plates or a platter, atop the fig leaves if using, and serve with a bowl of the mint cream. Garnish with sprigs of mint on the side.

NOTE: Do not be tempted to remove the flavorful fat from the prosciutto. The perfect slice of prosciutto has one edge with some of the white fat left intact.

TO DRINK: Champagne, Billecart-Salmon brut rosé
Champagne, Laurent-Perrier brut rosé

CURED PORK CROSTINI WITH SWEET POTATO BRANDADE

SERVES 8

Crostini—toasted or grilled bread topped with a flavorful bite—have become a standard hors d'oeuvre or little appetizer. This one combines two southern classics: sweet potatoes and pork. In the South of France, a traditional brandade of salt cod, potatoes, and garlic, bound with olive oil, is often used as a spread on a crostini. Here, we improvise and use cured pork instead of cured fish, and local sweet potatoes instead of white potatoes. You can substitute roasted or grilled pork tenderloin and still have delicious results, but if you have the time, try this cure.

FOR THE BRINE

½ cup sugar

½ cup Kosher salt

4 garlic cloves, crushed

8 peppercorns, crushed

4 allspice berries, crushed

1 star anise, crushed

1 dried hot chile pepper

4 cups water, preferably spring water

1 pound pork tenderloin, trimmed and silverskin removed

2 large sweet potatoes, peeled and quartered

½ head garlic (about 8 cloves), peeled

Kosher salt and freshly ground black pepper to taste

¼ cup cubes (½-inch) slab bacon

1 teaspoon extra virgin olive oil

2 teaspoons olive oil

FOR THE CROSTINI

Eight ¼-inch-thick slices baguette

1 tablespoon extra virgin olive oil

Kosher salt and freshly ground black pepper

Cilantro sprigs for garnish

In a medium saucepan, combine the sugar, salt, garlic, peppercorns, allspice, star anise, chile pepper, and water and bring to a boil. Reduce the heat and simmer for 15 minutes.

Pour the brine into a narrow nonreactive container that is deep enough to keep the pork tenderloin submerged. Let the brine cool completely in the refrigerator, then add the pork, cover, and let cure overnight, or for up to 2 days, in the refrigerator.

Put the sweet potatoes and garlic in a medium saucepan and cover with water by 2 inches. Add a good pinch of salt and bring to a simmer. Cook until the potatoes are very tender, about 30 minutes.

Meanwhile, preheat the oven to 425°F.

While the sweet potatoes are cooking, cook the bacon in a sauté pan over medium heat until crisp, about 8 minutes. Set the pan aside.

Drain the sweet potatoes and puree them through a food mill or ricer. Transfer the puree to a heatproof bowl or the top of a double boiler and add the bacon and its rendered fat, along with the extra virgin olive oil and salt and pepper. Stir vigorously to combine. Keep the potatoes warm, covered, over a pan of simmering water or the bottom of the double boiler.

Remove the pork from the brine and pat dry. In a heavy ovenproof sauté pan, heat the 2 teaspoons olive oil over high heat. Sear the pork, turning as necessary, until browned on all sides. Place the pan in the oven and cook until the pork is medium (an internal temperature of 145°F), 10 to 15 minutes. Transfer the pork to a rack to rest. (Leave the oven on.)

Place the baguette slices on a baking sheet, brush with the olive oil, and sprinkle with salt and pepper. Toast in the oven for 5 minutes.

Spoon a little sweet potato brandade on top of each crostini, spreading it evenly. Thinly slice the pork and arrange a few slices on top of each crostini, allowing the colorful brandade to show around the edges for an attractive presentation. Garnish each with a few sprigs of cilantro and a grind or two of black pepper and serve.

NOTE: Any extra brandade can be covered and refrigerated for several days. Reheat gently before using.

TO DRINK: Beaujolais, Morgon LaPierre
Beaujolais, Côte de Brouilly Château Thivin

From day one, we have featured Cullman sweet potatoes as a way of promoting local farmers. People chuckled a bit at first. They were somewhat accustomed to the habit of ascribing provenance to certain European goods, but they were certainly not accustomed to seeing Cullman sweet potatoes in bold type on the menu. And they may not have been quite ready for my pairing of local sweet potatoes with day-boat grouper, or the way in which such a dish pays homage to the sweet potato and concurrently lays claim to a rationale for the place of Gulf-caught fish on a north Alabama menu.

I believe that the people of Cullman are now proud of the fact that we list Cullman sweet potatoes on the menu. I'm proud of the small town I'm from. I think of myself as a country boy at heart. Among natives of Alabama, Birmingham will always be the big city, and with that association comes a tendency toward pretension. I'm cognizant of that, and I look to local goods like sweet potatoes as a means of grounding my menu in a historical reality.

It certainly helps that the sweet potatoes are as good as they are. Cullman sits at a slightly higher elevation than Alabama's other sweet potato–growing regions, on a little bit of a sandy plateau, and its "microclimate" contributes to the quality of its sweet potatoes. Years and years ago, back when I started poking around at the farmers' market trying to find good, local sources for vegetables and fruits, one of the most interesting discoveries was that a lot of farmers from my old hometown of Cullman still come down to Birmingham to sell their goods. Throughout the 1960s and 1970s, Cullman was the most important agricultural county in Alabama. Granted, a lot of that had to do with the poultry industry's predominance in northern Alabama, but Cullman farmers were also known for their excellence in raising all kinds of truck-farming staples, from strawberries to collard greens to sweet potatoes. When I walked the aisles at the market and introduced myself, people would say, "Now are you young Doc Stitt's son, or old Doc Stitt's son?" They knew my people, and that mattered to me.

I take a great deal of pride in serving Cullman produce, but it wasn't always easy. In the past, the farm extension services seemed to be in bed with the DuPonts and the Monsantos and the other chemical companies, but now sustainable agriculture is blossoming, and even for old-line dirt farmers in Cullman, the future looks promising. I have friends up around there who are now trying to develop niche markets for their free-range chickens and heirloom varieties of tomatoes.

Sustainable agriculture is flourishing throughout the country, from California to Maine, from the Hudson Valley of New York to Pennsylvania's Amish country. These farmers are quickly realizing that they can sell their products to discriminating restaurants. And I'm hopeful that we can develop similar success stories here in the Deep South. I'm on a mission: We've got to let the farmers know, let the grocery stores know, that we want them to raise and market the fruit and vegetable varieties that have the most flavor. It has been a losing battle for the last forty or so years. But I think it's a battle worth fighting. Just look to Cullman sweet potatoes for inspiration.

Produce offerings at the Alabama Farmers' Market

CRABMEAT CROSTINI

SERVES 4

Thin slices of crustless bread, drizzled with olive oil, gently toasted, and topped with a heaping spoonful of luscious crabmeat make an ideal hors d'oeuvre or an elegant garnish for a bowl of Curried Pumpkin Soup (page 96).

These can also be made with cooked lobster or shrimp.

½ pound jumbo lump crabmeat, picked free of shells
    and cartilage
Grated zest and juice of ½ lemon
Juice of ½ lime
1½ tablespoons extra virgin olive oil
1 teaspoon finely minced chives
1 teaspoon finely minced chervil or parsley,
    plus 4 small sprigs for garnish
Kosher salt and freshly ground white pepper to taste
Four ½-inch-thick slices baguette, crusts removed

Preheat the oven to 375°F.

Combine the crabmeat, lemon zest and juice, lime juice, 1½ teaspoons of the olive oil, the chives, chervil, and salt and pepper in a medium bowl. Stir gently to combine, being careful not to break up the lumps of crabmeat. Taste and adjust the seasonings.

Brush the bread with the remaining tablespoon of olive oil and place the slices on a baking sheet. Toast in the preheated oven until just firm but not at all colored, about 3 minutes.

Spoon a generous mound of the crab onto each toast and garnish with a sprig of chervil.

VARIATIONS: Crabmeat Crostini with Green Mango: Cut ¼ of a green mango into ¼-inch dice and gently fold it into the crabmeat mixture.

Crabmeat Crostini with Apple: Core and peel 1 tart apple, and cut into ¼-inch dice. Sauté in about 1 teaspoon unsalted butter until slightly softened, about 2 minutes. Stir in a few minced tarragon leaves, 1 teaspoon extra virgin olive oil, and Kosher salt and freshly ground black pepper to taste. Let cool, then fold into the crab mixture.

TO DRINK: Vouvray, Champalou
    Riesling, Fritz Haag Brauneberger
    Juffer-Sonnenuhr Kabinett

HIGHLANDS SEAFOOD PLATTER

SERVES 2 TO 4

Thanksgiving and Christmas are ideal times to serve a seafood platter, because shellfish are at their briny best with a particularly good flavor during the winter months. The dramatic beauty of a frosty tray brimming with color adds to the festive mood of the season. Blue crab claws are an easy addition because they are sold precooked in one-pound containers, often labeled "crab fingers." Try to include at least three different selections: oysters, crab, and shrimp, for example. Or go wild and splurge with clams, periwinkles, lobster, and steamed, chilled mussels, to name other worthy candidates.

½ dozen Apalachicola oysters
½ dozen bluepoint, Malpeque, or Pemaquid oysters
¼ pound cooked blue crab claws
Juice of 1 lemon
Juice of 1 lime
Kosher salt and freshly ground black pepper
1 small bunch flat-leaf parsley, leaves removed and chopped
¼ pound boiled large shrimp (or ⅓ pound uncooked
    shrimp, boiled according to the instructions in
    the Note, page 67), peeled and deveined
1 recipe Cocktail Sauce (page 66)
1 recipe Mignonette Sauce (page 326)
Lemon wedges

Shuck the oysters, leaving them in the bottom shells (see page 347).

In a small bowl, toss the crab claws with the lemon and lime juices. Season with salt and pepper, sprinkle with the chopped parsley, and toss again to coat well.

Arrange the crab claws and the oysters on the half shell on a platter lined with crushed ice, then pile on the shrimp. Set small bowls of the cocktail and mignonette sauces on the platter and garnish with lemon wedges.

TO DRINK: Cheverny, Domaine du Salvard
    Champagne, J. Lassalle Imperiale Préférence

FRIED OYSTERS
WITH SPICY RÉMOULADE

SERVES 4 • PHOTOGRAPH PAGE 64

Out of all the attempts to present an exciting easy-to-eat hors d'oeuvre, few please quite like these simple, crisp, yet juicy morsels of, as Pat Conroy says, "the sea made flesh." We serve fried oysters "in the shell," with the sauce resting in the bottom and the oyster sitting on top. Pass the oysters while they are still warm, and enjoy immediately!

FOR THE RÉMOULADE

1 cup Homemade Mayonnaise (page 336)

1 tablespoon coarse mustard, such as Pommery

¼ cup chopped rinsed capers

2 tablespoons chopped cornichons

1 teaspoon chopped anchovy

2 tablespoons finely chopped blend of two herbs, such as
    flat-leaf parsley, chives, chervil, and/or tarragon

1 scant tablespoon finely diced shallot or grated onion

½ teaspoon paprika

Dash of hot sauce, such as Tabasco or Cholula

1 teaspoon sherry vinegar

Grated zest of 1 lemon

Juice of ½ lemon

FOR THE OYSTERS

3 cups peanut oil for deep-frying

2 cups cornmeal

¾ cup all-purpose flour

Kosher salt and freshly ground black pepper to taste

Cayenne pepper to taste

2 cups buttermilk

24 oysters, such as Apalachicola, Chesapeake, or bluepoint,
    shucked (see page 347), bottom shells reserved, scrubbed
    and dried (if you have the fishmonger shuck the oysters,
    be sure to have him save the bottom shells)

Put the mayonnaise in a medium bowl, add the mustard, capers, cornichons anchovy, herbs, shallot, paprika, hot sauce, vinegar, lemon zest, and lemon juice and stir to blend. Taste and adjust the seasoning; set aside.

Heat the oil in a large heavy saucepan over high heat until it registers 350°F on a deep-frying thermometer.

Meanwhile, combine the cornmeal, flour, salt and pepper, and cayenne in a shallow bowl. Put the buttermilk in another shallow bowl and add the oysters. One by one, transfer the oysters from the buttermilk to the cornmeal mixture, turning to coat thoroughly, and place the oysters on a rack set over a small baking sheet.

Place a spoonful of the rémoulade in each clean oyster shell and arrange on a serving platter.

Carefully drop the oysters, in batches of about 6 at a time, into the hot oil and cook, turning once or twice, until golden, 2 to 3 minutes. Transfer to paper towels to drain. Place the fried oysters in the shells and serve.

TO DRINK: Sancerre, Delaporte
             Pouilly-Fumé, Gaudry

Opposite: Fried Oysters with Spicy Rémoulade, page 63. *Above left:* Shrimp Cocktail, page 66. *Above right:* Pickled Shrimp, page 67.

SHRIMP COCKTAIL

SERVES 6 • PHOTOGRAPH PAGE 65

Shrimp cocktail was so popular in the 1960s and 1970s it became a cliché, but to see a chilled silver bowl filled with big, bright, shiny shrimp and a ruby red sauce thick with freshly grated horseradish remains a sight to behold. Crunchy perfectly cooked shrimp and refreshing sinus-numbing homemade cocktail sauce wow the taste buds while retaining elegance after all these years.

Always cook shrimp in the shell, then peel them; they will be much more flavorful if cooked with the shells still on. If you can get fresh shrimp with the heads on, cook and peel them, but leave the heads attached. Never rinse cooked shrimp to cool it, or you will lose the delicious flavorings from the court bouillon.

Court bouillon is a simple broth used to poach all sorts of fish and shellfish. Although it is quick to prepare, it is critical to simmer it for at least 15 to 20 minutes to develop its flavors before adding the seafood. The court bouillon can be used again to poach shrimp or other shellfish. Cover and refrigerate for a few days, or freeze for up to a month.

FOR THE COURT BOUILLON
8 quarts water, preferably spring water

1 onion, coarsely chopped

2 celery stalks, coarsely chopped

4 garlic cloves, crushed

3 bay leaves

6 peppercorns

1 dried hot chile pepper

1 lemon, sliced

4 flat-leaf parsley sprigs

4 thyme sprigs

Kosher salt

16 jumbo shrimp (10 to 15 count per pound)

FOR THE COCKTAIL SAUCE
1 cup Heinz ketchup

¼ cup freshly grated horseradish, or to taste

Juice of 1 lemon, or to taste

Juice of 1 lime, or to taste

3 shakes Worcestershire sauce

2 shakes hot sauce, such as Tabasco or Cholula

1 teaspoon cracked black pepper

Lemon wedges for serving

Fill a large pot with the water and add the onion, celery, garlic, bay leaves, peppercorns, chile pepper, lemon, parsley, thyme, and a large handful of salt (the water should approximate sea water in saltiness). Bring to a hard boil, then reduce to a simmer, cover, and cook for 15 to 20 minutes.

Add the shrimp and raise the heat to high. Once the court bouillon has returned to a simmer, remove from the heat and set aside, covered, for 5 minutes. Drain the shrimp in a colander, reserving the court bouillon for another use. Transfer the shrimp to a small baking sheet and refrigerate. When the shrimp are cool, peel and devein. (The shrimp can be prepared up to this point a day ahead. Cover the shrimp and refrigerate until chilled.)

To prepare the cocktail sauce, combine all the ingredients in a small bowl. Taste and adjust the seasoning, adding more horseradish, hot sauce, and/or lemon or lime juice to taste. Transfer to a small serving bowl. To serve, put the bowl of cocktail sauce in the center of a serving plate and arrange the shrimp and lemon wedges around it.

TO DRINK: Whatever suits your fancy—margaritas, shaken daiquiris, beer, or Champagne

PICKLED SHRIMP

SERVES 15 TO 20 AS AN HORS D'OEUVRE

PHOTOGRAPH PAGE 65

Another Lowcountry classic, pickled shrimp is a favorite hors d'oeuvre for entertaining. And it gets even better after a couple days' marinating. A nonreactive container, such as a glass canning jar, is best for holding the shrimp in the refrigerator. If you plan on keeping the shrimp in the fridge for more than a few days, however, it's best to sterilize your (heatproof) container first by boiling it in water for five minutes.

3 pounds boiled small to medium shrimp (see Note), peeled

2 medium onions, quartered and very thinly sliced

1 teaspoon celery seeds

1 cup extra virgin olive oil

6 garlic cloves, thinly sliced

4 lemons, thinly sliced

14 bay leaves

1 teaspoon fennel seeds

1 teaspoon mustard seeds

4 dried hot chile peppers

1 teaspoon freshly ground white pepper

1 teaspoon coriander seeds

¼ cup white wine vinegar

½ cup fresh lemon juice

Combine all the ingredients in a large bowl and toss thoroughly. Pack everything into a large glass jar, cover, and refrigerate overnight to allow the flavors to come together.

Serve as an hors d'oeuvre with toothpicks and napkins.

NOTE: To cook shrimp, fill a large pot with water and add 1 onion, quartered, 1 celery stalk, cut into pieces, 1 lemon, sliced, and 4 flat-leaf parsley sprigs. Bring to a boil over high heat, reduce the heat, and simmer for 15 to 20 minutes.

Add a tablespoon of salt and the shrimp. As soon as the water returns to a simmer, remove from the heat. The shrimp will have just begun to curl and have turned a bright pink. Do *not* allow the water to boil, or the shrimp will be tough. Drain—but do not rinse the shrimp, or the flavor will go right down the drain. Reserve the broth, if desired. Allow the shrimp to cool.

TO DRINK: Pinot Grigio, Tiefenbrunner

MARIE'S HERBED COTTAGE CHEESE DIP AND CRUDITÉS

SERVES 8

Packed with herbs—in particular, dill and chives—this colorful dip is crunchy with lots of diced carrots and cucumbers. This healthy snack was my mother, Marie's, staple hors d'oeuvre. It's even better the next day, so make extra to keep in the refrigerator. Serve with the crudités, along with crackers or chips if you like.

FOR THE DIP (MAKES 3 CUPS)

2 cups cottage cheese

2 tablespoons mayonnaise (Hellmann's or Best Foods is fine)

1 heaping teaspoon Dijon mustard

1 tablespoon red wine vinegar

½ teaspoon freshly cracked black pepper

1 scant tablespoon chopped chives

1 scant tablespoon chopped dill

1 scant tablespoon chopped flat-leaf parsley

2 scallions, finely chopped

1 cucumber, peeled, halved lengthwise, seeded, and cut into tiny dice

2 small carrots, peeled and cut into tiny dice

2 celery stalks, cut into tiny dice

½ red bell pepper, cored, seeded, and cut into tiny dice (optional)

FOR THE CRUDITÉS

2 red bell peppers, cored, seeded, and cut into ½-inch-wide strips

4 carrots, peeled and cut into 3-by-½-inch strips

2 celery stalks, cut into 3-by-½-inch strips

2 cucumbers, peeled, halved lengthwise, seeded, and cut into 3-by-½-inch sticks

To make the dip, place all the ingredients in a mixing bowl and stir to combine. Taste and adjust the seasoning.

Serve with the crudités.

TAPENADE

MAKES 1 CUP

A coarse mixture of all things Mediterranean—olives, capers, anchovies, garlic, olive oil, and basil—tapenade is great spread on grilled bread slathered with goat cheese or topped with mozzarella or feta. Or use as an accompaniment for grilled fish, lamb, or beef.

One common mistake is to be heavy-handed with the garlic. Be sure to use a small garlic clove, or the garlic will dominate the other flavors.

3/4 cup mixed Niçoise and Kalamata olives, pitted
3 anchovy fillets, rinsed and drained
2 tablespoons capers, rinsed
1 small garlic clove, crushed
Juice of 1/2 lemon, or to taste
Freshly ground black pepper to taste
1/4 cup olive oil
2 tablespoons finely chopped basil

Pulse the olives, anchovies, capers, garlic, lemon juice, and pepper in a food processor until roughly chopped. Add the olive oil and process to a coarse puree. Transfer to a bowl. Taste and adjust the seasoning, adding pepper and/or lemon juice as desired. Add the basil and mix well. Cover and refrigerate until ready to serve (the tapenade will keep for at least 1 week).

Serve chilled or at room temperature.

VARIATION: Add 1 tablespoon cognac and 1 tablespoon Dijon mustard along with the lemon juice.

SPICED PECANS

MAKES 4 CUPS

Neither cloyingly sweet, nor overly salty, these nuts derive their heightened flavor from rosemary with a kick of cayenne pepper.

4 cups pecan halves
1 1/2 teaspoons Kosher salt
Pinch of freshly ground black pepper
1/4 teaspoon cayenne pepper
1 heaping teaspoon dark brown sugar
1 heaping tablespoon freshly chopped
    rosemary leaves
1 tablespoon melted butter
2 tablespoons olive oil

Preheat the oven to 350°F.

Place the pecans on a baking sheet and bake for 15 minutes. Remove from the oven. Season the pecans with the salt, pepper, cayenne, sugar, rosemary, butter, and olive oil. Toss together until the pecans are thoroughly coated. Return the pecans to the oven for another 2 to 3 minutes, until toasted and fragrant, but be careful not to overcook them.

FIRST COURSES

FAVORITE APPETIZERS

SAVORY SOUPS

HOMEGROWN SALADS

Spring Lettuces with Sweet Peas, Chives, Dill, and Mint, page 108 }

One of the very best

outdoor experiences I have ever participated in was an oyster roast held on the banks of a creek in the marshy lands beyond Charleston, South Carolina. It was the middle of winter—prime oystering time—the sky was gray, and a menacing formation of clouds was rolling in. Spanish moss hung heavy in the trees, and a hard wind was blowing. We were all bundled up, but still we hunched over the fire that burned before us, fighting to keep warm. It proved to be the ideal day to learn the rituals of the oyster roast.

One rule, which any good chef could understand, is that everybody brings his or her own knife. If you do not, you are looked down upon. Of course, your hosts would graciously find you one, but from that point on, you would be set apart. Luckily, I had brought my knife.

Before it came time to use that knife, the oysters were dumped onto a sheet of tin perched over a wood fire, covered with a wet burlap sack, and steamed until the shells eased open. Then the oysters were shoveled onto a special table, with a hole in the center for receiving the spent shells, and everyone, without the least bit of timidity, attacked the pile. For the rest of the afternoon, we held the same rhythm: Crack the shell open with your knife, dunk the oyster meat into a little melted butter, devour, and then repeat. After a dozen or three, you get the hang of it, and you begin to take pride in knowing how to wield the knife, in being able to fend for yourself among a throng of people working its way through bushel after bushel of local oysters. We ate with what I can describe only as uninhibited joy.

{ Baked Oysters with Slab Bacon and Wilted Greens, page 77

The simplicity of that feast, the unbridled, almost bacchanalian tenor of the event, gave me a new perspective on the Lowcountry. Until that time, I had known Charleston and environs as a place out of time, a rarefied city of wealth and art and architecture. I saw Charleston and the Lowcountry as a crown jewel of the South and I still do: It is one of the most diverse, the most beautiful areas of the South. And the culinary tradition—not to mention the wealth of culinary resources—is among the most sophisticated of any region in the country. But that day, along the creek bank, I came to know a different Lowcountry, a place where the best meal one could ever imagine was laid out on a rickety plywood table and available to anyone with a knife and a taste for oysters.

BAKED OYSTERS
WITH SLAB BACON AND
WILTED GREENS

SERVES 6 • PHOTOGRAPH PAGE 74

This is our spin on a traditional New Orleans–style oyster preparation. Typically the oysters are topped with spinach enriched with cream, garlic, and Pernod, the licorice-flavored liqueur. Ours rely on the earthy taste of leeks, shallots, and lots of herbs.

30 oysters, such as Apalachicola, bluepoint, Pemaquid,
    or Malpeque

2 pounds spinach (or about 3 cups trimmed watercress
    or mixed herbs and lettuces)

1 tablespoon extra virgin olive oil

3 ounces slab bacon, cut into small dice

2 leeks, trimmed, cleaned, quartered, and thinly sliced

1 shallot, quartered and sliced

2 garlic cloves, finely chopped

Grated zest and juice of 1 lemon

2 cups medium-coarse bread crumbs (see page 347)

8 tablespoons (1 stick) unsalted butter, melted

Grated nutmeg to taste

Kosher salt and freshly ground white pepper to taste

1 small handful *each* chervil, chives, flat-leaf parsley,
    and tarragon, stemmed if necessary and finely chopped
    (about ¼ cup chopped herbs)

Rock salt for serving

Lemon wedges for garnish

Position a rack in the top of the oven and preheat the oven to 500°F.

Shuck the oysters, leaving them in the bottom shells, (see page 347) and set on a baking sheet. Cover with plastic wrap and refrigerate.

Bring to a boil a large saucepan three-quarters full of generously salted water. Meanwhile, prepare an ice bath (see page 346). When the water has come to a boil, add the spinach and blanch for 30 seconds. Drain and immediately transfer to the ice water. When the spinach is cool, drain well and squeeze dry. Finely chop and set aside.

Combine the olive oil and bacon in a large sauté pan and cook over medium heat until the bacon has rendered its fat but is not yet crisp. With a slotted spoon, transfer the bacon to paper towels to drain. Add the leeks, shallot, and garlic to the pan and cook over low heat until just softened. Transfer the vegetables to a large bowl and add the blanched spinach, bacon, lemon zest and juice, bread crumbs, melted butter, nutmeg, and salt and white pepper. Stir well. Stir in the herbs, then taste and adjust the seasoning.

Gently place 1 tablespoon of the bacon mixture on each oyster to loosely cover the top.

Place the oysters on a bed of rock salt on an ovenproof serving platter. Place on the top shelf of the oven and bake until the topping is golden, about 6 minutes. Garnish with lemon wedges and serve immediately.

TO DRINK: Sancerre, Reverdy

        Chardonnay, Witness Tree

SPICY BAKED OYSTERS
WITH CARAMELIZED ONIONS

SERVES 4

This is so simple, yet there is an almost magical explosion on the palate when briny oysters collide with sweet onions, salty pork, and spicy hot chile. Cover the oysters with the caramelized onions and treat everything else with discretion, adjusting the amounts to suit your own taste. Less is more. More is dangerous.

1 tablespoon olive oil
2 onions, quartered and thinly sliced
Kosher salt and freshly ground black pepper

Rock salt for serving

24 oysters, such as Apalachicola, bluepoint, Pemaquid,
    Chesapeake, or Malpeque, shucked and left in the
    bottom shells (see page 347)
8 tablespoons (1 stick) unsalted butter
Coarsely ground dried hot chile or cayenne pepper to taste
6 to 7 very thin slices pancetta, cut into twenty-four 1½-inch
    squares, or 6 slices bacon, preferably center-cut,
    cut into 4 pieces each
1 cup medium-coarse bread crumbs (see page 347)

Preheat the oven to 450°F.

Heat the oil in a medium skillet over medium-high heat. Add the onions and cook, stirring often, until golden, about 15 minutes. Season with salt and pepper and set aside.

Make a bed of rock salt on a baking sheet and arrange the oysters on top. Top each with a little of the sautéed onion—just enough to cover. Place a teaspoon of butter and a good pinch of chile on each, then top with a square of pancetta (or bacon) and a scattering of bread crumbs to finish.

Bake until the pancetta is slightly crispy, the bread crumbs golden, and the oysters heated through, 10 to 12 minutes.

TO DRINK: Champagne, Veuve Clicquot
        Frosty mugs of beer

STONE CRAB CLAWS WITH
CRUDITÉS AND BAGNA CAUDA

SERVES 4 • PHOTOGRAPH PAGE 80

Stone crabs, in season from October through May, are a beautiful delicacy not to be missed. Joe's Stone Crab Restaurant in Miami Beach helped popularize stone crab claws. It serves them with either a sweet honey-mustard sauce or drawn butter, and their steadfast seasonal appearance has garnered a devoted following. However, as much as we enjoy those sauces, the Italian garlic-oil concoction called bagna cauda packs a powerful punch and is a perfect match for crudités as well.

2 to 3 pounds medium or large fresh stone crab claws
½ pound (2 sticks) unsalted butter
½ cup extra virgin olive oil
3 garlic cloves, pounded to a paste in a mortar
    (or chopped and mashed with a chef's knife)
3 anchovies, pounded to a paste in a mortar
    (or chopped and mashed with a chef's knife)
Kosher salt and freshly ground black pepper
1 red bell pepper, cored, seeded, and cut into
    1-inch-wide strips
1 yellow bell pepper, cored, seeded, and cut into
    1-inch-wide strips
½ fennel bulb, cut into small wedges about 1 inch thick
2 celery stalks, cut into 3-inch pieces
Lemon wedges

Crack the claws with the back of a knife or a small hammer and remove some of the shells, being careful not to smash the meat. (We leave some of the shells on for an appealing presentation.)

Combine the butter, olive oil, garlic, and anchovies in a saucepan and heat over low to medium heat until the butter is melted and the sauce is very fragrant. Season with salt and pepper. Transfer the bagna cauda to a small bowl.

Arrange the vegetables and crab claws on a platter and nestle the bowl of warm sauce in the center. Garnish with lemon wedges and dig in!

TO DRINK: Sierra Nevada Pale Ale
        Pinot Grigio, Zenato

SHRIMP AND CRAB TOWERS

SERVES 6 • PHOTOGRAPH PAGE 81

The vertical look of this dish certainly feels like a restaurant-style presentation, but it's all part of the appeal. For the molds, we use 2½-inch PVC (available at your local hardware store), cut into 3-inch lengths (and sterilized in a dishwasher or very hot water); other options include cleaned tomato paste cans with both ends removed or other open-ended cylindrical containers. If you would rather not improvise the molds, just arrange the components side by side on the plate, for a composed salad. We vary the ingredients—cubed sushi-grade tuna can replace the shrimp, roasted peppers can stand in for the tomatoes, even a zesty ceviche could be an element. Agrumato lemon oil is made in southern Italy by pressing local lemons along with the olives. It is a wonderful addition to any pantry, but you can garnish the towers with additional Lemon Mayonnaise instead, if necessary.

1 recipe Sherry Vinaigrette (page 330)

1 scant tablespoon chopped chives, tarragon,
    or flat-leaf parsley

¾ pound jumbo lump crabmeat, picked free of shells
    and cartilage

2 medium tomatoes, halved, seeded, and cut into ¼-inch dice

Kosher salt and freshly ground black pepper

¼ pound medium shrimp (21 to 25 count per pound) boiled,
    (see Note, page 67) peeled, deveined, and cut into
    ¼-inch dice

1 heaping tablespoon Lemon Mayonnaise (page 336),
    plus additional for serving if desired

Juice of ½ lemon

2 avocados, peeled, pitted, cut into ¼-inch cubes,
    and tossed with a little lemon juice

Generous handful of mixed lettuce and herb leaves,
    such as arugula, mizuna, watercress, chervil,
    cilantro, parsley, and/or dill

Chervil or cilantro sprigs for garnish

Agrumato lemon oil (see Sources, page 352) or additional
    Lemon Mayonnaise (thinned with a little warm water)

In a small bowl, mix the vinaigrette with the herbs. In another small bowl, gently toss the crabmeat with 1 tablespoon of the vinaigrette; set aside. In a third small bowl, combine the tomatoes with 1 teaspoon of the vinaigrette and season with salt and pepper; set aside, reserving the remaining vinaigrette for another use. In yet another bowl, toss the shrimp with a spoonful of the mayonnaise and the lemon juice; set aside.

Place a mold in the center of one plate and fill with 2 tablespoons avocado and 2 tablespoons crabmeat, packing it down tightly with the back of a small spoon. Repeat the layering with 2 tablespoons avocado, 2 tablespoons crabmeat, 2 tablespoons tomato, and finally 2 tablespoons shrimp, pressing each layer down firmly with the back of the spoon. Unmold by gently lifting the ring while pressing down on the top of the tower. Repeat to make 5 more towers.

Garnish the plates with the lettuces and herbs and drizzle a little lemon oil or more lemon mayonnaise around each tower.

VARIATION: Steamed chilled shellfish, such as clams, make an excellent garnish.

TO DRINK: Mâcon-Villages, Denogent
        Grüner Veltliner Smaragd, Prager

Stone Crab Claws with Crudités and Bagna Cauda, page 78

Shrimp and Crab Towers, page 79

CRAB CAKES

SERVES 8

This recipe came about more than fifteen years ago through my collaboration with longtime kitchen staffers Verba Ford and Dolester Miles—and a little instruction from the *Time-Life Good Cook* series. The crab cakes hadn't been on our menu long before lines started to form outside Highlands on Thursday mornings at 11:30. (Nowadays those craving crab cakes for lunch can visit Bottega Café on Mondays and Chez Fonfon on Thursdays.) This was the one and only day we offered these plump, tender, golden, crackling-crisp buttery cakes filled with moist, just-picked blue crabmeat. No bell peppers or mayonnaise here; these are not Maryland crab cakes, or anybody else's. Our secret is the freshest combo of jumbo lump and crab claw meat mixed with melted butter, bound with eggs, and flavored with lots of lemon, parsley, shallot, nutmeg, and cayenne. Another key element is perfect bread crumbs: crumbs that are neither too old nor too fresh, neither too dry nor too moist. They must be ground just right. French baguettes, one to two days old, make perfect crumbs with ideal texture. Verba, Dol, and I are quite proud of our crab cakes.

Serve with a tender lettuce or herb salad.

2 pounds blue jumbo lump and claw finger crabmeat
    (see page 139), picked free of shells and cartilage
1½ cups medium-coarse bread crumbs (see page 347)
6 tablespoons unsalted butter, melted and cooled
2 large eggs, beaten
2 tablespoons chopped shallots
1 tablespoon chopped scallion
2 tablespoons chopped flat-leaf parsley
Grated zest of 1 lemon
2 tablespoons fresh lemon juice
Pinch of grated nutmeg
Pinch of cayenne pepper
Kosher salt and freshly ground black pepper to taste

2 large eggs
2 tablespoons water
1½ cups medium-coarse bread crumbs (see page 347)
2 tablespoons clarified butter (see page 347), or as needed
Lemon wedges
1¼ cups Beurre Blanc (page 338)

In a large bowl, combine the crabmeat, bread crumbs, butter, eggs, shallots, scallion, parsley, lemon zest, lemon juice, nutmeg, cayenne, and salt and pepper. Toss lightly to combine. Taste and adjust the seasoning as needed. Divide the mixture into 8 equal portions and shape into 1-inch-thick patties, being sure not to press them too firmly.

In a small shallow bowl, beat the eggs, then stir in the water. Put the bread crumbs in a shallow dish. Carefully dip each cake into the egg, then into the bread crumbs, and place on a rack.

In a large sauté pan, heat the clarified butter over medium-high heat almost to the smoking point. Add the crab cakes, being sure not to overcrowd the pan; you may have to use two pans or cook the cakes in two batches, using additional butter. Cook the cakes until golden brown on the first side, 3 to 4 minutes. Turn and cook just until brown on the second side, about 3 to 4 minutes longer.

Place the crab cakes on serving plates, garnish with plenty of lemon wedges, and drizzle the beurre blanc over the cakes.

TO DRINK: Chardonnay, Au Bon Climat
    Albariño, Fillaboa

CRAB AND RICE SALAD

SERVES 6 TO 8

This refreshing and luxurious dish combines our Gulf Coast jumbo lump crabmeat with a bit of lemony mayonnaise on top of rice salad flavored with roasted pepper, olives, and herb vinaigrette. Some sliced raw mushrooms add a nice contrast, and a few lettuce leaves complete the picture. Sliced avocados would add richness and make a more substantial salad. This salad also makes an elegant lunch.

1 pound jumbo lump crabmeat, picked free of shells
    and cartilage
2 tablespoons Lemon Mayonnaise (page 336)
    or substitute Hellmann's or Best Foods
Fresh lemon juice to taste
Kosher salt and freshly ground black pepper
1 heaping cup chilled cooked basmati rice
1 red bell pepper, roasted (see page 345), peeled,
    seeded, and cut into ½-inch squares
12 to 16 oil-cured black olives, such as Niçoise,
    pitted and cut in half
4 to 5 button mushrooms, trimmed and thinly sliced
2 scallions, thinly sliced
1 tablespoon flat-leaf parsley leaves
1 tablespoon torn basil leaves
2 tablespoons Sherry Vinaigrette (page 330)
Fresh lime juice, a few dashes of hot pepper sauce,
    such as Tabasco or Cholula, and/or a few tender
    sprigs of cilantro, minced (optional)
A large handful of small lettuce or herb leaves for garnish

Toss the crabmeat with the mayonnaise in a small bowl. Season with lemon juice and salt and pepper.

Place the rice in a medium bowl, add the roasted pepper, olives, mushrooms, scallions, parsley, and basil and toss to combine. Add the vinaigrette and season with salt and pepper and toss again. Taste and adjust the seasoning—you may want to add some lime juice and even a little hot pepper sauce or cilantro, depending on your taste.

Place a nice mound of the rice on each plate and top with the crabmeat. Garnish with the lettuces or herbs.

TO DRINK: Prosecco, Nino Franco
        Albariño, Fillaboa

SEARED TUNA WITH CELERY AND BUTTER PEA SALAD

SERVES 4

The contrasting textures of the buttery smooth tuna, the crunchy celery, and the earthy beans provide a tantalizing combination. Toasting the peppercorns and fennel seeds awakens their flavors and releases their deep aromas. Butter peas, a delicate shell pea somewhere between fresh black-eyed peas and butter beans, are a favorite choice, but canned chickpeas are a dependably good alternative. If truffles are unavailable, or not in the budget, substitute a julienne of button mushrooms with a drizzle of truffle oil.

Fresh black truffles are generally available from December to March. Try to find out ahead of time when your purveyor (see Sources, page 352) expects the next shipment of truffles to arrive, then purchase them the moment they come in. Their heady aroma begins to fade after just a few days. But frozen or canned truffles are always an acceptable alternative.

1½ teaspoons peppercorns

1 teaspoon fennel seeds

One 8-ounce piece of center-cut tuna loin, about 3 by 3 by 4 inches (see Note)

Kosher salt

2 teaspoons olive oil

FOR THE SALAD

2 celery stalks, cut lengthwise in half and sliced ¼ inch thick, leaves reserved for garnish

1 cup cooked butter peas (see recipe on page 15 for cooking instructions) or drained and rinsed canned chickpeas

1 red bell pepper, roasted (see page 345), peeled, seeded, and cut into ½-inch dice

One 1- to 2-ounce black truffle (see headnote) or 3 large button mushrooms, trimmed, cleaned, and cut into julienne strips

1 shallot, finely minced

Grated zest and juice of 1 lemon

Freshly ground black pepper

2 tablespoons extra virgin olive oil

1½ teaspoons red wine vinegar

1½ teaspoons black truffle oil, or more if desired

Toast the peppercorns and fennel seeds in a small skillet over medium heat just until fragrant, about 3 minutes. Transfer to a mortar and crush with the pestle, or crush under a heavy skillet. Spread the peppercorns and fennel seeds on a small plate. Roll the tuna "brick" in the spices and press with the heel of your hand so they adhere. Season the tuna with salt.

Heat a small heavy sauté pan over high heat. Add the olive oil and sear the tuna on all sides, 3 to 4 minutes total; it will still be very rare inside. Transfer the tuna to a rack set over a plate to rest.

To prepare the salad, combine the celery, peas, roasted pepper, truffle, shallot, and lemon zest in a medium bowl and season with salt and pepper. Toss with the extra virgin olive oil, vinegar, lemon juice, and truffle oil.

Slice the tuna crosswise into ⅛-to-¼-inch-thick slices and arrange like a sunburst in a circle on each of four serving plates. Place the salad in the center and garnish with the reserved celery leaves. Drizzle the tuna with any remaining dressing from the bowl, or a little extra truffle oil, if desired.

NOTE: You may need to order the tuna ahead. Ask the fishmonger to cut a rectangular "brick" from a "loin" of tuna.

TO DRINK: Vouvray, Champalou
Riesling, Domaine Weinbach Réserve Personelle

FRIED QUAIL WITH CORNMEAL CRUST AND SCRAMBLED EGG SALAD

SERVES 4

An unlikely marriage: the old southern standby of fried quail and an innovation on a Tuscan salad introduced to me by my friend Cesare Casella of Beppe restaurant in New York.

FOR THE QUAIL

½ cup all-purpose flour

½ cup cornmeal

Kosher salt and freshly ground black pepper

Cayenne pepper

1 large egg

½ cup buttermilk

4 boneless quail, legs and breast separated, rinsed and patted dry

Peanut oil for frying

FOR THE SALAD

2 thick bacon slices, finely chopped

4 large eggs, beaten

Kosher salt and freshly ground black pepper

2 cups mixed young lettuces

3 tablespoons Sherry Vinaigrette (page 330)

In a small bowl, combine the flour and cornmeal and season with salt, pepper, and cayenne; set aside. In a medium shallow bowl, beat the egg. Add the buttermilk and season with salt, pepper, and cayenne. Whisk thoroughly to combine. Place the quail in the buttermilk and let stand while you cook the bacon for the salad.

Heat a sauté pan over medium-high heat and cook the bacon until semi-crisp. With a slotted spoon, transfer the bacon to paper towels to drain. Set the pan aside.

Heat 1 inch of oil in a deep medium skillet over high heat until it reaches 350°F on a deep-frying thermometer. Remove the quail from the buttermilk and dredge in the flour mixture, shaking off the excess. Carefully drop the quail legs into the hot oil and fry, turning once, until golden, 3 to 4 minutes. With a slotted spoon, transfer to paper towels to drain. Add the quail breasts to the hot oil and cook, turning once, just until golden, about 3 minutes.

Transfer to the paper towels to drain.

Meanwhile, return the pan with the bacon drippings to the stove. Add the eggs, season with salt and pepper, and cook, stirring to scramble until just set. Remove from the heat.

In a medium bowl, toss the lettuces with the sherry vinaigrette and season with salt and pepper. Add the scrambled eggs to the salad and toss to combine.

Divide the salad among four plates. Place the quail atop the salads and finish with a scattering of crisp bacon.

TO DRINK: Pinot Noir, Saintsbury

Beaujolais, Morgon Breton

RABBIT LOIN SALAD

SERVES 4

Appetizers that combine a little meat with a distinctive salad are a delectable way to start a meal. Follow this appetizer with a seafood course or a hearty braise using the rabbit leg, or make a double portion for a luncheon main course. Walnut and truffle oils are two extraordinary staples, and we like the two combined here, but you could certainly use just one or the other. Truffle oil is all the rage these days, but it is often used excessively when just a few drops will do. Walnut oil is fragile and once opened will quickly turn from aromatic to rancid due to oxidation: Buy it in small bottles or tins, store it in the refrigerator, and once one is open, use it within a few weeks.

Ask your butcher to bone out the rabbit loins called for here and reserve the legs, shoulders, and flanks for another preparation, such as Rabbit Stuffed with Apple Duxelles (page 230). Or just order the loins from a specialty butcher or purveyor. If rabbit is unavailable (see Sources, page 352), you could substitute chicken-apple sausage, such as those readily available from Aidells (see Sources, page 352), for the loins, or use boneless chicken breasts cut into long strips.

4 boneless rabbit loins (see headnote)

3 tablespoons plus 1 teaspoon olive oil

1 whole thyme or marjoram sprig, plus 2 thyme or
    marjoram sprigs, leaves removed and chopped

Kosher salt and freshly ground black pepper

1 cup quartered mushrooms, such as chanterelle or cremini

1 large shallot, finely minced

2 tablespoons sherry vinegar

2 tablespoons walnut oil

2 teaspoons truffle oil

2 cups mixed lettuces, such as frisée, watercress, arugula,
    and radicchio

½ cup walnut halves, toasted (see page 346)

1 pear, quartered and thinly sliced

1¼ cups coarsely crumbled blue cheese

In a shallow dish, toss the rabbit loins with 2 teaspoons of the olive oil and the thyme sprig, and season with salt and pepper. Allow the rabbit to marinate for 10 to 20 minutes.

Heat a medium sauté pan over high heat, then add 2 teaspoons olive oil. Add the loins and sear over medium-high heat, turning once, until just golden, about 3 minutes per side. Transfer the loins to a rack set over a plate to rest. Add the mushrooms to the pan and sauté over medium heat for 2 minutes, or until they begin to release their moisture. Add half of the shallot, season with salt and pepper, and sauté for a minute more. Remove the pan from the heat, and cover to keep warm.

To prepare the vinaigrette, combine the remaining shallot, the chopped herbs, and sherry vinegar, and season with salt and pepper in a small bowl. Slowly whisk in the walnut and truffle oils and the remaining 2 tablespoons of olive oil. Taste and adjust the seasoning. Toss the lettuces with the vinaigrette.

Slice the rabbit loins on the diagonal. Mound the lettuces in the middle of each plate, and arrange the rabbit slices around the edges. Garnish with the mushrooms, walnuts, pear, and blue cheese. Drizzle any remaining vinaigrette over the rabbit slices.

TO DRINK: Chinon, Jouget
        Savennières, Domaine des Baumard

Granddaddy White never owned a tractor. He plowed walking behind mules until he was seventy years old. They were always big dark bay mules, and he had a kind of love/hate relationship with them. When my brother, David, and I were young, he would pull us along on a sled behind the mules, bumping over the terraced rows and across the field. I have a very clear memory of him walking up in the middle of the day, after he had been working for a few hours, bringing a mule around to the well by the farmhouse, and that mule would drink a whole bucket of water in no time. I loved to see and hear those hardworking mules slurp and practically inhale the clear well water.

My grandfather's use of mules was not born out of some hidebound allegiance to the old ways. He was a smart and efficient farmer who had won several awards from Auburn University for having the best cotton or corn or potatoes. I remember hearing stories about how, during the Depression, when a lot of people didn't have much to eat, my grandparents were fortunate enough to be able to feed anybody and everybody they could.

They always had a big vegetable patch, with beans planted between the corn so that they could climb up the stalks. There were always tomatoes and okra too, and sometimes asparagus. The garden was really my grandmother's domain—mules were forbidden, as was most anyone or anything else—but my grandfather was allowed access, for he, in his own quiet way, loved the garden as much as she did. And he contributed to the wealth of that garden by periodically spreading aged manure over the soil—rich from the mules and cows, stockpiled in the back of the barn for three or four years until it had reached its peak.

In addition to being a prolific gardener, my grandmother kept chickens and, periodically, guinea hens and quail. The guinea hens were very loud and squawked when anybody came up, but Grandmother loved fooling with those birds. "Little bitties, bitties, bitties, bitties," she called. For a short while they had a couple of pigs, and I would feed them the table scraps. And then there was the Jersey cow that Granddaddy would milk, allowing us to watch from a corner of the barn. I remember Grandmother churning the cream into butter.

There was a little potato house where my grandparents would store their root crops, and a corncrib where the crop was stored until they ground it up to feed the chickens. And there was an old smokehouse too.

When we were growing up, we would spend weekends on the farm. The house had a big swing on the porch, and during the summer we would spend hours out there rocking, trying to catch a breeze. Come wintertime, it would get so cold that Grandmother would put hot water bottles in our beds to warm us. Back then, she did her cooking on a coal stove, and she always made biscuits in the morning while listening to country music or gospel on the radio.

When I look back, my time on the farm seems idyllic. My grandparents valued their own products, their own produce, their own birds and pigs—they really weren't so sure about things that came from the grocery store. How could they trust something they hadn't raised with their own hands? I don't think I realized it then, but they taught me many of the values I now hold dear.

RAVIOLI WITH SWEET POTATOES, MUSTARD GREENS, AND COUNTRY HAM

SERVES 4

This version of ravioli could only be found south of the Mason-Dixon Line, yet I'd bet some northern Italians might claim it as their own. And, indeed, one of the most traditional tortelloni stuffings, made with autumn squash, is not too dissimilar to the sweet potato filling used here. Substitute a little wilted rapini and prosciutto di Parma for the greens and ham, and you'd think you were in Bologna.

FOR THE DOUGH (MAKES ½ POUND)
1¾ to 2 cups all-purpose flour
2 extra-large eggs
½ teaspoon extra virgin olive oil

FOR THE FILLING
½ cup mashed sweet potatoes (see Note)
1 cup ricotta, preferably fresh
½ tablespoon finely sliced chives
½ tablespoon chopped flat-leaf parsley

1 cup coarsely chopped mustard greens
1 tablespoon bacon fat or olive oil
1 ounce country ham or prosciutto, cut into julienne strips
Kosher salt and freshly ground black pepper
1 tablespoon unsalted butter
1 tablespoon freshly grated Parmigiano-Reggiano,
    plus extra for serving

Mound the flour on a large wooden board or marble slab to form a peak with a well in the center, like the crater of a volcano. Place the eggs and olive oil in the well and, using a fork, mix them together, gradually bringing in a little flour from the sides. Continue adding the flour gradually until the dough comes together and all the flour has been incorporated. Knead the dough, flouring the work surface as necessary, until it is smooth and elastic, 5 to 7 minutes; it still will be a bit sticky. Wrap it in plastic and refrigerate for 30 minutes to 1 hour.

Combine the mashed sweet potatoes, ricotta, and herbs in a bowl, stirring well to blend.

Remove the dough from the refrigerator and divide it into 4 equal portions. Roll each portion through your pasta machine from the widest to the thinnest setting, laying the ribbons of dough out on a floured work surface. Cut the dough into 4-inch squares. Place 1 tablespoon of filling in the center of each square, then moisten the outer edges of the square with a dampened fingertip. Bring the opposite corners together to form a triangle and press the edges together firmly to ensure a good seal.

Prepare an ice bath (see page 346). Blanch the mustard greens in a large saucepan of boiling water for 1 minute. Drain and transfer to the ice bath to stop the cooking. Drain well and squeeze dry, then chop. Set aside.

Bring a large stockpot of salted water to a boil. Meanwhile, heat the bacon fat in a small saucepan over medium heat until it melts (or heat the oil until hot). Add the mustard greens and briefly sauté to coat in the fat. Add the ham, stirring to incorporate, and season with salt and pepper. Remove from the heat and cover to keep warm.

Add the ravioli to the pot of boiling water and cook until tender, about 3 minutes. Remove the ravioli with a slotted spoon and add to the warm greens and ham. Add the butter and a small ladleful of the hot pasta water and gently toss until the butter is melted and incorporated. Taste and adjust the seasoning.

Transfer the ravioli and greens to a platter and sprinkle with the Parmigiano. Serve additional cheese and cracked black pepper at the table.

NOTE: Bake 2 sweet potatoes in a 375°F oven for 1 hour, or until tender. Peel and mash; reserve any extra for another use.

TO DRINK: Greco di Tufo, Feudi di San Gregorio
    Tocai Friulano, Schiopetto

A soup course is almost

always welcome. The simplicity of aromatic sweet vegetables slowly simmered with a fragrant chicken broth makes me very happy. Soups are a healthy way to transfer seasonal vegetables into soul-satisfying dishes. A summer variation on a Provençal *soupe au pistou*—chock-full of peppers, onions, new potatoes, zucchini, and tomatoes topped off with a pecan pesto—can be a perfect lunch or an ideal late supper. A winter "take" would incorporate more root vegetables—parsnips, carrots, sweet potatoes, turnips, and greens. And, if no *pistou* is available, a drizzle of the fruitiest olive oil is all you need. Seafood chowders are always a hit; just remember to use the freshest ingredients—this is not a time to incorporate something less than pristine. Another great tip to keep in mind is that a combination of bacon, potatoes, and onions happily complements almost any type of fish or shellfish. Just finish with a touch of cream.

Soups require time but little else—gentle cooking of something as simple as leeks, pumpkin, and potato with chicken broth—yet score a home run for the cook. As I mention in the following pages, a beef shank (or other shank) adds a depth of flavor unequaled by fancy ingredients. And a dollop of pecan pesto improves most any soup and just about everything else it might garnish.

Beef Shank and Vegetable Soup, page 103

CURRIED PUMPKIN SOUP

SERVES 8 TO 10

As this soup cooks, the kitchen will quickly fill with the tantalizing aroma of leeks stewing in butter with pumpkin, curry, and spices. Crabmeat Crostini (page 62) floated atop the soup adds a luxurious contrast to this humble but silky creation. Of course, the soup is also delicious served on its own.

2 tablespoons unsalted butter
2 onions, sliced
2 leeks, trimmed, cleaned, and thinly sliced
1 carrot, peeled and sliced
1 Granny Smith apple, peeled, cored, and sliced
1 tablespoon mild curry powder
¼ cinnamon stick, 2 cloves, and 3 allspice berries,
        tied in cheesecloth to make a sachet
1 pound butternut squash, peeled, seeded, and sliced
1 pound peeled pie pumpkin, sliced
1 sweet potato, peeled and sliced
6 cups water, preferably spring water
1 cup heavy cream
Snipped chives for garnish
8 to 10 Crabmeat Crostini (page 62)

Melt the butter in a large saucepan over medium heat. Add the onions, leeks, carrot, and apple and sauté over medium-low heat until the onions are translucent, about 15 minutes. Add the curry, spice sachet, and the remaining vegetables. Pour in the water and bring to a gentle simmer, for about 45 minutes, until the vegetables are very soft.

Remove the spice sachet and puree the vegetable mixture in a food mill. To give the soup a silky-smooth texture, pass through a fine-mesh strainer. Transfer the soup to a saucepan. Add the cream and taste and adjust the seasoning. Heat gently just until warmed through.

Ladle the soup into bowls and garnish with the chives and crabmeat crostini, floating one on top of each bowl.

TO DRINK: Riesling, Pikes Clare Valley

LATE-SUMMER TOMATO SOUP

SERVES 4

Ripe red apple tomatoes have to be summer's quintessential ingredient and as the season winds to a close, those last precious gems fresh off the vine are incomparably delicious in this simple soup—the pure essence of tomato. Be sure to allow the tomatoes to macerate with the salt for at least an hour before proceeding. Serve with tiny cubes of summer vegetables and a drizzle of the fruitiest of olive oils.

10 ripe tomatoes, cut into 8 wedges each
1½ garlic cloves, crushed
Kosher salt
3 tablespoons good-quality red wine vinegar such as
        the Spanish garnacha vinegar from L'Estornell
1 tablespoon sherry vinegar
1 teaspoon sugar
About 2 tablespoons extra virgin olive oil
Dash of hot sauce, such as Tabasco or Cholula
Four ¼-inch slices baguette
Freshly ground black pepper
2 small firm cucumbers, peeled, halved lengthwise, seeded,
        and cut into ⅛-inch dice
2 red bell peppers, cored, seeded, and cut into very small dice
½ red onion, cut into ⅛-inch dice
Slivered basil leaves for garnish

Place the tomatoes in a ceramic, glass, or stainless steel bowl and toss with the crushed garlic and 1 tablespoon salt. Cover and set aside at room temperature for 2 to 4 hours.

Pass the tomato mixture through a food mill (or puree in a food processor and then pass through a strainer) and return it to the bowl. Whisk in the vinegars, sugar, 2 tablespoons of the olive oil, and the hot sauce. Season to taste. Cover and refrigerate for 2 hours, or until very cold.

Preheat the oven to 350°F.

Place the bread on a small baking sheet and brush lightly with olive oil. Toast in the oven for 5 minutes, or until lightly golden. Season with salt and pepper.

In a medium bowl, combine the cucumbers, peppers, and onion.

To serve, ladle the soup into chilled bowls and place a crouton in the center of each. Place a mound of the vegetables on top of the crouton. Garnish with basil and drizzle with olive oil.

ROASTED CORN
AND CRAWFISH CHOWDER
SERVES 6

There is a fleeting spell somewhere between late spring and early summer when sweet yellow corn is just coming to market, and, simultaneously, the crawfish season is coming to a close. We take advantage of this short window by combining the two in this uncommon chowder. Small fresh shrimp or lump crabmeat would make fine substitutes for the crawfish. Roasting the corn deepens its flavor—even the cobs contribute to the broth—and the seafood adds a deceptive richness to what is really a light soup.

Fresh crawfish tail meat is one of Louisiana and America's great seafood ingredients. Crawfish tail meat is boiled picked crawfish with fat, the golden yellow essence, which enriches this sublime Cajun chowder.

4 ears corn, shucked

2 tablespoons unsalted butter

2 tablespoons olive or corn oil

2 leeks, trimmed, cleaned, and thinly sliced

2 medium sweet onions, such as Vidalia or Texas Sweets,
    finely diced

2 celery stalks, finely diced

2 garlic cloves, 1 minced, 1 crushed

2 bay leaves

A few thyme sprigs, plus 3 thyme sprigs, leaves removed,
    for garnish

A few basil stems, plus 6 basil leaves, thinly slivered,
    for garnish

2 cups Chicken Broth (page 339) or canned low-sodium broth

2 cups Seafood Broth (page 341) or 2 additional cups
    chicken broth

4 new potatoes, peeled and finely diced

½ to 1 pound crawfish tails (see Sources, page 352)

2 scallions, thinly sliced

Kosher salt and freshly ground white pepper to taste

Cayenne pepper to taste

2 tomatoes, seeded and diced

4 chives, thinly sliced, for garnish

Prepare a hot grill or preheat the broiler. Grill or broil the corn, turning occasionally, until blackened and charred, about 6 to 8 minutes. Cut the kernels off the corncobs, reserving the cobs, and set both aside.

In a large nonreactive casserole, heat 1 tablespoon of the butter and 1 tablespoon of the oil over medium heat. Add the leeks, onions, celery, and minced garlic and sauté until softened, about 10 minutes. Add the bay leaves, thyme, basil, and corncobs, reduce the heat, cover, and cook gently for 10 minutes.

Add the chicken broth and seafood broth, bring to a simmer, and simmer, partially covered, for 10 minutes. Add the potatoes and simmer, partially covered, for 20 minutes more or until tender. Remove from the heat.

Meanwhile, in a large sauté pan, heat the remaining 1 tablespoon each butter and oil. Add the crushed garlic and stir and toss until fragrant, 1 to 2 minutes. Add the crawfish tails, scallions, salt and white pepper, cayenne, and corn kernels and sauté for 3 minutes, or until just tender. Remove from the heat and cover to keep warm.

Remove the corncobs from the soup and scrape them with a knife over the pot to extract any juices. Taste and adjust the seasoning.

Divide the crawfish, corn, and tomatoes among six warm soup bowls, placing a mound of each in each bowl. Pour the broth over and garnish with the thyme, basil, and chives.

TO DRINK: Pinot Blanc, Etude
        Pinot Blanc–Pinot Gris, Au Bon Climat

When I was living in the South of France, after about ten days or so of rising at dawn to pick grapes, and after what seemed an eternity of backbreaking work fueled by snacks of cheese and bread and lunches in the fields, I had an Alabama epiphany. (There's nothing like being 4,791 miles away to give you a fresh perspective on home.) I began to ponder the cycle of life. Dirty and bone tired, I came to appreciate what it meant to be a cog in the harvest, what it meant to be attuned to the cycle of the seasons. I felt a connection to my home, to the farms of Cullman, Alabama. I felt this connection to the farmwork of mankind.

I admire the European tradition of the harvest festival, and I wish for the days when such festivals were still a part of our lives. I was born in the mid-1950s, in a transitional time, when the sense of pride in farming was slipping quickly away. The closest thing we had to the harvest festivals of Provence was the Cullman County Fair. That was the time for the judging of the jams and the jellies, the time to determine who had the finest steer and the best sheep. The fair mattered, but it was past its prime. My parents and I might have still marveled at the beauty of a pair of matched mules or the majesty of a Jersey cow, but in many ways, society had come to view such appreciations as vestiges of the past. My grandparents might have still cared about who put up the best blueberry jelly or the best fig jam, but, in large part, somewhere along the way our culture had lost its appreciation for the spiritual aspect of celebrating the bounty of the harvest.

But a few years back, just when I was on the verge of writing off the possibility that such celebrations could matter in modern-day Alabama, the farmers' market movement took hold here in Birmingham. And now, each Saturday during the summer, farmers from throughout the state offer just-picked fruits and vegetables for sale on the grounds of the old Dr Pepper syrup plant in the Lakeview neighborhood.

I've served on the board of directors for the market, and I have reaped many benefits from the association. I now see the Pepper Place Market as a center for a new kind of harvest celebration. On any given Saturday there might be a jazz band playing. Or a twangy country band. I've even heard bagpipers. And as the clerical workers, the doctors and lawyers, the waiters and bartenders, the teachers and children, mingle in the aisles, I've come to appreciate the market as a celebration in its own right.

What's more, I've come to believe that one of the roles of a chef today is to breathe new life into traditions. When the first peaches of the season arrive, I want trumpets to play. I want horns blasting. I want to see people dancing in the street when we harvest our first Alabama strawberries. I want people to herald their coming in the same way that the people of France celebrate the arrival of Beaujolais Nouveau. Come to think of it, that is what I see when I look across the Pepper Place parking lot on a Saturday morning. I hear music. I see dancing. I see people celebrating the bounty of the Alabama soil.

FIELD PEA AND OKRA SOUP

SERVES 10

When June arrives, so does an almost unending flow of fresh peas and beans at our southern farmers' markets. One of the best ways to enjoy them is in a simple soup—a healthy, inexpensive, and soul-satisfying meal with infinite variations. Here you could use butter beans instead of peas, or add sweet corn, or maybe a few pole beans or wilted greens. This particular combination came about when I stumbled upon the tiniest green "white crowders" that had been picked a little too early for optimum yield, which made them all the more delicate and savory to me. Instead of the pesto, or *pistou*, that garnishes soups in the Mediterranean, we finish this with a little herb-marinated diced tomato. Serve hot Corn Bread (page 26) on the side.

1 tablespoon olive oil

2 onions, finely diced

2 carrots, peeled and finely diced

2 celery stalks, finely diced

1 leek, trimmed (green top reserved for bouquet garni), cleaned, and finely diced

1 red bell pepper, cored, seeded, and finely diced

2 ears corn, shucked and kernels removed

Freshly ground black pepper

2 garlic cloves, 1 finely minced, 1 crushed

3 flat-leaf parsley sprigs, 3 thyme sprigs, 2 bay leaves, and reserved leek top, tied together to make a bouquet garni

2 cups field peas, such as crowders, pink-eyes, or lady peas (see page 251), rinsed

6 cups Chicken Broth (page 339) or canned low-sodium broth, or vegetable stock or water (preferably spring)

Kosher salt

1 cup sliced okra (1- to 2-inch-thick slices)

2 tomatoes, seeded and diced

4 sprigs marjoram, savory, or basil, leaves removed and torn into little pieces

1 tablespoon extra virgin olive oil

Heat the olive oil in a large casserole over medium heat. Add the onions, carrots, celery, leek, bell pepper, corn, season with pepper, and cook over medium-low heat for 5 minutes, or until the vegetables begin to soften. Add the minced garlic and cook for another 5 minutes, or until the garlic is fragrant and the vegetables are soft. Add the bouquet garni, peas, broth, and a good pinch of salt and bring to a simmer over medium-high heat. Skim any foam that rises to the surface and simmer gently, partially covered, for about 25 minutes.

Add the okra and cook for 5 minutes more. Taste and adjust the seasoning.

While the soup is simmering, combine the tomatoes, crushed garlic, herbs, and extra virgin olive oil in a small bowl and season with salt and pepper. Toss together and allow the flavors to marry for about 10 minutes.

Ladle the soup into warm soup bowls and place a small spoonful of the tomatoes in the center of each one.

TO DRINK: Bass Ale
Sierra Nevada Pale Ale

WATERCRESS AND
NEW POTATO SOUP

SERVES 6

Freshly picked watercress has a vibrant green color and peppery taste. I have childhood memories of gathering it in the wild from clear spring waters near my family home. Be sure to add the watercress only at the last minute—if you add it too soon, the color of the soup will fade to an unappetizing green.

Kosher salt and freshly ground white pepper

3 bunches fresh watercress, stems removed and washed,
    6 sprigs reserved for garnish

3 tablespoons unsalted butter

2 leeks, quartered, cleaned, and sliced

5 new potatoes, peeled, 4 thinly sliced, 1 diced

2 cups Chicken Broth (page 339) or water, preferably
    spring water

1 cup heavy cream

Bring 2 quarts of water to a boil in a large pot and add a couple of teaspoons of salt. Meanwhile, prepare an ice bath (see page 346). Toss the watercress into the boiling water and blanch for 1 minute, then drain and immerse in the ice water to shock. When it is cold, remove from the ice bath, squeeze dry, and finely chop.

Place one-third of the watercress in a blender, add ½ cup water, and puree until very smooth, 3 to 4 minutes. Set aside.

In a large casserole or stockpot, melt 1 tablespoon of the butter over medium heat. Add the leeks and cook over low heat for 10 to 15 minutes, until soft; do not let the leeks color.

Add the sliced potatoes and broth and bring to a simmer. Cover and cook gently for 30 minutes, or until the potatoes are very tender. Season with salt and pepper. The soup can be made a few hours ahead to this point. Cover and refrigerate, then reheat before proceeding.

Meanwhile, blanch the diced potato in a saucepan of boiling salted water until just tender. Drain and set aside.

Add the cream to the soup and bring back to a simmer. Add the chopped watercress and simmer for 3 minutes. Transfer the soup to a blender or food processor and blend until well pureed. Strain through a fine strainer, then return to the casserole and bring to a simmer. Cut the remaining 2 tablespoons butter into small cubes and swirl into the soup bit by bit. Pass the pureed watercress through a fine strainer into the soup, pressing hard to extract all of the green essence.

Divide the diced potato among six soup bowls and ladle in the hot soup. Garnish each serving with a sprig of watercress.

TO DRINK: Savennières, Château d'Epiré

BEEF SHANK
AND VEGETABLE SOUP

SERVES 6, WITH LEFTOVERS • PHOTOGRAPH PAGE 94

This quintessential winter soup combines a meaty broth—made from flavorful beef shank, prized for its rich marrow—with a load of seasonal vegetables. Accompanied by Corn Bread (page 26), this soup makes a substantial winter lunch or late supper. Embellish with a dollop of pecan pesto, our regional take on the beloved Niçoise standard. This flavorful pesto is also wonderful with pasta or served with Hoppin' John (page 9). Leftover braised beef shanks are fantastic mixed with a Sauce Gribiche (page 326) and served cold as part of a salad.

FOR THE BROTH

1 tablespoon olive oil

2½ pounds beef shank, in slices about 2 inches thick

1 onion, quartered

1 carrot, peeled and quartered

1 celery stalk, quartered

1 parsnip, quartered

1 turnip, quartered

5 thyme sprigs, 5 flat-leaf parsley sprigs, 1 bay leaf,
   and reserved leek top (from below), tied together
   to make a bouquet garni

2 quarts Chicken Broth (page 339) or canned low-sodium broth

FOR THE SOUP

1 tablespoon unsalted butter

1 medium onion, finely diced

3 carrots, peeled and finely diced

2 medium turnips, peeled and finely diced

1 leek, trimmed, cleaned, and finely diced

2 parsnips, peeled and finely diced

1 celery stalk, finely diced

FOR THE PECAN PESTO

2 garlic cloves

10 pecan halves, toasted (see page 346)

1 bunch flat-leaf parsley, leaves removed and finely chopped

2 tablespoons thinly sliced chives

2 tablespoons thyme leaves

2 tablespoons freshly grated Parmigiano-Reggiano

Grated zest of 1 lemon

Kosher salt and freshly ground black pepper to taste

¾ cup extra virgin olive oil

Heat the oil in a large stockpot over medium-high heat. Add the beef shanks and brown well on all sides. Add the vegetables, bouquet garni, and chicken broth, bring to a simmer, and simmer gently until the meat is tender, about 2 hours. Remove from the heat and strain the broth; reserve the meat. (The broth can be refrigerated for up to 3 to 4 days; refrigerate the meat separately.)

To prepare the soup, in a large casserole or stockpot, melt the butter over medium-low heat. Add the diced vegetables and sweat until tender, about 15 minutes. Add the beef broth and simmer gently to marry the flavors, about 20 minutes more.

Meanwhile, remove the shank meat from the bones, discarding the fat. Shred the meat and add it to the soup.

To prepare the pesto, with the pestle, grind the garlic into a paste in a mortar. Crush the pecans into the garlic paste, then add the parsley, chives, and thyme and grind them in. (If necessary, the pesto can be made in a small food processor.) Transfer to a bowl and stir in the Parmigiano, lemon zest, and salt and pepper. Sparingly add the olive oil. Taste and adjust the seasoning.

Ladle the piping-hot soup into large soup bowls and pass the pesto at the table for your guests to add to taste. Serve with corn bread.

TO DRINK: Valpolicella, Allegrini

Beaujolais, Côte de Brouilly Château Thivin

Salads are a window to the soul of a chef. They are about delicacy and restraint, about what's in season, about adding only what is vital, nothing extraneous. The quality and freshness of the ingredients are paramount to a superb salad. The subtle harmony and balance of the components say a lot about the chef. For me, the addition of a small handful of tender herbs for each serving adds a freshness that takes a salad from just ho-hum to downright spectacular. And when I stress a specific vinegar (or other acid)—L'Estornell's red wine vinegar, a Spanish garnacha vinegar with an exquisite punch; the distinctive sherry vinegar from Don Bruno; or a true aged balsamic vinegar—it is because acidity is of the utmost importance. Acidity is something that many Americans shy away from, but as cooking has become more sophisticated, we have come to appreciate the crispness and brightness it brings. Apple cider vinegar mixed with a little honey lends a sweet-sour essence to foods that is eye-opening. Vinegars from Banyuls add a portlike richness, and our southern cane vinegar adds a unique aroma that everyone enjoys.

Pardis and I have become accustomed to our backyard *potager,* or "little kitchen garden," and almost every family meal is highlighted by an excursion outdoors to gather a few sprigs of basil, dill, or mint, or a handful of the tiny but powerful leaves of selvetica arugula. Herbs and lettuces are the easiest of all the gardening enterprises, requiring the least amount of time and work, so I urge you to try and develop your own little patch outside your back door, or in a window box, or even in a few small pots on a fire escape, if that's all that space will allow.

Besides the tender little leaves from our home garden, I adore watercress, peppery and intensely green; frisée, with its pale white heart deepening to chartreuse green at the tips; and the crunchy hearts of romaine. These are the standbys of which I never tire. True Bibb lettuce, or Kentucky limestone, is another favorite, but we can rarely find it these days. The hydroponics and

{ **Poached Egg Salad with Red Wine Sauce, page 109**

Warm Cabbage Salad with Goat Cheese and Corn Bread Crostini, page 126

the huge-leafed variety do not offer much joy. Even though arugula has become rather ubiquitous,

I would be happy to have a daily plate of it dressed with a great olive oil and a splash of red wine

vinegar, and garnished with shaved Parmigiano-Reggiano or a chunk of creamy Fourme d'Ambert.

The small pickling or Kirby cucumbers, firm and crisp and picked before the seeds have

matured, as well as the thin-skinned Persian type, are our favorites. We peel them in zebra stripes, halve them lengthwise, and remove with a spoon any seeds that have developed. Thinly sliced and sprinkled with salt, these cucumbers are one of our preferred snacks and salad accompaniments.

Torn mint, tarragon, basil, or cilantro leaves, tender leaves of romaine, a slab of feta, and a few black olives tossed together and doused with a good vinaigrette is an all-time classic. Here are some of our other favorite salad accoutrements:

Slow-roasted pecans tossed with pecan or olive oil and aggressively seasoned
    with salt and freshly ground black pepper

Toasted walnuts tossed with walnut oil and generously seasoned with salt and pepper

Roasted beets, sliced or quartered, depending on size, doused with vinegar

Grilled red onions drizzled with extra virgin olive oil

Boiled new potatoes, halved or quartered, depending on size

Shaved radishes

Thinly sliced sweet carrots

Avocado slices with lime juice and salt

Shaved fennel

Lentils, chickpeas, and field peas, or shell beans

Leftover roasted lamb, chicken, beef, or fish

All of the above are worthy components for building a composed salad. Composed salads, as Richard Olney taught me, are one of the most useful of all dishes. Created from tasty bits of leftovers, they become meals that are standard fare for weekend lunches or late-night suppers. Keep your salad ingredients washed, dried, and chilled (except tomatoes) and toss everything with your homemade vinaigrette right at the table. Make salads a celebration.

WATERCRESS SALAD WITH SHAVED MUSHROOMS AND RADISHES

SERVES 4 • PHOTOGRAPH PAGE 70

My fascination with watercress began as a child, when my mother and I foraged each spring in the north Alabama hills, where bubbling springs provided the perfect environment for the peppery cress. At that time, in the mid-1960s, most of the lettuce available was shipped from California, so this locally picked green was almost magical to me. It has never lost its appeal. My mother would turn it into wonderful salads or layer it in sandwiches for lunches at our Cullman home. This is just one of many ways we showcase this Alabama gem at Highlands.

1 heaping tablespoon Pommery or other coarse-grain mustard
½ cup Sherry-Honey Vinaigrette (page 330)
2 small bunches radishes with tops, washed
½ cup thinly sliced firm button mushrooms
1 shallot, finely minced
Kosher salt and freshly ground black pepper
2 bunches watercress, tough stems removed, washed and dried
Herb blossoms, such as chive or thyme, for garnish

In a small bowl, whisk together the mustard and vinaigrette. Set aside 4 radishes with tops for garnish. Trim the remaining radishes and thinly slice them. Place the sliced radishes, mushrooms, and shallot in a medium bowl, season with salt and pepper, and toss with 1 tablespoon of the vinaigrette mixture. Set aside for 10 minutes.

Toss the watercress with the remaining dressing and divide it among four salad plates. Top with the sliced radishes and mushrooms. Garnish with the whole radishes and herb blossoms. Serve immediately.

VARIATION: Add a chunk of Humbolt Fog or other goat cheese or a wedge of blue cheese.

TO DRINK: Soave Classico Superiore, Pieropan
Arneis, Ceretto

SPRING LETTUCES WITH SWEET PEAS, CHIVES, DILL, AND MINT

SERVES 4 • PHOTOGRAPH PAGE 73

Herb leaves are a standout when used as a major component in a salad. Pile them on and mix them up—replace the dill with chervil or basil if it suits your fancy. Spring lettuces to try here include watercress, arugula, frisée, mâche, oak leaf, little Bibb, and romaine. Add cubes of mozzarella, wedges of feta, or matchsticks of Comté if you like.

1 heaping cup spring lettuce mix (see headnote), trimmed, washed, and dried
1 cup coarsely chopped herbs, such as mint, dill, chives, and parsley
½ cup sweet English peas, blanched in boiling salted water until tender, cooled in an ice bath, and drained
A few pea tendrils (optional)
¼ cup Sherry Vinaigrette (page 330)
Kosher salt and freshly ground black pepper

Combine the lettuces, herbs, peas, and pea tendrils, if using, in a large bowl and gently toss with the vinaigrette. Season with salt and pepper and serve.

VARIATION: Add some sliced boiled or steamed new potatoes and sliced scallions.

TO DRINK: Riesling, Domaine Weinbach
Riesling, Allan Scott

POACHED EGG SALAD WITH RED WINE SAUCE

SERVES 4 • PHOTOGRAPH PAGE 104

Every time I eat this salad, I am amazed by how delicious it is with its wine-drenched sauce full of smoky bacon, mushrooms, and garlic, and warm egg yolk that mixes with the tangy vinaigrette-tossed bitter lettuces. I prepare this dish with leftover red wine braising liquid, when I have it on hand. The next time you make the Red Wine–Braised Rabbit (page 228) or the Red Snapper with Ham Hock–Red Wine Sauce (page 161), save any remaining sauce for this salad. Or simply make the sauce from scratch (as in the recipe below) to create this elegant first course; it's also a great lunch or light supper.

FOR THE RED WINE SAUCE

1 cup red wine
¼ cup Madeira
1 shallot, finely minced
1 cup Beef or Chicken Broth (page 340 or 339) or
    canned low-sodium broth
8 tablespoons (1 stick) unsalted butter, cut into small pieces
Kosher salt and freshly ground black pepper
Drop of sherry vinegar

FOR THE EGGS

1 tablespoon white wine vinegar
Generous pinch of Kosher salt
4 large organic or "free-range" eggs

FOR THE SALAD

Six 1-inch-thick slices baguette, cut into 1-inch cubes
1 tablespoon olive oil
Kosher salt and freshly ground black pepper
½ cup cubed (1-inch) slab bacon
1 cup quartered mushrooms, such as cremini, button,
    or wild mushrooms
2 shallots, finely minced
2 cups mixed young lettuce, such as frisée, watercress,
    and oak leaf, trimmed, washed, and patted dry
¼ cup Sherry Vinaigrette (page 330)

To make the sauce, combine the red wine, Madeira, and shallot in a small saucepan, bring to a simmer over medium-high heat, and simmer until reduced by three-quarters. Add the broth and again simmer to reduce by three-quarters. Reduce the heat to low and whisk in the butter bit by bit. Season with salt and pepper and the vinegar. Remove from the heat and cover to keep warm.

Fill a medium to large saucepan with water. Add the vinegar and salt and bring to a boil over high heat, then reduce the heat to a simmer. Prepare an ice bath (see page 346). Break an egg into a saucer and gently slip it into the barely simmering water. With a slotted spoon, carefully pull the billowing egg white's edges toward the yolk. Add the remaining eggs in the same way, and cook until the whites are firm but the yolks are still soft, about 5 minutes. Remove the eggs with a slotted spoon and place in the bowl of ice water to stop the cooking. Carefully remove, pat dry, and set aside on a plate. Set the saucepan aside.

Meanwhile, preheat the oven to 400°F.

Arrange the bread on a baking sheet, drizzle with the olive oil, and sprinkle with salt and pepper. Bake for 3 to 4 minutes, until lightly toasted. Set aside.

In a large heavy sauté pan, cook the bacon until it has rendered much of its fat and is semi-crisp, about 6 minutes. With a slotted spoon, transfer the bacon to paper towels to drain. Add the mushrooms to the pan and sauté until just tender, about 3 minutes. Add the shallots and sauté for 30 seconds. Add the red wine sauce and heat through, then reduce the heat and simmer.

Reheat the egg poaching liquid. Carefully trim away any excess egg whites. Place the eggs in the simmering water for a few seconds, just to warm through. Remove the eggs with a slotted spoon and blot dry on a kitchen towel.

Meanwhile, toss the lettuce with the vinaigrette and mound it on four plates. Place a warm egg in the center of each, scatter the bacon and croutons about, and spoon the mushrooms and red wine sauce over all.

TO DRINK: Beaujolais, Côte de Brouilly Chanrion
    Pinot Noir, Au Bon Climat

Tomato season begins early in Alabama, and if we're lucky, it can sometimes last until the first frost of early November. Summer lunches on my own time consist of either a composed tomato salad or some assemblage of a tomato sandwich. I prefer firm, acidic varieties, much like the Italians, who hold a fondness for tomatoes with a streak of green underripeness showing through the skin. Over the years, commercially raised tomatoes in Alabama have been whittled down to a single variety, Mountain Pride, which is easy to grow, extremely prolific, easy to harvest, and able to withstand the bumps and bruises of shipment. The downside is that it is mediocre at best in terms of flavor. That is why we seek out the small pickup trucks at the farmers' market loaded with Better Boys, Early Girls, Atkinsons, German Pinks, Brandywines, and other tomatoes grown for their full flavor, as well as some of the so-called heirloom varieties. For me, many of the heirlooms, especially the yellow varieties, lack that spark of acidity that I favor. The other tomatoes I love are the cherries, especially Sweet 100s, Supersweet 100s, and Sunburst. Last year one of the best salads on our menu was called White Truck Tomato Salad, because we were directed to the best tomatoes in the market by a simple directive: "Go see that guy in the white truck down on the corner."

Small, firm pickling or Kirby cucumbers are a great accompaniment for any tomato salad or sandwich. Sea salt, freshly ground black pepper, and olive oil or mayonnaise are permanent players, and basil is often involved. Fresh mozzarella, feta, and mild fresh goat cheeses are always welcome. Sweet onions macerated in vinegar are an extra treat.

No tomato should ever have seen the inside of a refrigerator. When stored at below fifty degrees, a tomato's cellular structure begins to collapse and its aroma and flavor are severely compromised. Instead, line them up on a kitchen windowsill where you can bask in their cheery hue and will be enticed to include them in whatever you're preparing.

Old-fashioned Tomato Salad, page 114 ⟩

OLD-FASHIONED
TOMATO SALAD

SERVES 4 • PHOTOGRAPH PAGE 113

The old-fashioned salad I grew up with is a vinegary mix of tomatoes cut into chunks, with some sliced cucumbers and onions all tossed together with a little fresh dill. This presentation is just a bit more refined. Make this only when the ingredients are perfect, in July or August, and tomatoes and cucumbers are at their best. Choose varieties such as Brandywine, Big Beef, Atkinson, German Pink, or Green Zebra. Use small pickling-type cucumbers, such as Kirby or thin-skinned Persian. Avoid tomatoes that have been refrigerated—their flavor will have suffered substantially.

For a heartier version of this salad, add some blanched or boiled little green beans, tiny beets, and/or just-dug new potatoes.

2 small Kirby cucumbers, skin removed in wide zebralike stripes
Sea salt
1 small sweet onion, such as Vidalia, cut into thin rings
2 tablespoons cider-honey vinegar (2 tablespoons cider vinegar
    plus ½ teaspoon honey) or red wine or sherry vinegar
4 to 8 nice tomatoes—a variety of flavorful types in different
    colors, sizes, and shapes, cored and thickly sliced
About 1 cup cherry or grape tomatoes, preferably an assortment,
    halved
3 tablespoons finest-quality extra virgin olive oil
Freshly ground black pepper
A handful of fresh herbs, such as chives, dill, mint sprigs,
    and basil leaves coarsely chopped

If the cucumbers are small enough that the seeds have not fully developed, simply slice them thin. If the seeds are noticeable, cut the cucumbers lengthwise in half and, with a small spoon, remove the seeds; then slice. Toss with a good pinch of sea salt in a small bowl and place in the refrigerator to macerate for 15 minutes.

Meanwhile, toss the thinly sliced onion with 1 tablespoon of the vinegar in a bowl and refrigerate for 15 minutes. (Macerating the onion slices both crisps them and tames their pungency.)

Arrange the sliced tomatoes attractively on a large platter. Scatter the cherry tomatoes over and around them.

To serve, drain the cucumbers and squeeze to remove any excess liquid. Toss with the onion slices and scatter over the tomatoes. Drizzle over the remaining 1 tablespoon vinegar and the olive oil, season with salt and pepper, and toss the herbs over everything.

TO DRINK: Sancerre, Delaporte
            Sancerre, Reverdy

WALTER'S SALAD

SERVES 4

This composed salad was named for one of our dear friends, a larger-than-life character by the name of Walter Perry, who shared a striking resemblance to Ernest Hemingway. He had one of the greatest appetites for life, food, and drink that I have ever encountered. He fascinated me with his stories of dining at the famous Fernand Point in France in the 1950s. He would pontificate on the merits of starting the day with a Ramos gin fizz, or perhaps some old Chartreuse, which is probably how he began another quirky habit—using orange flower water as his standard cologne. Walter would arrive in his canary-yellow Lincoln convertible dressed to the nines—linen suit, Jermyn Street shirt, and Panama hat. He insisted on copious amounts of anchovy in his salads, and he was never one to hold back on the olive oil. We didn't dare think about slicing his onions thinly.

6 large ripe beefsteak tomatoes, cut into thick slices
8 slices fresh goat cheese, such as Montrachet
12 to 20 anchovies to taste, rinsed
1 large red onion, cut into thick slices and separated into rings
Sea salt and freshly ground black pepper to taste
½ cup extra virgin olive oil
2 tablespoons red wine vinegar
1 large bunch basil, leaves removed

Arrange the tomatoes on a large platter in a slightly over-lapping fashion to make an oval. Place the goat cheese down the center. Drape the anchovies over the tomatoes along the edges of the goat cheese. Scatter the onion rings on top. Season the salad with sea salt and pepper. Drizzle everything with the olive oil and sprinkle with the vinegar.

Just before serving, tear the basil leaves into large pieces and scatter about.

TO DRINK: A not-too-dry Bombay martini
Bandol Rosé, Château de Pibarnon

TOMATO SALAD WITH CORN BREAD, BACON, AND BUTTERMILK VINAIGRETTE

SERVES 6

July and August are the prime months for tomatoes in Alabama. Our local farmers find that Better Boys, old-fashioned Atkinsons, German Pinks, Brandywines, and red and yellow cherry tomatoes all do well in our hot, humid climate. This salad combines tomatoes with a few of our favorite southern ingredients—corn bread, bacon, butter-milk, and watercress.

2 thick slices bacon, cut into ¼-inch-wide strips
Corn Bread (page 26), cut into four 3-inch rounds
    (reserve the remainder for another use), or 4 slices
    sourdough bread, each cut into a 3-inch round
2 pounds beefsteak tomatoes, cut into thick slices
2 pounds cherry tomatoes, halved
¼ cup Sherry Vinaigrette (page 330)
Kosher salt and freshly ground black pepper
1 bunch watercress, trimmed, washed, and dried
2 small firm Kirby cucumbers, peeled in zebra stripes
    and thinly sliced
¼ cup Buttermilk Vinaigrette (page 331)

Preheat the oven to 250°F.

Cook the bacon in a medium skillet until crisp. Pour off the fat and reserve for another use, such as corn bread, if desired. Set the bacon aside in the hot skillet to keep warm.

Meanwhile, place the corn bread rounds on a small baking sheet and warm in the oven (or toast the sourdough bread).

Toss the tomatoes with the sherry vinaigrette in a large bowl, season with salt and pepper, and divide among four salad plates. Toss the watercress in the vinaigrette remaining in the bowl and place to the side of the tomatoes. Pile on the cucumbers. Place a corn bread (or sourdough) round on top of each salad, scatter the bacon around, and drizzle the whole salad with the buttermilk vinaigrette.

TO DRINK: Arneis, Giovanni
Vouvray, Pichot

SMOKED TROUT SALAD WITH BLOOD ORANGES, AVOCADO, AND FRISÉE

SERVES 4

Contrasting textures and colors collide with unctuous and bitter flavors in this winter salad: Meaty smoked trout and creamy avocado contrast with bright, tart blood oranges and crisp, slightly bitter frisée. We use pecan-smoked fillets, but Ducktrap Farms's (see Sources, page 352) is an excellent, fruitwood-smoked trout available nationally. Besides being rubylike fruit gems, the beautiful blood orange suprêmes are much more tart than navel oranges. That acidity really brightens up a salad. If blood oranges are unavailable, you can substitute navel oranges, but add a squeeze of lemon to the suprêmes.

2 smoked trout fillets, halved lengthwise and each half
    separated into 4 pieces
1 avocado, pitted, quartered, and peeled, and each quarter
    cut crosswise into 4 pieces
2 blood oranges, cut into suprêmes (see page 346;
    you will need 16 suprêmes)
¼ cup Sherry Vinaigrette (page 330)
Kosher salt and freshly ground black pepper
1 bunch frisée, trimmed, washed, and dried
1 small bunch watercress, tough stems removed,
    washed and dried

Place the smoked trout on a platter and place the avocado next to the trout. Put the blood oranges in a small bowl. Drizzle 2 tablespoons of the vinaigrette over everything and season with salt and pepper.

Combine the frisée and watercress in a bowl, toss with the remaining 2 tablespoons vinaigrette, and season with salt and pepper. Divide the greens among four salad plates. Encircle each salad with 4 pieces of smoked trout, 4 pieces of avocado, and 4 blood orange suprêmes, alternating them. Serve immediately.

TO DRINK: Riesling, Mosel Kabinett Fritz Haag
    Riesling, Trefethen

CORN BREAD PANZANELLA

SERVES 8

We offer a regional interpretation of this Italian salad, bringing golden, savory corn bread to a Mediterranean standard. The corn bread can be made a day or two in advance and kept in a plastic zipper bag. The vegetables can be prepared several hours ahead, but toss everything together just before serving.

1 red bell pepper

1 yellow bell pepper

1 recipe Corn Bread (page 26)

3 tablespoons red wine vinegar

2 tablespoons sherry vinegar

Kosher salt to taste

Freshly ground black pepper to taste

¾ cup extra virgin olive oil

6 tomatoes, halved, seeded, and cut into 1-inch chunks

1 small red onion, quartered lengthwise and thinly
      sliced crosswise

½ cup Kalamata olives, pitted and halved

2 Kirby cucumbers, peeled, halved lengthwise, seeded,
      and cut into ¼-inch-thick slices

½ cup loosely packed basil leaves

½ cup loosely packed mint leaves

½ cup loosely packed flat-leaf parsley leaves

Roast the red and yellow bell peppers directly on the burner of a gas stove over high heat, turning occasionally with tongs, until the skins are blackened, 10 to 12 minutes. (Or place on the broiler rack and broil, turning until charred.) Transfer the peppers to a bowl and cover tightly with plastic wrap. Set aside for 20 minutes to cool and steam (this helps separate the skin from the flesh).

Preheat the oven to 400°F. Cut the corn bread into ¾-inch cubes. Spread in one layer on a baking sheet. Toast until the edges are golden, about 10 minutes. Remove the sheet from the oven and allow the corn bread to cool.

When the peppers are cool enough to handle, peel them. Remove the stems and seeds. Cut the peppers into 1-inch squares.

Combine the vinegars and salt and pepper in a large bowl. Slowly whisk in the olive oil in a steady stream until thoroughly incorporated. Add the tomatoes, onion, and olives, tossing to coat. Marinate for 10 to 15 minutes.

Add the roasted peppers, cucumbers, basil, mint, and parsley to the tomatoes, tossing well. Add the croutons to the bowl and toss to moisten them evenly. Taste and adjust the seasoning. The salad should be bright with acidity from the vinegars. Serve immediately.

TO DRINK: Bandol rosé, Domaine Tempier
      Bandol rosé, Château de Pibarnon

I strive to serve food that celebrates the seasons, food that honors this day that we're alive, this moment in time. Here in the South—where spring comes so early and summer lasts so long, where fall blazes so bright and winter wanes so desolate—I have the perfect opportunity to educate our guests about the imperative of seasonality.

I want people to take comfort in a winter stew of oxtails, or an autumn rabbit stuffed with apples, or a distillation of springtime like soft-shell crabs with pea tendrils, brown butter, bacon, and shallots. That's the essence of the tale I tell through the food at Highlands.

I am a cook who really does ride the ebb and flow of the local market. Nowadays most people think nothing of buying grocery store tomatoes from Mexico, their fish shipped frozen from Chile. I believe that part of my role and responsibility is to reeducate people about what is seasonal, to say, by way of my cooking, "By God, you need to eat asparagus every chance you can for the month and a half when those green spears are at their peak!" I want to do the same thing with apples and pears and figs and watermelons and tomatoes and corn and okra.

There is a certain myopic quality to our cooking: We stay focused on what's truly seasonal. Sure, sometimes we have to cheat, but, at its best, our restaurant celebrates the first picking of a crop, whether it is just-dug creamer potatoes that taste of the earth or collard greens harvested after the first autumn frost, when they are at their sweetest. A large part of my job is knowing about availability. Growing up in rural Alabama, I came to know the seasonal cycle of crops. But finding the best crops is more about intellect. It's about having a produce Rolodex in my head. It's about having the intuitions of a farmer, about feeling the oncoming low-pressure front in my bones and knowing what that means for this week's pick of vegetables. I know when lady peas are at their peak, and I know that the full moon in August means the tomatoes will ripen more quickly. Conversely, I have to know when the beans are starting to play out, and when the best thing I can do for dinner is a ragout of new potatoes. It's about knowing seasons by way of crops.

Sweet potatoes and Concord grapes, butternut squash and pecans, signal the arrival of fall—not to mention pumpkins and late watermelons, and maybe just a few more artichokes. By December, the winter greens are flourishing: collard, mustard, kale, and turnip. In February, the shad run, and we serve all the shad roe we can get. And beets and turnips and other root vegetables. Ditto endive and sorrel. By late winter, maybe early spring, we will begin to get the first Vidalia bulbs.

My commitment to seasonality was informed by my time in France. At the markets in the South of France I observed a sense of hyper-seasonality, a kind of excitement among the townspeople about the debut of just-picked vegetables. Seeing that excitement gave me the confidence and enthusiasm to come back to Alabama and try to cook with that kind of commitment and enlightened passion. I resolved that if chefs could cook that way in France, I could cook that way in Alabama. I could help nurture our local gardeners and, along the way, educate my guests about the joys of seasonally focused cooking. Twenty years later, I'm still at it. If I have succeeded—and I believe that I have—then the credit must, in large part, be attributed to that produce Rolodex that turns in my head.

Autumn Beet Salad with Spiced Pecans, Pears, and Fourme D'Ambert, page 125

CURED DUCK SALAD

SERVES 4

The duck in this hearty salad is actually a duck confit, duck leg that is cured for two days in the refrigerator and then slowly cooked in duck fat until very tender. Here it is tossed with some crunchy green beans, walnuts, and shallots. Make your own duck confit (save the duck breasts for another meal, seared until medium rare and sliced over creamy grits) or buy prepared duck confit (see Sources, page 352).

FOR THE DUCK

4 duck legs, with skin, trimmed of excess fat, rinsed, and patted dry

¼ cup Kosher salt

6 juniper berries, toasted (see page 346) and crushed

6 peppercorns, crushed

2 thyme sprigs

2 garlic cloves, crushed

2 cups duck fat (see Sources, page 352)

FOR THE SALAD

6 shallots, cut lengthwise in half

2 tablespoons honey

1 tablespoon duck fat or olive oil

6 small white new potatoes, cut into ½-inch cubes, cooked in boiling salted water until tender, drained, and patted dry

½ cup walnut halves, toasted (see page 346)

1 cup green beans cut into 2-inch pieces, blanched in boiling water just until tender, cooled in an ice bath, drained, and patted dry

1½ teaspoons sherry vinegar

Kosher salt and freshly ground black pepper to taste

1 bunch watercress, trimmed, washed, and dried

1 tablespoon olive oil

4 thin slices sourdough bread, toasted

2 ounces soft goat cheese or farmer's cheese

Put the duck legs in a baking dish. Combine the salt, crushed spices, thyme, and garlic and rub all over the duck legs. Cover and allow to cure for 2 days in the refrigerator.

Preheat the oven to 200°F.

Melt the duck fat in a deep heavy skillet or casserole in the oven. Rinse the salt off the duck and pat dry.

Immerse the duck in the duck fat, cover, and cook for 3½ hours. Remove the duck from the oven and let cool. (The duck can be refrigerated, covered with its fat, for several days, or even weeks.)

Combine the halved shallots and honey in a small saucepan, add just enough water to cover the shallots, and bring to a boil. Reduce the heat and simmer until the shallots are tender and glazed, 5 to 6 minutes. Remove from the heat and set aside.

Remove the duck legs from the fat and pick the meat from the bones, discarding the skin (or reserve it for cracklin's; see page 26). Shred the meat into bite-sized pieces.

In a medium sauté pan, heat the 1 tablespoon duck fat over medium heat. Add the potatoes, walnuts, shallots, and duck meat and toss them in the fat until they are hot. Add the green beans, vinegar, and salt and pepper and taste for seasoning.

Toss the watercress with the olive oil. Spread the toasted bread with the cheese. Put a handful of watercress on each plate, flanked by a portion of cured duck salad, and top the salad with a crouton.

TO DRINK: Corbières rosé, Domaine de Fontsainte
Artadi Artazuri

AUTUMN BEET SALAD WITH SPICED PECANS, PEARS, AND FOURME D'AMBERT

SERVES 4 • PHOTOGRAPH PAGE 121

The autumn flavors of beets, pecans, and pears combine to make a salad we are happy to serve and eat from October through December. The sweetness of the beets and pears is offset by the strong blue cheese and tart vinaigrette.

FOR THE BEETS

4 small beets, stems trimmed, gently washed
Kosher salt and freshly ground black pepper
1 teaspoon extra virgin olive oil
Splash of red wine vinegar

¼-pound slab bacon, cut into 1-inch lardons (see page 218)

FOR THE SALAD

Scant 3 cups mixed lettuce, such as baby romaine, lolla rosso,
    and frisée, trimmed if necessary, washed and dried
Kosher salt and freshly ground black pepper to taste
3 to 4 tablespoons Sherry Vinaigrette (page 330)

2 Bartlett pears, quartered, cored, and thinly sliced lengthwise
½ cup Spiced Pecans (page 68)
Scant ¼ pound Fourme d'Ambert or other blue cheese,
    such as Roquefort or Stilton, cut into 4 wedges

Preheat the oven to 350°F.

Place the beets on a square of foil, season with salt and pepper, and drizzle with the olive oil and vinegar. Wrap them in the foil and bake until tender, 45 to 60 minutes. Allow them to cool, then peel and cut each beet into eighths.

Place the bacon lardons in a large pan and cook over medium heat until just rendered and barely crisp, about 4 minutes. Set aside and keep warm.

In a medium bowl, toss the mixed greens with the salt, pepper, and vinaigrette to taste.

Place a mound of salad on each plate. Scatter the beets, pears, lardons, and pecans around and arrange a wedge of cheese on each plate.

TO DRINK: Prosecco, Le Colture
       Spumante, Bellavista Franciacorta Cuvée Brut

WARM CABBAGE SALAD
WITH GOAT CHEESE
AND CORN BREAD CROSTINI

SERVES 4 • PHOTOGRAPH PAGE 106

This "wilted salad" comes from a tradition of tossing a variety of greens (or, as here, reds) with hot bacon fat and sizzling vinegar and serving them while still warm. Spinach is good served this way, but this cool-weather version is heartier, crunchier, and, with no spinach to clean, easy to make.

⅓ cup bacon lardons (1-by-1½-inch-thick strips)
   (see page 218)

1 tablespoon extra virgin olive oil, plus a little extra

3 garlic cloves, smashed with the side of a knife

1 dried hot chile pepper

2 cups very thinly sliced red cabbage

1 tablespoon sherry vinegar, or to taste

Kosher salt and freshly ground black pepper

4 Corn Bread (page 26) "planks"—4 inches long and
   about ½ inch wide (reserve the remaining corn bread
   for another use)

¼ cup soft fresh goat cheese, such as Coach Farms

¼ cup pecans, toasted (see page 346)

Preheat the oven to 425°F.

In a large sauté pan, cook the bacon in the 1 tablespoon olive oil over medium heat until it has rendered its fat but is not quite crisp, about 5 minutes. Remove the bacon with a slotted spoon and set aside to drain on paper towels.

Add the garlic cloves to the pan and cook until light golden and fragrant, about 1 minute. Toss in the chile pepper and sauté for 10 to 20 seconds, until the chile infuses the oil with its spice. Add the cabbage and sauté until just softened, 3 to 4 minutes. Add the sherry vinegar and toss, then season with salt and pepper. You may wish to add a little extra vinegar—the salad should be just a bit tart.

Meanwhile, drizzle the corn bread with a little olive oil and spread the goat cheese on top. Place the bread on a baking sheet and warm in the oven, about 3 minutes.

Remove the garlic cloves and chile pepper from the cabbage and discard. Mound the cabbage on four salad plates. Add the bacon and pecans to the hot pan and toss over high heat until sizzling, then quickly scatter over each salad. Garnish with the corn bread crostini.

TO DRINK: Gewürztraminer, Kuentz-Bas
   Pinot Gris, Trimbach

ARUGULA SALAD WITH RED ONION AND PARMIGIANO-REGGIANO

SERVES 4

Ever since I first tasted arugula, I've been hooked. Travels to Provence and Italy fueled my love for this spicy green, which now has a strong presence in our home garden. *Rucola selvetica* is a variety to search out, although it is slower growing than others and not nearly as prolific; I adore its intensely peppery bite and dense texture.

1 shallot, finely minced
3 tablespoons balsamic vinegar
1 tablespoon red wine vinegar
Kosher salt and freshly ground black pepper
1/2 cup extra virgin olive oil
1 red onion, sliced into rings about 1/2 inch thick
2 large bunches arugula, trimmed, washed, and dried
1/2 cup *each* of watercress, Bibb lettuce, and frisée,
    trimmed, washed, and dried (optional)
4 ounces Parmigiano-Reggiano, shaved into shards
    with a vegetable peeler

To make the vinaigrette, in a small bowl, combine the shallot with the vinegars, a pinch of salt, and pepper to taste and let macerate for 15 minutes. Slowly whisk in the olive oil. Taste and adjust the seasoning.

Heat a medium skillet over high heat until hot. Add the onion and cook, turning once, until charred and just tender, about 4 minutes on each side. Transfer to a plate to cool.

Combine the arugula, mixed lettuces, and charred onion in a bowl and season with salt and pepper. Toss with the vinaigrette and divide among four salad plates. Scatter some of the Parmigiano over each serving.

TO DRINK: Arneis, Ceretto
    Sauvignon Blanc, Honig

FIG AND PEANUT SALAD WITH ARUGULA AND MINT

SERVES 4

Unexpected companions, figs and peanuts are exceptional together in this salad dressed with raspberry vinaigrette and mint. This is one of those creations that splendidly combine many different textures—the crunch of peanuts, the plumpness of figs, and the mix of tender, sweet, and peppery greens. Serve this delectable salad before a course of grilled lamb or pork.

12 ripe black, brown, or green figs
1 shallot, finely minced
1 scallion, finely chopped
8 mint sprigs, 4 finely chopped, 4 left whole
1 tablespoon raspberry vinegar
1/4 cup peanut oil
Kosher salt and freshly ground black pepper
1 bunch arugula, trimmed, washed, and dried
1 head Bibb lettuce, cored, washed, and dried
3/4 cup raw peanuts, toasted (see page 346)

Cut off the fig stems and discard. Slice each fig crosswise into 4 or 5 slices and set aside.

Combine the shallot, scallion, chopped mint, and vinegar in a small bowl. Whisk in the peanut oil and season with salt and pepper.

In a large bowl, toss the greens with the vinaigrette. Arrange the salad on plates and top with the figs and peanuts. Garnish with mint sprigs.

TO DRINK: Prosecco, Nino Franco

FISH & SHELLFISH

Sautéed Red Snapper with Sweet Pea and Fava Bean Pilaf, page 159 }

Highlands is famous

for its seafood—which surprises many people since Birmingham is an inland city. We are the first stop for seafood trucks coming up from Panama City, Destin, Bayou La Batre, and Bon Secour—the areas of the Gulf that are our summer playgrounds. One supplier comes up every Tuesday and Friday, another provides our Wednesday shipment, and another arrives every Saturday. This almost daily activity is akin to trading stocks and bonds. We are in the enviable position of being able to pick only the very freshest seafood every day. When Highlands first opened, we shocked many purveyors because a third to a half of what we received was returned as subpar quality. If the seafood did not shine, we would simply change the menu that day and focus on something else. That remains our philosophy, and we still return a considerable amount of fresh fish and shellfish that does not meet our standards. Our purveyors may not always agree, but they respect our passion.

We are motivated by the seasonality of the Gulf Coast fishing industry. When we hear that the cobia are making their run along our coast, we jump to showcase cobia in the most spectacular ways we can, because we know that its appearance is fleeting. The same holds true for so many other varieties that may appear for a time, wane as another species makes its appearance, and then return again. That means we go with the flow. We create our menu around the most pristine, impeccable fish we can get our hands on. This should hold true for the home cook as well. Be willing to adjust your game plan. If you're planning a dinner party around salmon, but your fishmonger says that the red snapper is just in and is some of the freshest he's seen—go with it, improvise your menu around it, and always make a point to choose the freshest, best fish you can get.

I love shellfish—little clams, mussels, oysters, shrimp, crawfish, and scallops—and I love cooking them. We often combine a bit of shellfish with a small portion of fish—a great but doable extravagance. Frogmore stew, seafood pirlau, paella, and bouillabaisse are dishes I treasure. One common mistake is incorporating too many ingredients, so be confident that a few impeccable ingredients are better than several average ones.

I feel great after having fresh seafood for dinner. I am convinced that I sleep better and am a little clearer headed the next day—of course, this could be an index of consuming less red wine. . . .

SEAFOOD PIRLAU

SERVES 4

The ragouts of rice called "pirlaus" are a specialty of the South Carolina Lowcountry, originating from a time when rice was the basis of the local agriculture. Pirlaus are simple, old-fashioned rice stews made with anything from vegetables to chicken to this seafood one with shrimp, clams, scallops, and grouper. While similar to paella—both can be made with limitless combinations of meats, shellfish, and vegetables—pirlau is typically soupier, often includes stewed meats, and has never known a thread of saffron. This pirlau showcases the freshest shellfish and fish, but feel free to include some sausage, ham, or seasoned vegetables as well.

2½ cups Chicken Broth (page 339) or canned low-sodium broth
12 medium to large shrimp, peeled and deveined, shells
    reserved for stock
1 cup basmati rice
3 tablespoons olive oil
2 tablespoons unsalted butter
1 large onion, finely diced
2 celery stalks, finely diced
1 red bell pepper, cored, seeded, and cut into 1-inch squares
2 to 3 slices bacon, finely diced and cooked just until crisp
    (optional)
2 garlic cloves, finely chopped
1 bay leaf, 1 thyme sprig, 1 basil sprig, and 1 flat-leaf parsley
    sprig, tied together to make a bouquet garni
1 dried hot chile pepper
4 tomatoes, peeled, seeded, and chopped (or substitute one
    14-ounce can tomatoes, seeded and chopped)
Kosher salt and freshly ground black pepper
Four 3-ounce pieces grouper or other firm fresh fish fillet,
    skin removed
4 dry-packed scallops (see Note)
8 small littleneck clams, scrubbed
½ cup dry white wine
1 tablespoon chopped flat-leaf parsley
A few basil leaves, torn
½ lemon

In a medium saucepan, bring 2 cups of the broth to a simmer. Add the reserved shrimp shells and cook for 10 minutes. With a slotted spoon, remove the shells from the pan and add the rice. Stir with a wooden spoon, cover, and cook over low heat until the rice is tender and most of the liquid has been absorbed, 15 to 18 minutes. Transfer to a large shallow bowl and cover to keep warm.

While the rice is cooking, heat 1 tablespoon each of the olive oil and butter in a large sauté pan over medium heat. Add the onion, celery, bell pepper, and bacon, if using, and gently cook until the vegetables are softened, about 10 minutes. Raise the heat to medium-high, add the garlic, and cook for 2 minutes, or until aromatic, stirring frequently. Add the bouquet garni, chile, and tomatoes, stir thoroughly, and cook for 5 minutes more to marry the flavors. Remove the bouquet garni and chile, season with salt and pepper, and set aside.

Heat 1 tablespoon of the olive oil in a Dutch oven over medium heat. Sear the fish pieces on both sides until the edges just begin to turn opaque but the fish is not cooked through, about 2 minutes per side. Transfer to a rack set over a platter. Increase the heat to high and sear the scallops, turning once, until the edges just begin to turn opaque, about 1 minute per side. Transfer to the rack with the grouper. Add the clams and white wine to the Dutch oven and bring to a hard boil. Add the shrimp, cover, and cook until the clams open and the shrimp are firm, about 4 minutes. Discard any clams that have not opened.

Add the fish and scallops, the tomato mixture, and the rice to the dutch oven, along with the remaining ½ cup broth and any juices that have accumulated on the platter. Toss in the remaining 1 tablespoon each butter and olive oil to enrich the sauce. Add the parsley, basil, and a big squeeze of lemon and gently warm, stirring to combine. Serve in shallow bowls.

NOTE: Scallops are often soaked in a preservative solution of tripolyphosphate to prolong shelf life, but this treatment causes them to lose both their own juices and their sweetness. Avoid these scallops if possible and instead seek out "dry-packed" scallops or diver scallops, neither of which is treated with preservatives—both are available at good fish markets.

TO DRINK: Soave, Gini
      Mâcon-Villages, Louis Jadot

OYSTER PAN ROAST
WITH CRAWFISH
AND BUTTERY CROUTONS

SERVES 4 AS AN APPETIZER

Although I often bake or fry oysters, I always return to the pan roast because there is a savory plumpness to the naked oysters heated until hot through and through. I cannot resist including a healthy portion of shallots, garlic, butter, lemon, and herbs, along with my cherished little crawfish tails (see Sources, page 352). In lieu of crawfish, substitute lump crabmeat or boiled and chopped shrimp (or cooked tiny shrimp). This dish comes together very fast, so have your guests seated at the table when you begin preparation.

5 tablespoons unsalted butter

2 shallots, finely minced

2 to 3 garlic cloves, crushed and finely minced

¼ cup dry white vermouth

16 to 20 oysters, shucked (see page 347) and every bit of their
    liquor reserved and strained, or ½ pint shucked oysters,
    drained, liquor strained and reserved

¼ pound fresh crawfish tailmeat (see headnote)

Kosher salt and freshly ground black pepper to taste

Juice of 1 lemon

Hot sauce, such as Tabasco or Cholula, to taste

8 slices crustless French baguette, toasted and buttered

Scant 1 tablespoon sliced chives

1 heaping tablespoon flat-leaf parsley leaves

1 heaping tablespoon chervil leaves

In a large nonreactive saucepan, melt a scant tablespoon of the butter. Add the shallots and garlic and cook over medium-low heat until aromatic and soft, about 1 minute. Add the vermouth and bring to a hard boil. Add the oysters, their liquor, and the crawfish, lower the heat to medium, and cook for about 2 minutes, turning the oysters over as they firm and curl.

Add the salt and pepper, raise the heat, and swirl in the remaining 4 tablespoons butter bit by bit. Add the lemon juice. Add the hot sauce and remove from the heat. Place the croutons in shallow bowls and immediately spoon the pan roast over, dividing the oysters evenly. Garnish with the fresh herb leaves and serve.

VARIATION: For additional seafood flavor, add 12 littleneck clams and steam for 2 minutes before adding the oysters.

TO DRINK: Chardonnay, Arcadian
        Champagne, Krug

FROGMORE STEW

SERVES 6

Somewhere between Charleston and Beaufort, South Carolina, there was a little community called Frogmore, which no longer exists. As my friend Hoppin' John Taylor describes in his superb book *Hoppin' John's Lowcountry Cooking*, this stew was a popular local feast in Frogmore. It is one of those great party dishes that gets everyone in a celebratory mood. Like an oyster roast or crawfish boil, the stew is usually served outside, with plenty of paper towels, lots of beer and wine, and uninhibited eating. It is packed full of corn on the cob, shrimp, spicy sausages, and whole crabs. We like the addition of garlic, tomatoes, new potatoes, and quartered sweet onions. In the Lowcountry, Wadamalaw Sweets, which are similar in mildness to Vidalias, would be the onion of choice.

3 tablespoons crab boil seasoning, such as Old Bay,
    or pickling spice (see Notes)
1 tablespoon Kosher salt
1 sweet onion, such as Vidalia, cut into 6 wedges
1 head garlic, halved crosswise
12 new potatoes, scrubbed and halved
4 tomatoes, seeded and chopped
1½ pounds andouille sausage (such as Aidells;
    see Sources, page 352), cut into 2-inch lengths
9 ears corn, shucked and halved
3 live blue crabs, cleaned and halved (see Notes),
    or 1 live lobster
3 pounds large to medium shrimp (in the shell)
Several thyme sprigs
1 small bunch basil, leaves removed

In a large stockpot, combine the crab boil seasoning, salt, onion, and garlic. Add 6 quarts water and bring to a boil over high heat. Toss in the potatoes and tomatoes, reduce the heat slightly, and cook for 10 minutes. Add the sausage, corn, and crabs and continue cooking at a gentle boil for 5 minutes (if using lobster, boil for 8 minutes). Add the shrimp and cook until they curl, about 4 minutes more. Drain in a colander, reserving the broth, if desired, for another use (such as chowder, fish soup, etc.). Mound the stew on a big platter and garnish with the thyme and basil.

NOTES: If you can't put your hands on Old Bay or another crab boil seasoning blend, create your own pickling spice: Combine 1 tablespoon mustard seeds, 1 tablespoon fennel seeds, 1 tablespoon coriander seeds, 1 teaspoon celery seeds, 2 star anise, 2 tablespoons black peppercorns, 2 scant tablespoons broken dried hot chile peppers, and 6 bay leaves. Wrap in a small square of cheesecloth and tie with kitchen twine. Remove at the end of cooking.

To clean a live crab, with either a steady hand or a pair of sturdy tongs, hold the crab firmly from the backside with its claws pointing away from you. Use caution, because crabs will quickly pinch you if given the chance. With calculated confidence and a gloved hand, twist off and remove the claws. Then pull the "apron," the taillike flap lying flat against the underside of the crab, up and back in order to pop off the "back," or top shell, of the crab. Cut the crab in half lengthwise and remove the gills. Rinse, and you are ready to cook. If you prefer, you can cook the crab whole in boiling water for two minutes before cutting and cleaning.

TO DRINK: Sancerre, Jolivet
    Ice-cold beer

When we talk about crab, we're talking about blue crab. These "beautiful swimmers" thrive all along the Gulf Coast, up and around Florida, and all the way to the Chesapeake Bay and beyond. At their most fragile, they come to us in their soft-shell stage, just after they have molted and left behind their old, calcified shells. Soft-shells are very vulnerable and once caught must be put in cages separate from hard-shells to prevent them from being eaten. Cleaned and cooked, soft-shells can be eaten in their entirety: Don't miss out on their goodness—eat every last bite. But do plan on eating them the day you purchase them, as they are extremely perishable.

The bulk of the blue crab catch, however, is hard-shells. The harvest hits its peak as the waters begin to warm in the spring, usually around April, and continues through the late fall, when the waters cool. There is a specific nomenclature for different kinds of crabmeat. At the top of the pecking order is "jumbo lump," which, as its name suggests, consists of the largest nuggets of crabmeat. It is luxurious and expensive—perfect for salads or sautéing to garnish fish—and by far the ultimate. "Lump crabmeat" consists of smaller shreds of crabmeat that require very careful picking over to remove the little fragments of shell and cartilage. Though not as beautiful as the large nuggets of the jumbo crabmeat, lump crabmeat is fine for crab cakes or for blending with jumbo lump to stretch it. "Claw meat" is basically shell-free crabmeat that comes from the picked claws. This meat is darker in color with a great flavor, perfect for sautéing or for crab cakes, and a good option for mixing with jumbo lump when cost is a concern. "Claw fingers" are the claws with part of the shell and the cartilage attached. They are typically fried as an appetizer or marinated, as we do, and served as part of a seafood platter, or on their own with a ginger sauce. The crabmeat and most crabs sold commercially have already been cooked. In Alabama and

Louisiana, live blue crabs are cooked in large pots of boiling water, while in Florida they are steamed. I do not have a strong preference either way as long as they're fresh.

Keep in mind that crabmeat is very perishable and should smell fresh and appetizing, not strong or loud. Use fresh crabmeat the day you buy it if you can; if not, keep it packed in ice. We have our own little rhythm at the restaurant—the crab is cooked on Tuesday at the coast, and we receive it Wednesday, to have fresh crab for the rest of the week. In ideal conditions, it will keep, packed in ice, for seven days. But, if you've ever tasted truly fresh, just-caught crab, you know it'll be eaten up long before then.

TOMATO AND CRAB TOWERS

SERVES 4 AS AN APPETIZER

There is a little drama in the presentation of these stacked towers and probably a little fear in the cook's heart that the architectural masterpieces may tumble, but using larger tomato slices on the bottom as a foundation and adding smaller slices as you ascend makes these savory columns of tomatoes and crabmeat in a lemony herb mayonnaise structurally sound. Alternate different kinds of tomatoes, such as Green Zebras or other varieties, with beefsteaks for contrast, and garnish with some tiny cherry tomatoes. Toss the tomatoes with a little sherry vinaigrette. We like to scatter a few micro-greens around the outside, but watercress, mâche, or arugula works just as nicely. You can use shrimp or lobster in place of the crabmeat, or, for a vegetarian version, sliced avocado.

3 large ripe tomatoes, cut into 1/3-inch-thick slices

8 cherry or grape tomatoes, quartered

1 shallot, very finely sliced

1/2 cup Sherry Vinaigrette (page 330)

Kosher salt and freshly ground black pepper

1/2 pound jumbo lump crabmeat, picked free of shells
    and cartilage

Grated zest and juice of 1/2 lemon

2 tablespoons mayonnaise, such as Hellmann's or Best Foods

4 chives, finely sliced

6 basil leaves, thinly slivered

A large handful of micro-greens, watercress, mâche, or arugula,
    trimmed if necessary, washed, and dried

You will need a total of 12 slices of tomato for the towers: 4 large ones for the bottom, 4 slightly smaller ones for the middle layer, and 4 slightly smaller ones for the top. Set these aside, and reserve the remaining slices for another use.

Combine the 12 tomato slices, cherry tomatoes, and the shallot in a bowl and toss with the vinaigrette and a pinch each of salt and pepper.

In another bowl, combine the crabmeat, lemon zest and juice, mayonnaise, chives, and basil, mixing with your fingers but being careful not to break up the larger lumps of crabmeat.

Arrange the 4 largest tomato slices on four plates. Top each with a dollop of crabmeat, spreading it with the back of a spoon to almost cover the tomato. Place 4 slightly smaller tomato slices on top and gently steady them so they are stable. Top with the remaining crabmeat and then with the last tomato slices. Scatter the cherry tomatoes around the towers. Toss the baby lettuces in the vinaigrette remaining in the tomato bowl and sprinkle them around the outside of the plates.

TO DRINK: Grüner Veltliner Federspiel, R. Pichler
    Tocai, Schiopetto

SOFT-SHELL CRAB
WITH BROWN BUTTER
AND BACON VINAIGRETTE

SERVES 4 AS AN APPETIZER • PHOTOGRAPH PAGE 140

After months of being without these heavenly creatures, we look forward to each spring, when the first soft-shell crabs appear. Their limited season and fragility make them an especially appreciated treat. In our kitchens, we're involved in an ongoing debate about the best preparation: sautéed or fried. The vote seems to lean toward fried, but I'm still on the fence. When it comes to delicacy and straightfor-ward purity of flavor, the sautéed crabs reign. But no matter how they're prepared, we love serving them on a bed of lamb's quarters—a vividly green and supremely mild weed, if you will, that pops up everywhere mid-spring and is a glorious partner to our warm bacon and brown butter vinaigrette. This combination of nutty brown butter, vinegar, and shallots makes for the perfect accompaniment to soft-shell crab—or any other shellfish, or fish, for that matter. You can substitute mâche or watercress for the lamb's quarters, if necessary.

FOR THE VINAIGRETTE (MAKES ¾ CUP)
½ cup Brown Butter (page 338)
2 shallots, finely minced
2 ounces apple-smoked slab bacon, cut into ½-inch cubes
1 tablespoon balsamic vinegar
1 tablespoon sherry vinegar
Juice of ½ lemon, or to taste
Kosher salt and freshly ground black pepper to taste

2 tablespoons clarified butter (see page 347)
½ cup all-purpose flour
Kosher salt and freshly ground white pepper
4 soft-shell crabs, cleaned (see Notes, page 138)
1 loosely packed cup lamb's quarters (or substitute mâche, watercress, or even flat-leaf parsley leaves)

To make the vinaigrette, heat the brown butter until hot. Pour into a small bowl, add the shallots, and let stand for 10 minutes.

Meanwhile, cook the bacon in a small skillet until crisp. Transfer to paper towels to drain.

In a small bowl, combine the vinegars, lemon juice, and salt and pepper. Slowly pour in the brown butter and shal-lots, whisking constantly until emulsified. Taste and adjust the seasoning, adding more salt and pepper or lemon juice as desired.

Preheat the oven to 200°F.

Heat a heavy sauté pan just large enough to hold the crabs in a single layer over high heat, then add the clarified butter. Meanwhile, in a shallow pan, season the flour with salt and white pepper. Dredge the crabs in the flour, shaking off any excess. When the pan is almost smoking, carefully put the crabs in belly side down, lower the heat to medium-high, and cook until light golden on the first side, 3 to 4 minutes. Turn over and cook 4 minutes more, or until golden. Transfer the crabs to a paper towel–lined platter and keep warm in the oven with the door ajar.

Pour out the excess butter from the pan, add the vinai-grette and bacon, and warm over high heat. Arrange a small bed of the lettuces on each of four serving plates and place a crab belly side up on each. Ladle a little of the warm vinaigrette over each.

TO DRINK: Chardonnay, Landmark
Chardonnay, Neyers Napa

PANFRIED SOFT-SHELL CRABS
WITH ALMONDS
AND LEMON BUTTER

SERVES 4 AS AN APPETIZER

Sweet, with a briny, true sea flavor, soft-shell crabs are one of the sea's greatest gifts to the table. I feel mighty lucky to be in such close proximity to these coastal gems. It makes cooking and eating them that much easier. The slivered almond, lemon, and butter sauce we serve with these pan-fried crabs may be a bit retro, but it has stood the test of time.

1 cup all-purpose flour
Kosher salt and freshly ground white pepper
Cayenne pepper
4 soft-shell crabs, cleaned (see Notes, page 138)
1 tablespoon clarified butter (see page 347)
8 tablespoons (1 stick) unsalted butter, cut into 1-inch pieces
2 shallots, finely minced
¼ cup white wine
1 tablespoon chopped flat-leaf parsley, plus parsley sprigs
    for garnish
Juice of 1 lemon, or to taste
½ cup slivered almonds, lightly toasted (see page 346)

Preheat the oven to 200°F.

Season the flour with salt, white pepper, and cayenne and spread in a shallow pan. Dredge the crabs in the flour, shaking off any excess.

Heat the clarified butter in a large sauté pan over medium-high heat. Panfry the crabs, in batches if necessary, turning once, until golden on both sides, about 6 to 8 minutes total. Transfer the crabs to a baking dish and place in the oven to keep warm while you prepare the sauce.

Wipe out the sauté pan and melt 1 teaspoon of the butter over low heat. Add the shallots and sauté briefly just to soften. Add the white wine, bring to a simmer over medium-high heat, and reduce by half. Reduce the heat to low and whisk in the remaining butter piece by piece. When all the butter has been incorporated, add the chopped parsley and lemon juice, and season with a little salt and white pepper. Taste and adjust the seasoning, adding more lemon juice if necessary.

Place the soft-shell crabs on a platter and spoon the sauce partially over each crab and then around them. Garnish with parsley sprigs, sprinkle with the almonds, and serve.

TO DRINK: Puligny Montrachet, Domaine Etienne Sauzet
    Les Combettes
    Rully, J. M. Boillot

The warm waters of the Gulf Coast are teeming with an amazing array of sea life. Freshwater marshes and rivers join and mix with the sea, creating pools of differing salinity and unique ecosystems. Mobile Bay and Apalachicola Bay, in particular, are natural hatching grounds for shrimp, crab, speckled trout, red snapper, grouper, and redfish. Old ships and scrap metal—an inland junkyard—are dragged out into the bay to create a barrier reef that, over time, becomes encrusted with barnacles, providing refuge for all sorts of sea creatures. It is from these waters that most of the fish we serve at Highlands come.

The Gulf is a magical place. Virtually every summer, usually in late August, a strange phenomenon called Jubilee occurs in the bay near the city of Fairhope, Alabama. Conditions have to be just right—overcast skies, winds out of the east, predawn darkness, a rising tide—but when they are, the oxygen-poor bottom waters rise up and push toward the shore, trapping all sorts of bottom dwellers such as flounder, blue crab, shrimp, and others in it. The fish and shellfish caught in this wave of water gasp and struggle at the surface for the oxygen the water lacks and in doing so slow down considerably. As soon as residents realize the event is occurring, shouts of "Jubilee, Jubilee!" can be heard in the middle of the night. Locals come out to pick up the land-bound fish with gigs and buckets. The fish that don't get caught head back to the murky depths after sunrise when, just as strangely, the water conditions return to normal.

We love the variety of the fish caught off this stretch of coast, fondly referred to as the Redneck Riviera. It's about the freshness and flavor of the fish as much as it is about the people who bring it to us. Lee "Fish," as we've come to call him, has been our crab and shrimp supplier for many years. He is from Bayou Le Batre, Alabama, a town that remains, at its very core, a fishing village with some three hundred shrimp boats trawling the waters off this spur of the Fort Morgan peninsula.

Lee deals in perishable commodities at a time when overseas competition is taking its toll on the U.S. shellfish industry. Pond-raised shrimp are being shipped from Asia to the States in record numbers. Inexpensive though they may be, they are also highly processed, and their healthfulness has come into question. Warm breeding ponds are ripe for bacterial growth, and the shrimp live in their own waste. Add to that the assorted chemicals pumped into the ponds to keep bacteria at bay and then the soaking of the shrimp in tripolyphosphate to preserve them during transport and temperature fluctuations. The shrimp absorb so much of the preservative that a pound of shrimp that has gone into the preservative weighs quite a bit more when it comes out—and you pay for it. Europe banned such preservative-treated seafood due to health concerns, and large U.S. grocery chains moved in to take the seafood at a much-reduced cost.

At Highlands, we serve only the freshest Gulf or East Coast shrimp, dry-packed scallops, (see Note, page 135), and wild fish from purveyors, such as Lee, whom we know and trust.

Today's Gulf fishermen also feel the squeeze from the booming tourist industry. While the seasonal occupants of these coastal towns love to eat the fishermen's catch, many favor limiting commercial fishing access along the coastline in a misguided effort to curtail boating traffic and support recreational fishermen. As developers continue to snatch up prime oceanfront property to satisfy the demand for time-shares and second homes, the commercial fishermen have been pushed aside. What folks are unable to see is that the fishermen are also conservationists, ecologists, and trustees of sorts. As it is they who rely on fish for their livelihoods, it is in their best interests to do their part to make sure the ocean remains healthy, the catch abundant, and the industry strong for future generations of fishermen. Some years back Paul Prudhomme created a craze for the dish he christened "blackened redfish"; the resulting demand for redfish was so great that it soon became overfished. So fishermen backed off and moved on to other varieties, and today the redfish has returned stronger than ever.

Highlands supports local fishermen by buying their catch. We know our suppliers and they know their sources. Lee, for instance, can tell you if a fish is "A Grade," meaning it has been held between thirty-two and thirty-eight degrees Fahrenheit from the moment it's caught until it reaches the retailer. Lee says that all fish are more or less created equal; it's the dealer who changes the grade based on his or her handling of it. Rely on visual cues of freshness as well. Really fresh fish should have a sheen—a shiny translucence—almost like a lacquer. "Fish look either happy or sad, bright or dull," says Lee. If the fish is cut into fillets, the flesh should spring back when lightly pressed. Don't be turned off by a fish that smells like fish. But if it has a disagreeable or ammonialike scent, move on. Try experimenting with different varieties too. What's "in" on restaurant menus today will be "out" tomorrow, and some trash fish or junk fish—those the fisherman tosses back because there is no market for them—have gotten their bad rap for all the wrong reasons. Mullet, for instance, have more than a bad name—they're also ugly to look at. Yet, when caught in the clear waters off the sandbars of the Gulf, they taste as good as the handsomest of fish.

Keep an open mind and expand your palate. Go to the fish market with the objective of buying the freshest fish, not a predetermined species. Buy what looks to be the brightest, shiniest, and freshest of the catch and then develop your menu accordingly. Keep in mind that the market with the most options is not necessarily the best—in fact, if your purveyor has only a couple of types of fresh fish, that's OK—he has probably been selective. Also, keep in mind the seasonality of seafood. Everything has both its best and its less than ideal time—never hesitate to ask your fishmonger questions.

FLOUNDER
WITH BREAD CRUMBS
AND SAUCE GRIBICHE

SERVES 4

A fresh fish fillet lightly coated with slightly coarse home-made bread crumbs and carefully sautéed until golden brown, the fish encased in crispness, light, perfectly moist, and juicy has got to be one of my favorites—and is one of the Highlands signature dishes. Flounder is the ideal fish, but speckled trout also is sublime, and most any other thin white fish fillets will work well. Serve the fish simply, with no other distraction. Precede it with a crab or shrimp salad or a vegetable gratin. End with a rich dessert, perhaps a Strawberry Milk Shake (page 292).

1 cup all-purpose flour

2 large eggs

1½ cups medium-coarse bread crumbs (see page 347)

Four 6- to 7-ounce flounder fillets

Kosher salt and freshly ground white pepper

1 tablespoon clarified butter (see page 347) or 1 tablespoon
    olive oil plus ½ tablespoon unsalted butter

Lemon wedges

Generous ¼ cup Sauce Gribiche (page 326)

Spread the flour in a small shallow pan or dish. Beat the eggs with 1½ teaspoons water in another small shallow pan or dish. Spread the bread crumbs in another narrow pan. Season both sides of the fillets with salt and pepper and dredge them in the flour, dusting off the excess. Dip the fillets one at a time into the eggs, coating both sides, then place on the bread crumbs and toss some of the crumbs over the fish; turn and press lightly so that the crumbs adhere. Place on a baking rack or pan.

Heat a large heavy sauté pan over medium-high heat, then add the clarified butter (or oil and butter). Once it is very hot, add the flounder skin side down. Reduce the heat to medium and cook until golden, about 4 minutes (do not turn too soon). Turn and cook until just opaque through-out, 3 to 5 minutes, depending upon the thickness; do not overcook. Transfer to a pan lined with paper towels, then transfer to a warm platter. Garnish with lemon wedges and pass the sauce at the table.

TO DRINK: Chablis, Savary

FLOUNDER WITH LADY PEA SUCCOTASH

SERVES 4

The delicacy of flounder fillets is complemented here by the tiny, tender, pale green lady peas, which are the most delicate of the pea world. The addition of lots of basil, dill, and chives to this nontraditional succotash makes a very simple dish very special. If lady peas are not available, substitute favas or sweet peas.

FOR THE SUCCOTASH

1/2 small red onion, cut into 1-inch-thick slices

1 cup cooked lady peas (or substitute pink-eyes, crowders, or cranberry beans; see the recipe on page 15 for cooking instructions), 1/4 cup pot liquor from the peas reserved

2 tomatoes, seeded and cut into 1/4-inch dice

2 ears corn, husked, boiled for 4 minutes, and kernels cut off the cob

1/2 small shallot, finely minced

4 basil leaves, torn into small pieces

4 sprigs dill leaves, coarsely chopped

A few chives, finely chopped

1 tablespoon sherry vinegar

Kosher salt and freshly ground white pepper to taste

3 tablespoons extra virgin olive oil, plus extra for drizzling if desired

FOR THE FLOUNDER

Four 6- to 8-ounce flounder fillets, skin on or skinless

1 tablespoon vegetable oil, such as canola

1 lemon, cut into wedges

To make the succotash, prepare a hot grill or preheat the broiler. Grill or broil the onion slices, turning once, until lightly charred on both sides, 3 to 4 minutes per side. Let cool, then cut into 1/4-inch-dice.

In a large bowl, combine the charred onion, peas, tomatoes, corn, shallot, basil, dill, and chives. Stir in the sherry vinegar and season with salt and pepper. Stir in the olive oil, taste, and adjust the seasoning. Set aside.

To prepare the fish, heat a heavy skillet just large enough to hold the fillets over medium-high heat. Season the fish with salt and pepper. Add the oil to the hot skillet and heat until shimmering. Reduce the heat to medium, place the fillets skin side up in the skillet, and cook until nicely golden on the first side, 3 to 4 minutes. Carefully turn the fish and cook until just done, another 3 to 4 minutes. (Peek inside one fillet to check for doneness—the thickest part should have turned to pearly white.) While the fish finishes cooking, add the succotash and pea pot liquor to a sauté pan and cook over medium heat until heated through. Transfer the fish to serving plates and serve with the succotash and the lemon wedges. Drizzle each fillet with a splash of olive oil if desired.

TO DRINK: Tocai Friulano, Schiopetto

Grüner Veltliner Smaragd, Prager

FLOUNDER WITH CLAM CHOWDER SAUCE

SERVES 4

We have an incredible source for Apalachicola flounder—Greg Abrams Seafood in Panama City, Florida. The fish are "gigged" instead of caught in a net, the more common method of fishing. Net-caught fish are often tumbled about from the net to the boat, bruising the delicate flesh. But gigged fish are sought out during the night with big flashlights, speared with a three-pronged "gig," and immediately iced for travel back to land. We usually receive them the very next day and affectionately refer to them as "stiff as a board," based on their impeccable freshness and resultant firmness. Greg's fishermen are especially proud of the superbig ones (six to eight pounds), described in the local vernacular as "big as a doormat." Any impeccably fresh firm-fleshed white fish, sole, halibut, or cod, will suffice for this dish.

The clam chowder sauce is a take on the comforting soup, which we have lightened here and made especially attractive by the addition of lots of bright green celery. The key to ensuring the vibrant color is to add the celery at the very last moment.

12 littleneck clams, well scrubbed and rinsed

2 tablespoons unsalted butter

1 shallot, finely minced

Several thyme sprigs

1 cup white wine

½ cup heavy cream

2 Yukon Gold potatoes, peeled, cut into ¼-inch dice, and cooked in boiling salted water just until tender

1 tablespoon vegetable oil

Four 6- to 8-ounce flounder fillets, skin on

Kosher salt and freshly ground white pepper

12 lardons (1-by-½-inch strips) apple-smoked bacon (see page 218)

A small handful of flat-leaf parsley or chervil sprigs, leaves removed

4 small celery stalks, peeled, cut into ¼-inch slices, and blanched in boiling salted water for 30 seconds

In a medium saucepan, combine the clams, 1 tablespoon of the butter, the shallot, and thyme and cook over medium heat, stirring occasionally, until the shallots are slightly softened and aromatic, about 2 minutes. Add the wine, cover tightly, and give the pan a good shake, then steam the clams until they open, about 6 minutes. With a slotted spoon, transfer the clams to a bowl and cover to keep warm. Strain the broth through a fine strainer or cheesecloth-lined sieve and reserve ¾ cup broth for the sauce.

In a medium saucepan, combine the reserved broth, the cream, and potatoes. Bring to a boil and reduce by half. Remove from the heat and cover to keep warm while you prepare the fish.

In a large sauté pan, heat the oil and the remaining 1 tablespoon butter until quite hot. Season the flounder with salt and white pepper and add skin side up to the pan. Reduce the heat to medium and cook until the edges of the fillets begin to lighten and the flesh is lightly golden on the first side, 3 to 5 minutes. Turn and cook until just opaque throughout, 3 to 5 minutes longer, depending on the thickness of the fillets.

While the flounder is cooking, cook the bacon in a sauté pan over medium heat until it has rendered its fat and is slightly crisp, about 5 minutes. Transfer to a paper towel to drain.

Add the clams, bacon, and parsley to the sauce and warm over low heat. At the last moment, add the celery, ladle the sauce into large wide bowls, and top with the flounder.

TO DRINK: Muscadet, Chereau-Carré

GRILLED COBIA
WITH BEET RELISH

SERVES 4

Cobia is a harbinger of spring along the Gulf Coast. Big, fast, and strong, these are prized sport fish. They usually run just off the second sandbar only a hundred yards off the shore and when the water turns warm in late March and early April, we look forward to this firm, white, mild-tasting fish appearing on the menu.

James Huckaby, avid fisherman, dear friend, and the former chef de cuisine at our sister restaurant Chez Fonfon, came up with this unusual relish of beets, celery, radish, cornichons, and walnuts. It's a perfect example of how some seemingly disparate ingredients, thoughtfully combined, can lend a subtle yet flavorful punch to delicate fish.

FOR THE RELISH
1 cup cooked diced (about ½-inch) beets (see Note)
½ cup diced (about ½-inch) radishes
½ cup thinly sliced celery
½ cup diced cornichons
¼ cup walnut halves, toasted (see page 346)
¼ cup packed leaves plus 1 tablespoon chopped
    flat-leaf parsley
1 tablespoon thinly sliced chives
1 shallot, finely minced
2 tablespoons sherry vinegar
1 tablespoon fresh lemon juice
½ cup extra virgin olive oil
Kosher salt and freshly ground black pepper

FOR THE COBIA
Four 8-ounce cobia fillets (or substitute grouper or
    wild striped bass, or swordfish or tuna steaks)
1 tablespoon extra virgin olive oil, plus extra for drizzling
Kosher salt and freshly ground white pepper

Prepare a hot grill. Oil the grill rack.

Meanwhile, prepare the relish: Combine the beets, radishes, celery, cornichons, walnuts, parsley, chives, shallot, vinegar, and lemon juice. Stir in the olive oil. Season with salt and pepper. Set aside.

Place the fish on a plate and rub both sides with olive oil. Season with salt and white pepper. Grill until the edges begin to turn opaque, 5 to 6 minutes. Turn and grill until just cooked through, about 5 minutes more; do not overcook: The fish should be between medium-rare and medium, or it will be dry.

Arrange the fillets on serving plates. Top with a large spoonful of the relish and a drizzle of olive oil.

NOTE: You will need 2 cooked medium beets. To bake them, trim and wrap in foil. Bake in a 350°F oven for about 1 hour, until tender. Let cool, then peel.

TO DRINK: Reisling Smaragd, Freie Weingärtner

SEA BASS IN FIG LEAVES WITH RATATOUILLE AND HERB AÏOLI

SERVES 4

Fig trees are inherently beautiful to me, and I love their scent when brushing up against the branches to harvest the fruit. Wrapping fish in fig leaves imparts a subtle herbaceous aroma as they grill and keeps the fillets remarkably moist. When you serve them, the lightly charred leaves fill the room with a haunting fig scent that is the essence of late summer. Try fresh (organic) grapevine leaves if fig leaves are not available.

Generous ¼ cup Aïoli (page 337)
1 heaping tablespoon *each* chopped basil, chives,
    and flat-leaf parsley
Four 7- to 8-ounce sea bass fillets (or substitute loup de mer,
    grouper, or snapper)
Kosher salt and freshly ground white pepper
4 large fresh (unsprayed) fig leaves, washed and soaked in
    water for 10 minutes (see headnote)
2 tablespoons unsalted butter, at room temperature
2 tablespoons olive oil
Ratatouille (page 264), at room temperature or gently warmed

Prepare a hot grill.

Combine the aïoli and herbs in a small bowl; set aside.

Season the sea bass fillets with salt and white pepper. Lay the fig leaves veined side up on a work surface and brush with the butter. Place a fillet in the center of each one. Fold the sides of each leaf over, fold up the bottom, and roll up, tucking in any loose edges, to make a tightly sealed package.

Brush each packet generously with olive oil and grill for 4 to 5 minutes per side. (Make a slit in one packet and peek inside: The fish should be just opaque throughout.) Transfer to a rack set over a platter to rest for a few minutes.

Place the ratatouille in the center of four dinner plates. Tear away some of each fig leaf to expose the sea bass, leaving it just partially wrapped, and place the fish alongside the ratatouille. (Serving the fish in the fragrant leaves makes a striking presentation, but they are not meant to be eaten.) Garnish the fish with the herb aïoli.

TO DRINK: Greco di Tufo, Feudi di San Gregorio
    Fiano di Avellino, Feudi di San Gregorio

SLOW-ROASTED GROUPER WITH HAM AND PUMPKIN PIRLAU

SERVES 6 • PHOTOGRAPH PAGE 156

Grouper comes in many varieties: yellow-edge, red, snowy, and black, to name a few. However, the Gulf of Mexico black grouper, fished from Louisiana to Tampa, with Panama City as the fishing epicenter, is our hands-down favorite. We serve the grouper with pirlau, an old-fashioned rice stew that originated in the Lowcountry of South Carolina. Pronounced "pur-loo" or, equally correctly, "pur-loh," its name may have been derived from the word *pilaf*. Start with the pirlau and while it's cooking, prepare the fish.

2 tablespoons unsalted butter
1 tablespoon olive oil
Six 6- to 8-ounce grouper fillets, skinned
Kosher salt and freshly ground white pepper
Ham and Pumpkin Pirlau (page 259)
1 lemon, cut into wedges

Preheat the oven to 275°F.

Heat a large heavy ovenproof sauté pan over medium heat. Add 1 tablespoon of the butter and the oil and heat until hot. Season the fish with salt and white pepper, slip it into the hot pan, and turn the heat to low. After 2 minutes, turn the fish over, add the 1 tablespoon remaining butter, and place in the oven. Once the butter has melted, baste the fillets and cook until just barely done—the flesh should be opaque and firm, but still moist, about 10 minutes, depending on the thickness. Transfer the fillets to a rack set over a platter to rest briefly and cover loosely to keep warm.

Meanwhile, reheat the pirlau if necessary.

Place a mound of pirlau on each plate and top with a fillet. Give each fillet a big squeeze of lemon and serve.

TO DRINK: Châteauneuf-du-Pape blanc, Domaine du
    Vieux Télégraphe
    Condrieu, Cuilleron

SLOW-ROASTED GROUPER WITH ROOT VEGETABLE, WALNUT, AND PARSLEY SALAD

SERVES 4 • PHOTOGRAPH PAGE 129

For many years, we relied on our hickory-burning grill to cook grouper; its firm, meaty texture makes grilling a breeze (more delicate fish can stick to the grill or fall apart). Recently, however, we have employed an unusual cooking technique with superb results. We sear one side of the fish over medium heat, then turn it and place the pan in a "slow" oven, about 250°F. The fish come out incredibly moist, tender, and delicate.

Note that it's important that the vegetables for the salad be cut to a uniform small dice to ensure even cooking—and an attractive presentation.

1 tablespoon Kosher salt
2 parsnips, peeled and cut into ½-inch dice
2 carrots, peeled and cut into ½-inch dice
2 turnips, peeled and cut into ½-inch dice
¼ rutabaga, peeled and cut into ½-inch dice

FOR THE VINAIGRETTE
1 shallot, finely minced
2 tablespoons white wine vinegar
1 teaspoon fresh lemon juice
Kosher salt and freshly ground black pepper to taste
7 tablespoons olive oil
2 tablespoons walnut oil

FOR THE GROUPER
Four 6- to 8-ounce black grouper fillets (or substitute swordfish, salmon, or wild striped bass)
Kosher salt and freshly ground white pepper
1 tablespoon olive oil
⅔ cup walnuts, toasted (see page 346)
1 cup flat-leaf parsley leaves, plus a few extra for garnish

Preheat the oven to 250°F.

To prepare the root vegetables, bring a medium saucepan of water to a boil. Prepare an ice bath (see page 346). Add 1 tablespoon salt to the boiling water, add the parsnips, carrots, and turnips, and blanch until just tender, 4 to 5 minutes. With a slotted spoon, transfer the vegetables to the ice bath to stop the cooking. Add the rutabaga to the boiling water and blanch until tender, 12 to 15 minutes. Meanwhile, with the slotted spoon, transfer the vegetables from the ice bath to a towel and pat dry. Refresh the ice bath with more ice.

While the rutabaga is cooking, prepare the vinaigrette: Combine the shallot, vinegar, lemon juice, and salt and pepper in a medium bowl. Whisk in the olive oil and the walnut oil. Taste and adjust the seasoning. Set aside.

When the rutabaga is tender, drain and transfer it to the ice bath to cool. Drain, transfer to the towel, and pat dry.

Season the fish with salt and white pepper. Heat an ovenproof skillet just large enough to hold all the fish over medium-high heat. Add the olive oil and heat until hot. Add the grouper and cook until lightly colored on the first side, about 3 minutes. Turn the fish over and place the skillet in the oven to finish cooking, until just barely opaque throughout (it will continue cooking a bit as you serve it).

To serve, place the fish on a warm serving platter. Toss the diced vegetables, walnuts, and parsley with the vinaigrette and scatter over and around the grouper. Finish with a sprinkle of parsley leaves.

TO DRINK: Grüner Veltliner Smaragd, Prager
Chablis, Raveneau

GRILLED GROUPER WITH ARTICHOKE–CHARRED ONION RELISH

SERVES 4

When I make my own late-night dinner, I probably prepare a version of this recipe more often than any other. I never tire of pairing impeccably fresh fish with a relish of grilled marinated vegetables. The relish is easy to prepare if you have leftover steamed artichokes on hand.

FOR THE GROUPER

Four 8-ounce black grouper fillets

1 tablespoon extra virgin olive oil

1 heaping tablespoon *each* chopped flat-leaf parsley, basil, and mint

Kosher salt and freshly ground white pepper

FOR THE RELISH

2 fresh firm artichokes

½ lemon

Kosher salt and freshly ground black pepper to taste

4 mint or thyme sprigs

About ½ cup extra virgin olive oil

2 red onions, cut into ½-inch-thick slices

1 garlic clove, crushed

1 tablespoon chopped mint, parsley, basil, or thyme

2 tablespoons sherry vinegar

1 shallot, finely minced

Chopped mint, parsley, basil, or thyme for garnish

Place the fish in a baking dish, drizzle with the olive oil, and sprinkle with the herbs. Cover and let marinate for 30 minutes to 1 hour.

To trim the artichokes, pull off the tough outer leaves of each one and cut off the stem. Cut off the top two-thirds of the artichokes. Then cut away all the dark green at the base of each one until you come to the pale green artichoke heart. Rub all cut areas with the lemon half and transfer to a bowl of cold water. Squeeze the remaining juice from the lemon into the bowl to acidulate the water and keep the artichoke hearts from turning brown.

Bring a small pot of water to a boil and add a small handful of salt, along with the mint sprigs and artichokes. When the water comes back to a boil, turn down the heat to a simmer and cook for about 20 minutes. Test for doneness by piercing an artichoke heart with a paring knife: It should be tender. Drain and let cool.

When the artichokes are cool, scrape out the fuzzy chokes with a teaspoon. Slice the artichokes into thin slices and toss with a little olive oil.

Meanwhile, prepare a hot grill or preheat the broiler. Grill or broil the onion slices, turning once, until charred on both sides, 3 to 4 minutes per side. Let cool.

Chop the grilled onions. Rub the inside of a small bowl (terra-cotta is great for this) with the crushed garlic. Add the chopped onions, herbs, vinegar, shallot, and salt and pepper. Stir in ½ cup olive oil, add the artichoke slices, and toss to coat.

If not grilling the fish, preheat the broiler or heat a heavy cast-iron skillet. Season the fish with salt and white pepper. Rub the grill or broiler rack with oil or add just enough oil to the skillet to film it. Cook the fish, turning once, until the edges begin to turn opaque, about 4 minutes per side. (If desired, turn the fillets 45 degrees halfway through cooking on the first side when grilling to create crosshatch grill marks.) Transfer the fish to four plates, spoon the relish over the grouper, and garnish with the fresh herbs.

TO DRINK: Roussanne, Qupé
  Châteauneuf-du-Pape blanc, Château de
  Beaucastel

Slow-Roasted Grouper with Ham and Pumpkin Pirlau, page 153. *Opposite:* Red Snapper with Provençal Tomato Sauce, page 158.

RED SNAPPER WITH PROVENÇAL TOMATO SAUCE

SERVES 4 • PHOTOGRAPH PAGE 156

The red snapper brought in from about one hundred miles on either side of Destin, Florida, are the best-of-the-best—this is our fishin' stomping ground. Snapper from these waters are known in the commercial fishing world as "the true American red snapper." Here we've created a simple sautéed snapper with a classic tomato sauce, infused with the flavors of the Mediterranean. We often use canned tomatoes for this sauce, which are far better than out-of-season tomatoes, but obviously, if you can get ripe fresh tomatoes, use them. Fennel seeds have their own distinctive flavor, but combine them with orange zest and garlic and you'll bring home the flavors of Provence.

FOR THE SAUCE

1 tablespoon olive oil

2 tablespoons finely diced onion

2 tablespoons diced reserved fennel stalks (see below)

2 tablespoons diced leek

3 garlic cloves, minced

1 teaspoon fennel seeds

One 28-ounce can peeled tomatoes, drained and chopped

1½ teaspoons sherry vinegar

1 teaspoon sugar

Kosher salt and freshly ground black pepper

About 1 tablespoon extra virgin olive oil

Grated zest of 1 orange

8 fingerling potatoes, cut lengthwise in half and cooked in
    boiling salted water until tender

3 tablespoons olive oil

1 fennel bulb, trimmed and cut into 8 wedges, stalks reserved
    for sauce, fronds reserved for garnish

Kosher salt and freshly ground white pepper to taste

Four 6- to 8-ounce skin-on red snapper fillets (or substitute
    other firm white-fleshed fish, such as wild striped bass,
    halibut, tilefish, or cobia)

Extra virgin olive oil for drizzling

Coarse sea salt

To prepare the tomato sauce, heat the olive oil in a medium saucepan over medium-high heat. When it's warm, add the onion, fennel, leek, and garlic and sauté over medium heat until tender, about 10 minutes. Add the fennel seeds, tomatoes, sherry vinegar, and sugar and bring to a simmer. Reduce the heat to medium-low and cook until the tomatoes have broken down and the flavors have developed, about 45 minutes.

Pass the mixture through a food mill or puree using a hand or regular blender or food processor. For an ultra-smooth puree, strain through a fine sieve, if desired. Return the sauce to the pan and season with salt and pepper; cover to keep warm.

Cook the potatoes in a small pot of boiling salted water until tender. Drain and cover to keep warm.

Meanwhile, in a medium sauté pan just large enough to hold the fennel in one layer, heat 1 tablespoon of the olive oil over medium heat. Add the fennel, along with a tablespoon of water, season with salt and pepper, and cook, turning once, until tender, about 12 minutes. Transfer the fennel to a bowl, add the fingerling potatoes, and season with a little salt and pepper. Toss with 1 tablespoon of the olive oil, and cover to keep warm.

Heat a sauté pan just large enough to hold the snapper over medium-high heat and add the remaining 1 tablespoon olive oil. Season the fish with salt and white pepper. Place skin side up in the pan and cook until the edges begin to turn opaque, about 4 minutes. Turn and continue cooking until just done (a knife inserted into the thickest part of the fish should reveal a pearly opaqueness), about 4 minutes more.

Meanwhile, reheat the tomato sauce over medium heat. Whisk in the extra virgin olive oil and the orange zest.

Spoon the sauce onto individual serving plates. Top with the warm fennel and fingerling potatoes and then the fish. Drizzle with a bit of extra virgin olive oil, sprinkle with sea salt, and garnish with the reserved fennel fronds, if desired.

TO DRINK: Condrieu, Guigal

Côtes-du-Rhône blanc, Château Saint-Cosme

SAUTÉED RED SNAPPER WITH SWEET PEA AND FAVA BEAN PILAF

SERVES 4 • PHOTOGRAPH PAGE 131

Spring green color and flavor marry with crisp snapper fillets for a delightfully healthy dish. Sweet peas and favas come into season at about the same time and I love to combine them with spring onions, leeks, and tender herbs in sautés, ragouts, or as here in a rice pilaf.

1¾ cups light chicken broth or spring water
Kosher salt
1 cup basmati rice
2 tablespoons butter or extra virgin olive oil
1 shallot, finely minced
4 spring onions, halved or quartered (or 2 leeks), glazed
   (page 255)
½ heaping cup sweet peas, rinsed under hot water if frozen or
   blanched and shocked if fresh
½ cup peeled fava beans, blanched for 1 minute and shocked
Four 6- to 8-ounce red snapper fillets, skin on and scaled
Freshly ground pepper
Small bunch mixed fresh herbs, such as mint and parsley,
   coarsely chopped
Zest of 1 lemon

Place the broth in a medium saucepan. Season with salt to taste and bring to a boil. Add the rice, stir, and reduce heat to the lowest setting. Cover and simmer the rice for about 16 minutes. Test for doneness and place in a warm serving bowl.

While the rice is cooking, heat 1 tablespoon of the butter over medium-low heat. Add the shallot and cook until softened, 2 to 3 minutes. Add the glazed onions, peas, favas, and 2 tablespoons of water to the pan. Cook until heated through.

Heat a sauté pan just large enough to hold the snapper over medium-high heat and add the remaining tablespoon butter. Season the fish with salt and pepper, place the fish in the pan skin side up, and cook until the edges begin to turn opaque, about 4 minutes. Turn and continue cooking until just done when a knife inserted into the thickest part of the fish reveals a pearly opaqueness, about 4 minutes more.

To serve, season the vegetables with salt, pepper, and the chopped herbs. Toss the rice with the peas, favas, and half the lemon zest, then spoon onto warm plates. Top with the snapper fillets and garnish with the remaining lemon zest.

RED SNAPPER WITH HAM HOCK–RED WINE SAUCE

SERVES 6

As much as I love fish with a light sauce, sometimes I want to treat fish more like a substantial cut of meat. By that I mean serving it with a hearty red wine sauce flavored with meat essence, such as reduced beef braising liquid or lardons of bacon, or, as here, ham hocks. This way, you get your healthy piece of fish but also get to enjoy the big flavor of a roast or braised meat. This dish is best made during the cooler months of the year, when a robust red wine might be what you crave. Grouper, halibut, wild striped bass, tuna, swordfish, or salmon can all be substituted for the red snapper. The sauce can be made up to a day in advance and refrigerated; it can even be frozen, ready for use anytime. Try Autumn Root Vegetable Puree (see page 266) or consider the Autumn Vegetable Ragout (page 270) alongside the snapper.

FOR THE SAUCE

1 teaspoon olive oil

1 large yellow onion, diced

1 carrot, peeled and sliced

1 celery stalk, sliced

2 bay leaves, 3 thyme sprigs, 5 flat-leaf parsley sprigs, and 1 leek top, tied together to make a bouquet garni

2 cups red wine

¼ cup ruby port

2 smoked ham hocks (see page 218)

4 cups Chicken Broth (page 339) or canned low-sodium broth

2 tablespoons unsalted butter

Salt and freshly ground black pepper to taste

Red wine vinegar or fresh lemon juice to taste

FOR THE RED SNAPPER

1 teaspoon olive oil

1 tablespoon unsalted butter

Six 6- to 8-ounce skin-on red snapper fillets, skin on

Kosher salt and freshly ground white pepper

Heat the oil in a large pot over medium heat. Add the vegetables and cook until slightly caramelized, about 15 minutes. Add the bouquet garni and then deglaze the pot with the red wine and port, stirring up any browned bits. Boil until the wine is reduced by three-quarters. Add the ham hocks and chicken broth and bring to a simmer. Simmer very gently for 2½ hours until the meat is quite tender; skim carefully as the stock simmers to remove any fat that rises to the surface.

Remove the ham hocks with tongs or a slotted spoon. Strain the stock, return it to the pot, and boil over medium-high heat until reduced to 1 cup. Remove from the heat.

Meanwhile, when it is cool enough to handle, remove the ham from the bone and tear into small pieces, discarding the fat, skin, and gristle; set aside. (The sauce can be made to this point up to 1 day ahead. Refrigerate the sauce and ham separately.)

In a large heavy sauté pan, heat the oil and butter over high heat until almost smoking. Season the fish with salt and white pepper and add to the pan skin side down. Lower the heat to medium and cook until the edges just begin to turn opaque, about 4 minutes. Turn and continue cooking until just opaque throughout, about 4 minutes more. Transfer the fillets to a rack set over a platter and cover to keep warm.

To finish the sauce, bring the reduced broth to a simmer and swirl in the butter bit by bit. Add the ham, and season the sauce with salt and pepper and vinegar or lemon juice.

Place the snapper fillets on dinner plates and spoon the sauce (and ham hocks) over and about.

TO DRINK: Côtes-du Rhône, Château du Trignon
Barbera d'Asti, Parusso

WILD STRIPED BASS
WITH CITRUS VINAIGRETTE

SERVES 4

Refreshing, vibrant, healthy and oh-so-pretty, this citrus vinaigrette is loaded with herbs—mint, cilantro, chervil, and chives—sure to ease the winter blahs. But since citrus fruits are available year-round, you can enjoy its bright flavors any time of year. If you can find it, try using triggerfish for this recipe. Its firm white meat has a sweet lobsterlike flavor. Grill, sauté, broil, or bake your fish—just have your *mise en place* ready for tossing the vinaigrette and herbs together at the last second.

FOR THE VINAIGRETTE
1 pink grapefruit, cut into suprêmes (see page 346)
1 blood orange, cut into suprêmes
1 navel orange, cut into suprêmes
1 lemon, cut into suprêmes
1 lime, cut into suprêmes
1 shallot, finely minced
2 tablespoons red wine vinegar
¼ cup plus 2 tablespoons extra virgin olive oil
Kosher salt and freshly ground white pepper

FOR THE STRIPED BASS
2 tablespoons extra virgin olive oil
Four 6- to 8-ounce striped bass fillets (or substitute other
     firm white-fleshed fish, such as triggerfish, halibut,
     cod, or snapper)
Kosher salt and freshly ground white pepper
½ cup loosely packed cilantro leaves
½ cup loosely packed mint leaves
¼ cup loosely packed chervil leaves (optional)
2 tablespoons finely sliced chives
½ pound jumbo lump crabmeat, picked free of shells
     and cartilage (optional)

To prepare the vinaigrette, combine the fruit in a medium bowl. Add the shallot, vinegar, and olive oil and toss to combine. Season with salt and pepper.

In a sauté pan just large enough to hold the fish in one layer, heat the 2 tablespoons olive oil over medium-high heat. Season the fish with salt and white pepper and sear on the first side until golden and the edges turn opaque, 3 to 4 minutes. Turn and cook until just cooked through, 4 to 5 minutes. Transfer to a warm serving platter and cover loosely to keep warm.

Add half of the herbs to the citrus relish, then add the crabmeat, if using, and toss just to coat with the vinaigrette. Scatter the mixture over the fish, garnish with the remaining herbs, and serve at once.

TO DRINK: Riesling, Domaine Weinbach Schlossberg-
          L'Inédit
          Riesling Smaragd, Freie Weingärtner

GRILLED TUNA
WITH ARTICHOKE AND
OLIVE VINAIGRETTE

SERVES 4

This dish brings our love of Provençal flavors to the table: the freshest fish, simply grilled, with a garnish of baby artichokes, Niçoise olives, and herb vinaigrette. In the spring, this is especially good with tiny creamer potatoes, crushed (see page 263) with some of the vinaigrette, and roasted wedges of Vidalia (or small bulb) onion served alongside. Almost any fish marries happily with these ingredients: You might consider red snapper, salmon, cobia, grouper, or striped bass as well.

Four 6- to 8-ounce tuna steaks
Extra virgin olive oil for drizzling

FOR THE VINAIGRETTE
6 baby artichokes
1 lemon, halved
Kosher salt
1 shallot, finely minced
1 tablespoon red wine vinegar
1 tablespoon sherry vinegar
1 teaspoon Dijon mustard
4 thyme sprigs, leaves removed and chopped
2 marjoram, savory, or oregano sprigs, leaves removed
**   and chopped**
Freshly ground black pepper
½ cup extra virgin olive oil
¼ cup halved and pitted Niçoise olives

Kosher salt and freshly ground white pepper
A handful of flat-leaf parsley leaves for garnish

Place the tuna on a platter and drizzle with a little olive oil. Set aside while you prepare the vinaigrette.

To prepare the artichokes, peel off the outer leaves. Cut off the top half of each one and then cut into quarters. As you work, drop the artichokes into a bowl of water acidulated with the juice of half the lemon.

Bring a medium saucepan of water to a boil over high heat and add 1½ teaspoons salt. Add the artichokes, reduce the heat to medium, and simmer briskly until tender, about 12 minutes. Drain and pat dry.

Prepare a medium-hot grill.

Meanwhile, prepare the vinaigrette: Combine the shallot, vinegars, and the juice from the remaining ½ lemon in a medium bowl. Whisk in the mustard and chopped herbs and season with salt and pepper. Set aside to allow the flavors to marry for 5 to 10 minutes.

To finish the vinaigrette, whisk in the olive oil. Correct the seasoning, then add the olives and artichokes, stirring to coat with the dressing.

Carefully rub the grill rack with an oiled paper towel. Season the fish with salt and white pepper, place on the grill, and cook until the edges begin to turn opaque, 3 to 4 minutes. Turn the fish and continue cooking until the tuna is rare to medium-rare, 2 to 3 minutes more.

Place the tuna on serving plates. Spoon the vinaigrette over the tuna and garnish with a scattering of parsley leaves.

TO DRINK: Pinot Bianco, Marco Felluga
        Tocai Friulano, Venica & Venica

POMPANO EN PAPILLOTE

SERVES 4

Fish cooked in parchment, or "en papillote," provides a most dramatic presentation and a stunning whoosh of "make you swoon" aroma as the crackling parchment paper is opened at the table. The paper packets capture the unique seafood essences along with the fragrance of sweet onion, herbs, and lemon to make an unforgettable dish. Only prepare "en papillote" with fish that is absolutely fresh and shiny bright—if pompano is unavailable, use red snapper, flounder, or any other relatively thin fish fillet (no more than ¾ inch thick).

5 tablespoons unsalted butter, plus butter for the papillotes, at room temperature

2 spring onions or 1 large sweet onion, such as Vidalia, finely sliced

Freshly ground white pepper

8 thin lemon slices

2 shallots, thinly sliced

Kosher salt

Heaping ¼ cup chopped chives and parsley, and chervil, basil, or dill

Four 6-ounce pompano fillets (skin left on or removed)

Preheat the oven to 475°F.

Melt 1 tablespoon of the butter in a medium sauté pan over medium heat. Add the onions, season with white pepper, and sauté until softened and fragrant. Remove from the heat and allow to cool.

Cut four 16-by-20-inch sheets of parchment paper. Fold each one crosswise in half and trace a "half heart" shape from near the top to near the bottom of the folded edges. Cut the traced shape and unfold the paper into a heart. Rub a little butter over one half of each heart, where the fish will lie, and place 2 slices of lemon on each one. Top with the sliced shallots and sautéed onions. Season with salt and white pepper, scatter a large pinch of herbs over each packet, and top each with a fillet. Season each fillet assertively with salt and pepper, sprinkle the remaining herbs over the fish, and dot each fillet with 1 tablespoon butter. Fold the parchment over so that the edges align and, beginning at the top, seal with small overlapping folds each about an inch long, making sure to seal the end securely. (The packets may be refrigerated for a few hours; return to room temperature before proceeding.)

Place the packages on a baking sheet and bake on the top shelf of the oven for 10 minutes. Transfer to serving plates and immediately take the plates to the table. With scissors or a knife, carefully open each papillote, and let your guests inhale deeply.

VARIATION: If you like, scatter a bit of peeled, seeded, and diced tomato over each fillet and drizzle a spoonful of reduced seafood broth over it before sealing the papillotes.

TO DRINK: Pouilly-Fumé, Minet
              Chablis, Dauvissat Vaillons

FARM BIRDS & GAME BIRDS

Chicken with Autumn Vegetables and Madeira, page 174 }

Whether it's a historical

connection to the feasts of days long gone or to the charm of a southern family seated together for a Sunday dinner of fried chicken, birds symbolize the beauty of gathering to share a meal at table. From quail and dove to squab and guinea hen, from domestic and wild duck to capon, woodcock, and even grouse, there are many birds to choose from. While a well-fed, naturally raised chicken is certainly one of my favorite things to prepare and eat, exotic birds often offer more excitement from the cook's and diner's perspectives.

In terms of preparation, there is always the question of whether one should remove the hindquarters of a bird and cook them separately, since they are often at their best slowly simmered in a moist braise of wine and broth, or just to go ahead and roast the bird whole, perhaps removing the breast as soon as it is cooked through and letting the rest of the bird continue cooking until it is done. The white meat of the breast goes quickly from being moist and supple to overdone and dry, often by the time the legs and thighs are just right. At the restaurant, when spit roasting a duck, we remove the breast when medium-rare and then continue cooking the rest of the bird on the spit for another thirty minutes or so. With pheasant and other game, we often remove the breast before cooking, wrap it in pancetta, bacon, or pork fat, and cook it at the last moment, when we have already braised the leg separately and stirred the meat into a risotto, pirlau, or ravioli. But for chicken, I am pleased to keep things simple, roasting it whole and savoring its inherent goodness—even if the breast is just a little bit overdone.

Game birds offer a subtlety and elegance that few others can equal. Probably the most sophisticated bird commonly available is the domesticated pigeon, or squab. *Pintade,* or guinea hen, is another personal favorite that is not quite as common but deserves to be. Not as forceful in flavor as squab, guinea hen is more like an old-fashioned farm-raised chicken, with just a little more funk—the meat is slightly darker than chicken, more like quail. I am on a mission to encourage people to try this exquisite farm favorite.

CHICKEN SAUTÉ
WITH LEMON, CAPERS,
AND BREAD CRUMBS

SERVES 4

As with crab cakes, the bread crumbs you use are a crucial component here. They should be fluffy and almost coarse, but not too dry or too fine. For perfectly sautéed chicken, there are a few things to keep in mind: Use a large heavy pan, and don't crowd the chicken, or it will steam rather than brown. On the other hand, do not use too large a pan, or the butter may burn. The butter should not be too hot—wait until the foam subsides before adding the chicken, but don't let the butter get smoking hot. And, finally, carefully monitor the heat to achieve that even gold color. Serve this dish with sautéed cherry tomatoes.

4 large boneless skinless chicken breast halves
Kosher salt and freshly ground black pepper
¼ cup all-purpose flour
2 large eggs
1 cup medium-coarse bread crumbs (see page 347)
1 tablespoon olive oil
5 tablespoons unsalted butter
1 shallot, finely minced
¼ cup dry white vermouth
2 tablespoons capers, rinsed
Juice of ½ lemon
1 tablespoon chopped flat-leaf parsley

Season the chicken on both sides with salt and pepper. Place the flour in a shallow pan or dish. In another dish, beat the eggs well. Place the bread crumbs in a third dish. One by one, coat the chicken breasts in the flour, vigorously shaking off any excess, then dip to coat both sides with the egg, and press firmly in the bread crumbs, turning to cover both sides. Place on a baking sheet and set aside.

Heat a large heavy sauté pan over high heat. Add the olive oil and 1 tablespoon of the butter. When the foam subsides, add the chicken, reduce the heat to medium, and cook until golden on the first side, about 4 minutes. Turn the chicken and continue cooking (you may need to lower the temperature a little) until golden on the second side and just cooked through; the juices should run clear when the chicken is pierced with a knife tip. Transfer the chicken to a rack set over a platter to rest and cover to keep warm while you prepare the sauce.

Pour out the excess oil from the sauté pan. Add the shallot and cook over medium heat until softened, about 1 minute. Add the vermouth and capers and reduce the liquid over high heat until only a glaze remains. Lower the heat slightly, add 2 tablespoons of the butter, and whisk vigorously to combine. Add the remaining 2 tablespoons of butter, whisking constantly and occasionally shaking the pan. Add the lemon juice, taste, and adjust the seasoning. Remove from the heat and stir in the parsley.

Arrange the chicken breasts on serving plates, spoon the sauce over, and serve immediately.

TO DRINK: Chardonnay, Talley Vineyards
Chablis, Verget

CHICKEN
WITH AUTUMN VEGETABLES AND MADEIRA

SERVES 8 • PHOTOGRAPH PAGE 169

This braise is basically a classic coq au vin, but here, the chicken gets infused with the autumnal flavors of the root vegetables, which in turn, take on the caramel and fruit of the amber-hued Madeira. Madeira is named for the Portuguese island where it is made. A fortified wine that is heated during the maturation process, it ranges from light colored and dry to dark and very sweet. The lighter versions are often apéritifs, while the darker, richer varieties can be served as a sweet post-dinner digestif. It is also excellent for cooking in both sweet and savory preparations. The flavor is so appealing that I like to use it as the deglazing liquid for all kinds of meats. The addition of country ham gives the braise a salty "porkiness," that as we southerners know, improves just about everything.

Madeira and country ham have been partners since Colonial days, when trading ships would pick up the fortified wine on the way to America. Unlike regular wine, which is more fragile, Madeira could withstand the journey over turbulent waters and the extreme temperature changes common in the hold of a sailing ship, arriving no less tasty for the wear. Many old menus include Madeira as an apéritif and as a dinner accompaniment.

While the chicken simmers, prepare the root vegetable puree and the glazed vegetables to round out the menu.

2 tablespoons olive oil

One 3- to 4-pound free-range chicken, rinsed and cut into
    serving pieces

Kosher salt and freshly ground white pepper

3 tablespoons unsalted butter

2 medium onions, diced

3 medium carrots, peeled and sliced ½ inch thick

1 cup medium-dry Madeira

1 cup white wine

2 cups Chicken Broth (page 339) or canned low-sodium broth

A few thyme sprigs

3 bay leaves

Autumn Root Vegetable Puree (page 266)

Autumn Vegetable Ragout (page 270)

2 thin slices country ham, cut into thin julienne strips

Preheat the oven to 325°F.

In a large heavy sauté pan, heat the olive oil over medium heat. Season the chicken with salt and white pepper. Raise the heat to medium-high and sear the pieces on all sides until golden brown, about 10 minutes. Transfer the chicken to a rack set over a baking sheet and set aside.

Wipe the pan clean with a paper towel. Melt 1 tablespoon of the butter in the pan over medium heat. Add the onions and carrots and cook until softened and golden, about 10 minutes. Add the Madeira and white wine, bring to a boil, and reduce by three-quarters. Add the broth, thyme, and bay leaves and bring to a simmer.

Place the chicken in a casserole and pour the simmering broth over it. Cover the chicken with parchment paper, then cover the pan with a lid or aluminum foil and braise in the oven until tender, about 15 minutes for the breast and 45 to 55 minutes for the dark meat. Remove the pieces as they are done and transfer to a rack set over a baking sheet.

Strain the braising liquid into a large saucepan and set the pan over medium-high heat, half on and half off the burner so you can easily skim off the fat as it rises to the cooler side of the pan. Reduce by about half, 10 to 15 minutes. Add the remaining 2 tablespoons butter bit by bit, swirling it into the sauce. Add the chicken to the pan and heat through.

Spoon the vegetable puree onto individual plates. Arrange the chicken next to the puree and then the glazed vegetables alongside. Garnish with the little strips of country ham.

TO DRINK: Pinot Noir, Littorai
            Vosne-Romanée, Domaine Mongeard
            Mugneret

CHICKEN WITH
WATERCRESS SAUCE

SERVES 4 • PHOTOGRAPH PAGE 166

Vibrant green watercress, tiny pink radishes, and plump young asparagus shoots combined with succulent, farm-raised chicken breasts form a quintessential springtime repast. If young turnips or tiny new potatoes are available, toss in a few, but the simplicity (and uncrowdedness) of this dish is quite beautiful. Years ago for one of Highlands's winemaker's dinners, we served a version of this with fat deepwater crawfish providing the same pink contrast to the green sauce and asparagus that the radishes do here.

I prefer to use "frenched" chicken breasts for this dish—these are boneless breasts with the meaty part of the wing and the skin left on. See page 349, or ask your butcher for frenched breasts. If you must substitute regular boneless breasts, the cooking time will be a bit less.

1 large bunch watercress, tough stems removed, blanched in
    boiling water for 1 minute, and cooled in ice water
1½ cups Chicken Broth (page 339) or canned low-sodium
    broth, boiled to reduce to 1 cup
3 tablespoons unsalted butter
4 large frenched chicken breasts (see headnote)
Kosher salt and freshly ground white pepper
8 large asparagus spears, trimmed, blanched in boiling salted
    water until just tender, and cooled in ice water
8 small radishes, trimmed and halved
2 medium spring onions, quartered and glazed (see page 346)
½ cup white wine
2 tablespoons heavy cream

Preheat the oven to 425°F.

Squeeze the watercress lightly to remove excess water. Place it in a blender and puree until smooth, 1 to 2 minutes (you may need to add a little of the reduced chicken broth to facilitate pureeing). Set aside.

Heat a large heavy ovenproof sauté pan over medium heat and add 1 tablespoon of the butter. Season the chicken with salt and white pepper, add skin side down to the pan, and cook until golden on the first side, 5 to 6 minutes. Turn the chicken and place the pan in the oven to finish cooking, 4 to 5 minutes more.

While the chicken is cooking, slice the asparagus into halves or thirds, depending on the size, and place in a medium saucepan, along with the radishes and spring onions. Add 1 tablespoon of the butter, season with salt and white pepper, and warm gently; keep warm over very low heat.

Remove the chicken from the pan and place on a rack set over a platter. Pour out any excess fat from the pan, set over high heat, and deglaze with the white wine, stirring up the browned bits. Boil until reduced by half. Add the (remaining) chicken broth and reduce by slightly over half. Add the cream and reduce slightly, about 30 seconds. Turn the heat down and swirl in the remaining 1 tablespoon butter and the watercress puree. Season to taste.

Spoon the sauce onto warm serving plates. Top with the chicken and arrange the asparagus, onions, and radishes around it. Serve immediately.

TO DRINK: Chardonnay, DuMol
        Chablis, Raveneau

BASQUE-STYLE CHICKEN WITH PEPPERS

SERVES 6

This recipe is a take on the cooking of Southwest France, particularly Basque cuisine, which relies on a wonderful array of peppers as well as garlic, ham, and olive oil. The chicken is simmered in white wine with massive amounts of red, yellow, and green (poblano) peppers, along with lots of garlic, tomato, and a fine julienne of ham. Everything is cooked in extra virgin olive oil with the punch of a little hot chile and finished with a shower of chopped parsley.

FOR THE BRAISE

1 tablespoon extra virgin olive oil
One 3- to 4-pound free-range chicken, rinsed and
    cut into serving pieces
Kosher salt and freshly ground black pepper
2 medium onions, sliced
4 garlic cloves, finely chopped
¼ pound prosciutto, country ham, or Bayonne ham
    (trimmings are fine), cut into julienne
One 28-ounce can peeled tomatoes, drained and chopped
2 cups white wine
3 thyme sprigs, 1 large marjoram sprig, 1 bay leaf, and
    1 leek top, tied together to make a bouquet garni
4 cups Chicken Broth (page 339) or canned low-sodium broth

FOR THE PEPPERS

1 tablespoon olive oil, or as needed
2 red bell peppers, cored, seeded, and cut into
    2-by-½-inch strips
2 yellow bell peppers, cored, seeded, and cut into
    2-by-½-inch strips
2 poblano peppers, cored, seeded, and cut into
    2-by-½-inch strips
4 garlic cloves, finely chopped
1 teaspoon hot Spanish paprika
¼ pound sliced prosciutto, country ham, or Bayonne ham,
    trimmed if necessary and cut into julienne
1 small bunch flat-leaf parsley, leaves removed and chopped
Several marjoram sprigs, leaves removed
1 dried hot chile pepper, finely crushed, or 1 teaspoon crushed
    red pepper flakes
Extra virgin olive oil for drizzling

Preheat the oven to 325°F.

In a large heavy sauté pan, heat the olive oil over high heat. Season the chicken generously with salt and pepper and brown over medium heat until golden on all sides, about 12 minutes. Transfer the chicken pieces to a rack set over a baking sheet.

Pour off all but about 1 tablespoon of fat from the pan. Add the onions to the pan and cook for 10 minutes, or until soft and golden. Add the garlic and ham and cook for another couple of minutes, until the garlic is fragrant and softened. Add the tomatoes and white wine and simmer for a few minutes to cook off the alcohol. Add the bouquet garni and the chicken broth and bring to a simmer.

Place the chicken in a casserole and pour the tomato broth over and around it. Place a piece of parchment paper directly on top of the chicken, cover the pan with the lid or aluminum foil, and place in the oven. After 15 minutes, check the breast pieces for doneness. When the juices run clear, remove and transfer the breasts to a rack set over a baking sheet. Continue cooking the dark meat until very tender, 30 to 45 minutes more. Transfer the remaining chicken to the rack and cover to keep warm.

Meanwhile, prepare the peppers: Heat the olive oil in a large sauté pan over medium-high heat. Add the pepper strips (you may need to sauté them in batches or in two pans) and sauté until lightly colored, about 5 minutes. Add the garlic and paprika and cook until the garlic is softened, about 1 minute. Add the ham and toss to combine. Set aside, covered, to keep warm.

Strain the braising liquid into a large saucepan, pressing hard on the vegetables to extract all of the essence. Place the saucepan over medium-high heat, half on the heat and half off so that you can easily skim away all of the fat while reducing it, and reduce the sauce by half. Add the chicken pieces to the reduced sauce and warm through. Add the pepper mixture, parsley, marjoram, hot pepper, and a splash of extra virgin olive oil. Taste and adjust the seasoning.

Transfer to a platter and serve.

TO DRINK: Collioure, Domaine du Mas Blanc Les
        Junquets
        Rioja Gran Reserva, Marqués de Cáceres

CHICKEN BREASTS WITH ZUCCHINI, FIELD PEAS, AND NEW POTATOES

SERVES 4

These summer ingredients work equally well with most any bird or meat, especially grilled leg of lamb. So heat up the grill or, as in this recipe, simply pan-roast a chicken breast (or leg of lamb, pork tenderloin, or veal steak) and serve with this bowl of intensely green, garlicky zucchini and peas in a basil-flavored broth. The zucchini almost resembles thin noodles and, when tossed with the peas and pestolike flavorings, it makes for a great, almost soupy vegetable accompaniment—think *soupe au pistou*.

3 small zucchini

3 tablespoons olive oil

Four 6-ounce boneless chicken breasts with skin,
    excess fat trimmed away

Kosher salt and freshly ground black pepper

1 garlic clove, finely chopped

1 cup cooked field peas, such as butter peas, lady peas, or
    pink-eyed peas (see page 251), with their cooking liquid
    (see page 15 for cooking method)

4 new potatoes, cooked in boiling salted water until tender,
    drained, and quartered (optional)

6 basil leaves

1 tablespoon unsalted butter

Juice of ½ lemon, or to taste

Preheat the oven to 375°F.

Trim the zucchini and cut them in half. Using the julienne blade on a mandoline or other vegetable slicer, cut only the outer part of the zucchini lengthwise into thin strips, stopping before you reach the seedy core and turning the zucchini as you go. (Alternatively, using a sharp knife, slice off the skin and about ¼ inch of the flesh underneath it in wide strips, then cut these into thin julienne strips.) Set aside.

Heat 1 tablespoon of the olive oil in a heavy ovenproof sauté pan over medium-high heat until simmering. Season the chicken breasts with salt and pepper, place skin side down in the pan, and sauté until golden on the first side, about 5 minutes. Turn the breasts and place the pan in the oven to finish cooking, 5 to 6 minutes. Transfer the chicken to a rack set over a platter and cover loosely with foil to keep warm.

Meanwhile, heat 1 tablespoon olive oil in a large sauté pan over medium heat until warm. Add the garlic and sauté for 30 seconds. Add the zucchini and toss until softened, about 3 minutes. Add the peas and about ½ cup reserved pea broth (or chicken stock or water) and bring to a simmer. Add the potatoes, if using. Tear 4 of the basil leaves into pieces and add to the peas, then add the remaining tablespoon of olive oil and the butter and whisk to combine. Season with the lemon juice and salt and pepper to taste.

Divide the vegetables and broth among large shallow serving bowls. Place a chicken breast atop each. Garnish with the remaining basil, torn into pieces.

TO DRINK: Bandol rouge, Domaine Tempier
    Dolcetto d'Alba, G. Conterno

ROAST CHICKEN
WITH SPRING VEGETABLES

SERVES 4

One of my fondest food memories is of the roast farm chicken I purchased from a charcuterie in a little valley in Provence, not far from Vidauban. The bird was filled with a vast amount of herbs (thyme, savory, marjoram, tarragon, parsley, and rosemary), and the inside had been rubbed with more sea salt and freshly ground black pepper than most people would use for five birds. It had been basted with a mixture of melted butter and chicken fat as it roasted, giving it a crispy juiciness and an incredible flavor. Local red wine washed down herb-saturated bite after bite. Be generous with the herbs here—you want a heaping cup in all.

When preparing a whole chicken, I like to sprinkle it both inside and out with sea or Kosher salt and place it in the refrigerator, loosely wrapped with a kitchen towel, for a few hours or overnight. This "cure," which helps dry the bird, promotes a crisp skin and a more intense flavor.

One 3- to 3½-pound free-range chicken, excess fat removed from neck and body cavity and reserved
Coarse sea salt or Kosher salt
8 large thyme sprigs
5 large savory sprigs
5 large marjoram sprigs
5 large flat-leaf parsley sprigs
4 large tarragon sprigs
3 large rosemary sprigs
Coarsely ground black pepper
1 tablespoon extra virgin olive oil
1 head garlic, cut crosswise in half
3 lemon slices
2 tablespoons unsalted butter
2 carrots, peeled and cut into 3-inch sections
4 asparagus spears, trimmed
2 spring onions, halved lengthwise

Rinse the chicken inside and out and pat dry. Sprinkle inside and out with salt, loosely wrap in a kitchen towel, and set on a plate. Refrigerate for at least a few hours, or overnight.

Preheat the oven to 325°F. Remove the bird from the refrigerator.

Coarsely chop the thyme, savory, marjoram, parsley, tarragon, and rosemary, including stems, and place in a small bowl. Add about 1 tablespoon sea salt, 1 tablespoon pepper, and the olive oil and mix to combine. Rub the mixture into the chicken's cavity. Put the garlic and lemon slices in the cavity, and tie the legs together with kitchen twine.

In a small saucepan, melt the butter with a little of the reserved chicken fat over low heat. With a basting brush, coat the skin of the chicken with some of the butter and fat. Season with more pepper.

Place the chicken on a rack in a roasting pan and roast for 30 minutes, basting the bird several times with the remaining butter mixture.

Add the carrots, asparagus, and onions to the roasting pan and continue to cook until the juices from a pricked thigh run clear, about 45 minutes to 1 hour, continuing to baste the bird frequently with pan juices. The internal temperature of the thickest part of a thigh should reach 165°F (it will continue to rise to between 175° and 180°F after it is removed from the oven). Transfer the bird to a platter and let rest breast side down for 15 minutes. Cover the roasting pan and keep the vegetables warm. Remove the string, carve the chicken, and serve with the vegetables.

Keep in mind that the savory bits of the salty pepper-and-herb-infused portions are absolutely delicious, so be sure to nibble on the back and rib bones before discarding.

TO DRINK: Roast chicken is undoubtedly the finest single dish to show off the beauty and versatility of almost any wine—from dry white (e.g., Chardonnay) to a semi-dry white (Alsatian Riesling) to fruity and soft red (Beaujolais) to big intense red (Cabernet or Rhone style). Take your pick.

My father, like his father before him, was a doctor. I think he chose not to hunt because they had both treated one too many a local hunter who lost a finger to a shotgun blast. Though our family was not keen on guns, I do remember going on an occasional dove shoot with some of my high school buddies and stumbling around a field while trying to spot some quail.

Thanks to my close friendship with Bill and Hatton Smith, quail hunting has since come to be a bigger part of my life. The Smiths, who own Royal Cup Coffee of Birmingham, enjoy an annual two-week midwinter lease on one of the great plantations of south Georgia—Gillionville. And each year, they invite a few of their friends and business acquaintances down for a three-day hunt.

During the latter years of the nineteenth century, Gillionville was the country home of the governor of Georgia. The estate boasts a timelessness that I have rarely felt elsewhere in the South. Situated a mile or two off the highway, reachable only by a red clay road lined with one-hundred-year-old oaks, the house boasts a huge fireplace in every room, while the spread encompasses six thousand acres and is outfitted with classic mule-drawn wagons, grand Tennessee Walking horses, and the finest dogs you could imagine.

I come to Gillionville to hunt, but I also come to revel in the pace of life in rural south Georgia. Hunt days start early. Breakfast is very traditional: scrambled eggs, bacon, sausage, grits, biscuits, homemade jams and preserves. After fortifying ourselves for the day, and after shooting a bit of skeet, we head for the fields.

On the hunt, tromping along, the pines towering high above, you can't help but marvel at the teamwork of the dogs: It's a beautiful phenomenon to behold. That said, even though the dogs do all the work of pointing and flushing, quail hunting does require skill and athletic ability on the part of the hunter. It's no small task to hoist your gun up there and to bring down some quail. And if you miss, there's hell to pay, courtesy of your fellow hunters. I often miss. But I take solace in the grace of the experience, in the peerless beauty of a quail in flight, arching skyward from a thicket of millet or Egypt grass, quick with the wild thunder of wing beats.

As much as I love to hunt quail on a winter morning in south Georgia, I won't deny that a large part of the appeal of a trip to Gillionville has to do with the unabashed luxury of the place. Upon your return from the field, someone immediately takes your gun and cleans it. And more than likely, a lunch of fried quail is waiting. After lunch, we might go fishing or take a nap before the afternoon hunt. Evening events are a bit more formal. Men are required to wear a coat and tie. It's a time to drink bourbon and tell stories of the hunt.

On the day we leave, we hunt only in the morning. We end our trip with an outdoor feast, spread on tablecloth-draped picnic tables beside a hardwood fire on which the cooks prepare grilled quail, along with a salad and dessert.

Back at the restaurant, we often stuff quail with corn bread and pecans and rub them with lots of fresh thyme and butter. The pairing of pecans and quail is one of those natural affinities. Like a pork dish with prunes from Normandy, the taste of quail is, for me, a taste of place, one that came to me while tromping through the fields of Gillionville.

ROAST QUAIL
WITH APPLES AND PECANS

SERVES 4 AS AN APPETIZER • PHOTOGRAPH PAGE 185

Throughout the season, quail is always on the Highlands menu. Because of their size, quail make a perfect appetizer. We stuff them with ham, tasso, chicken liver, foie gras, crawfish, or corn bread. Our quail come from a farm in South Carolina, but most butchers or specialty markets sell semi-boneless quail, ideal for stuffing. The flavor of good, tart apples and aged balsamic vinegar makes a wonderfully savory, yet light, wintertime first course.

2 firm tart apples, such as Fuji, Braeburn, or Granny Smith

1 teaspoon olive oil

1 carrot, peeled and diced

1 celery stalk, diced

2 shallots, diced

1 cup crumbled Corn Bread (see page 26)

¼ cup Chicken Broth (page 339) or canned low-sodium broth

4 tablespoons unsalted butter, melted

2 thyme sprigs, leaves removed

½ cup pecans, lightly toasted (see page 346), half roughly
    chopped

Kosher salt and freshly ground black pepper

4 semi-boneless quail (see headnote), wing tips trimmed,
    rinsed and patted dry

1 tablespoon canola or olive oil

2 cups mixed lettuce, such as oak leaf, lolla rosa, arugula,
    and/or mizuna, trimmed, washed, and dried

¼ cup Balsamic Vinaigrette (page 331)

Preheat the oven to 450°F.

Quarter and core the apples. Dice half of them and set aside. Thinly slice the remainder lengthwise and set aside.

In a medium sauté pan, heat the olive oil over medium-high heat. Add the carrot, celery, shallots, and diced apples and sauté until softened, about 5 minutes. Transfer to a bowl and add the crumbled corn bread, then add the chicken broth, melted butter, thyme, and chopped pecans and toss thoroughly with your hands to combine. Season with salt and pepper.

Sprinkle the cavity of each quail with salt and pepper, then stuff a little of the corn bread mixture inside. Season the outside of the quail with salt and pepper and tie the legs together with kitchen twine.

Heat the oil over high heat in a heavy ovenproof sauté pan just large enough to hold the quail without touching each other. Add the quail and sear, turning occasionally, until golden, 4 to 6 minutes. Transfer the pan to the oven and roast the quail, for 6 to 9 minutes; the breast meat should still be a rosy color.

Meanwhile, in a medium bowl, toss the lettuce with the remaining apples and pecans and just enough of the vinaigrette to coat.

Remove the string from the quail. Arrange the salad on serving plates and place the quail alongside. Drizzle a little more vinaigrette over each quail and serve.

TO DRINK: Chinon, Jouget
           Pinot Noir, Bethel Heights

Roast Quail with Apples and Pecans, page 183 ⟩

GRILLED QUAIL
WITH ROSEMARY AND GARLIC

SERVES 6

After a long day of quail hunting, we made a crackling fire in the large stone fireplace of our cabin, rigged up a grill over the hickory embers, and cooked our prize. White Bean and Collard Green Gratin (page 258) is a nice accompaniment to the quail.

12 farm-raised quail or cleaned wild quail
12 juniper berries
4 large rosemary sprigs, leaves removed and coarsely chopped
4 garlic cloves, finely chopped
½ cup extra virgin olive oil
Kosher salt and freshly ground black pepper
Rosemary sprigs or a small bunch of watercress, trimmed,
    washed, and dried, for garnish

Split each quail down the back and remove the backbone (kitchen shears are very handy for cutting down both sides of the backbone, or use a large chef's knife). Press down on the breastbone firmly with the heel of your hand, slightly crushing it to flatten the bird. Rinse the quail and pat dry.

Heat a small dry skillet over medium heat until almost smoking. Add the juniper berries and toast, shaking the skillet occasionally, for 2 minutes. Remove the berries from the skillet and finely chop.

In a small bowl, combine the juniper berries, rosemary, garlic, and olive oil. Transfer one-quarter of this marinade to another small bowl and reserve. Place the quail in a glass or ceramic dish and massage the remaining marinade into the meat. Cover and marinate for 2 to 4 hours in the refrigerator.

Prepare a hot grill.

Generously season the quail with salt and pepper on all sides. Place breast side down on the grill and cook until golden brown, about 5 minutes. Turn and cook for about 5 minutes more; the breast meat should still be rosy.

Divide the quail among serving plates and drizzle with the reserved marinade. Garnish with rosemary sprigs and serve.

TO DRINK: Pinot Noir, Calera
    Bourgogne rouge, Domaine Laurent

GRILLED QUAIL
WITH BUTTERNUT SQUASH
AND DRIED FIG RISOTTO

SERVES 4

When cooking these birds on the grill, include some hardwood on the fire to lend a hint of wood smoke to the meat. The autumn flavors of butternut squash and dried figs provide a pleasing unctuous contrast to the charred smoky quail. With each season, change the risotto—say, sweet peas and asparagus in spring and eggplant and tomatoes in summer.

2 tablespoons olive oil
2 rosemary sprigs, leaves removed and chopped
A few thyme sprigs, leaves removed and chopped
2 garlic cloves, crushed and chopped
Kosher salt and freshly ground black pepper
8 semi-boneless quail (see headnote, page 187),
    wing tips trimmed, rinsed and patted dry
Butternut Squash and Dried Fig Risotto (page 272)

In a shallow bowl or baking dish, combine the oil, rosemary, thyme, garlic, and salt and pepper to taste. Add the quail and massage the herb mixture into them. Cover with plastic wrap and refrigerate for 2 to 3 hours (or set aside at room temperature for 1 hour).

Prepare a hot grill. Bring the quail to room temperature if it has been refrigerated.

Grill the quail until just done, about 4 minutes on each side; the breast meat should still be a rosy color. Transfer to a cutting board and season with salt and pepper. Cut the quail into quarters and serve hot atop the risotto.

TO DRINK: Barbera d'Asti, M. Chiarlo
    Barbera d'Alba, Scavino

QUAIL STUFFED WITH CORN BREAD AND FIGS WITH MOLASSES VINAIGRETTE

SERVES 4

Paired with the watercress salad dressed with molasses vinaigrette, this corn bread–stuffed quail has become a southern signature at Highlands. Most good butchers sell quail with the breastbone and backbone removed. These "semi-boneless" quail make for easy stuffing and even easier eating. This recipe can serve as a base for countless others. Pecans are often included, but everything from sweetbreads to leftover ham to mustard greens can make for a memorable stuffing. Leftover corn bread is hard to beat as the basis for this stuffing, but other leftover bread such as brioche or focaccia works well too. Just crumble, moisten with a little broth and melted butter, and flavor with a little sautéed mirepoix, as here. Consider adding a little something exotic, such as seared foie gras, or something more down-home such as cubes of sautéed bacon.

FOR THE STUFFING

½ cup Chicken Broth (page 339) or canned low-sodium broth

6 large dried figs, stems removed and cut into ¼-inch dice

1 tablespoon unsalted butter

1 medium carrot, peeled and cut into ¼-inch dice

1 medium celery stalk, cut into ¼-inch dice

2 shallots, cut into ¼-inch dice

2 cups crumbled Corn Bread (page 26)

2 tablespoons unsalted butter, melted

2 heaping tablespoons ham cut into ¼-inch dice

2 thyme sprigs, leaves removed

Kosher salt and freshly ground black pepper to taste

FOR THE QUAIL

8 semi-boneless quail (see headnote), wing tips trimmed, rinsed and patted dry

Kosher salt and freshly ground black pepper

1½ teaspoons olive oil

1 tablespoon unsalted butter

FOR THE SALAD

2 tablespoons red wine vinegar

1 tablespoon molasses

Kosher salt and freshly ground black pepper to taste

¼ cup olive oil

2 bunches watercress, trimmed, washed, and dried

¼ cup pecans, toasted (see page 346)

Preheat the oven to 450°F.

First prepare the stuffing: In a small saucepan, bring the broth to a boil. Add the figs, remove from the heat, cover, and set aside. In a small sauté pan, melt the 1 tablespoon butter. Add the carrots, celery, and shallots and sauté until tender, 10 to 12 minutes. Remove from the heat.

In a large bowl, combine the corn bread, melted butter, ham, thyme leaves, sautéed vegetables, figs, broth, and salt and pepper. Taste and adjust the seasoning. Set aside.

Season the cavities of the quail with salt and pepper and fill them with the corn bread stuffing, packing it loosely. Season the skin with salt and pepper. Tie the legs together with kitchen twine.

Heat a heavy ovenproof skillet over high heat. Add the oil and butter to the skillet and heat until hot. Add 4 quail and sear, turning occasionally, until golden brown all over, 4 to 6 minutes. Repeat with the remaining 4 quail. Remove from the skillet and place in a roasting pan. Place the pan in the oven and roast for 6 to 8 minutes; the breast meat should still be a rosy color.

Meanwhile, whisk together the vinegar, molasses, and salt and pepper in a small bowl. Slowly whisk in the olive oil. Toss the watercress and pecans with half the vinaigrette. Adjust the seasoning if necessary.

Remove the string from the quail, and arrange on plates. Serve the salad alongside, drizzling the quail with the remaining vinaigrette.

TO DRINK: Pinot Noir, Arcadian Sleepy Hollow
Morey St. Denis Domaine Dujac

GUINEA HEN BREASTS WITH OLD-FASHIONED ONION SAUCE AND TRUFFLES

SERVES 4

The French have long appreciated the complex, rich flavors and refined texture of guinea hen, and it is a favorite on menus throughout southern France and northern Italy as well. Moister than pheasant, yet not as plump as a free-range chicken, these farmed birds marry well with southern staples such as smoky cured pork and sweet onions. Here, however, we rely on the truffle's exotic perfume. If truffles are unavailable, substitute sautéed mushrooms drizzled with a few drops of truffle oil. Sauce soubise, the classic French onion sauce, adds an unusual subtle and superb flavor to the dish. Consider serving some wilted Swiss chard or wedges of roasted spring bulb onions on the side.

1 small black truffle (see Sources, page 352), thinly sliced
2 guinea hen breasts, skin on, boned and split
    (or substitute free-range chicken breasts)
1 small white onion, thinly sliced
1 carrot, peeled and thinly sliced
4 thyme sprigs
1 tablespoon plus 2 teaspoons olive oil
3 to 4 tablespoons unsalted butter
2 yellow onions, thinly sliced
1 cup Chicken Broth (page 339) or canned low-sodium broth
2 tablespoons basmati rice
Kosher salt and freshly ground white pepper
½ cup heavy cream
Grated nutmeg to taste

Carefully slide several slices of truffle under the skin of each breast half. Wrap the remaining sliced truffle in plastic wrap and refrigerate. (Use the truffle within two to three days or freeze it for up to six months.)

To prepare the marinade, combine the white onion, carrot, thyme, and the 2 teaspoons of olive oil in a medium bowl. Add the breasts and turn to coat. Marinate for 1 hour at room temperature, or refrigerate for as long as overnight.

To prepare the onion sauce, heat a medium saucepan over low heat. Add 2 tablespoons of the butter and the yellow onions and cook, stirring from time to time, until the onions are softened but have not taken on any color, about 15 minutes. Add the broth and rice, season with salt and white pepper, and bring to a simmer. Reduce the heat and cook slowly until the rice is very soft, about 30 minutes.

Meanwhile, season the guinea hen breasts with salt and pepper. Heat a sauté pan just large enough to hold them over medium heat. Add the 1 tablespoon olive oil, then add the breasts and sear until golden on the first side, about 5 minutes. Turn and cook over medium-low heat until just cooked through, 8 to 10 minutes more. Transfer to a rack set over a plate and cover to keep warm.

Pass the onion mixture through a food mill and return it to the saucepan. Add the cream and nutmeg and return to a gentle simmer. Taste and adjust the seasoning.

To serve, swirl the remaining 1 to 2 tablespoons butter into the onion sauce to enrich it. Spoon the sauce onto serving plates. Place a guinea hen breast on top of each and garnish with the reserved truffles.

TO DRINK: Bâtard-Montrachet, Domaine Etienne Sauzet
Pinot Noir, Au Bon Climat Isabelle

DUCK TWO WAYS

SERVES 4

Duck provides the ideal opportunity to incorporate two different cooking techniques. The legs are perfect for slowly braising, while the breast can be pan-roasted relatively quickly until just medium-rare. The braise may be prepared several hours in advance, and the legs can then be reheated in the strained and reduced braising liquid. The breasts benefit from being marinated while the legs braise and are then pan-seared separately and put on to cook at the last moment. I recommend trimming most of the duck fat off the breast and scoring the remaining skin in a crosshatch pattern (duck fat makes for delicious sautéed onions and potatoes, so be sure to save it), but if you prefer the bare minimum of fat, simply remove all of the skin and fat from the breast and proceed from there. We use figs, both fresh and dried, here, but many other fruits, such as cherries, peaches, or pears make a tasty addition. Also try dried fruit, rehydrated in some warm water, if fresh are not in season.

2 ducks, such as Pekin (Long Island)

3 allspice berries

2 star anise

A small piece of cinnamon stick

6 peppercorns

Reserved duck fat or 1 tablespoon olive oil

Kosher salt and freshly ground black pepper

1 onion, finely chopped

1 carrot, peeled and finely chopped

2 tablespoons molasses

1 cup red wine

4 dried figs, stems trimmed and quartered

2 cups Chicken Broth (page 339) or canned low-sodium broth

3 thyme sprigs, 3 flat-leaf parsley sprigs, 2 bay leaves, and
    1 leek top, tied together to make a bouquet garni

4 fresh figs, stems trimmed and cut into ½-inch dice

2 mint sprigs, leaves only

1 teaspoon Steen's pure cane syrup (see Sources, page 352)
    or apple cider vinegar

1 teaspoon olive oil

1 tablespoon unsalted butter

Sherry vinegar (optional)

To prepare the duck, first remove the legs by slicing through the hip joint. Trim away the excess fat from all sides, reserving for another use (see headnote). Remove the breast by slicing down along either side of the ridge of the breast plate to release the meat from the bone. The wing will remain attached to the carcass. (Reserve this for making duck stock. The carcass can be frozen until ready to use.) Trim away as much of the fat as possible on all sides of the detached breast meat and, again, reserve this fat for another use. Score the remaining skin in a ¼- to ½-inch crosshatch pattern. Be careful not to cut into the flesh.

Coarsely grind the allspice, star anise, cinnamon stick, and peppercorns together in a coffee mill or spice grinder. Rub the ground spices into the duck breasts, cover, and let marinate in the refrigerator for at least 2 hours, or overnight.

Preheat the oven to 325°F.

Heat a little of the duck fat trimmings in a large cast-iron skillet until some of the fat is rendered, then pour off all but about 1 tablespoon fat from the skillet. Alternatively, heat the olive oil. Season the duck legs with salt and pepper and sear over medium-high heat, turning occasionally,

until golden brown on all sides, about 15 minutes. Transfer to a rack set over a baking sheet to rest while you prepare the braise.

Add the onion and carrot to the skillet and cook, stirring occasionally, until well caramelized, about 15 minutes. Add the molasses, red wine, and dried figs and simmer until the liquid has reduced by half. Add the chicken broth and bouquet garni and bring to a boil.

Place the duck legs in a casserole or baking dish and pour the braising liquid and vegetables over them. Place a piece of parchment paper directly on the duck and then cover the casserole with the lid or aluminum foil. Place in the oven to cook at a gentle simmer (reduce the temperature if necessary—do not let the braise cook too fast, or the meat will be tough) for 1 to 1¼ hours, or until tender: The meat should offer very little resistance when pricked with a fork. Remove from the oven and allow the legs to rest in the braising liquid for 10 to 15 minutes, then remove to a rack set over a platter and cover to keep warm.

Strain the broth into a small saucepan, pressing down on the vegetables to extract all of their juice. Place the saucepan half on and half off the heat (this will make skimming the fat from the surface easier) and bring to a boil over high heat. Boil, skimming frequently, until reduced by half.

Meanwhile, in a small bowl, toss the fresh figs with the mint, syrup, olive oil, and a little salt and pepper.

Heat a large cast-iron or other heavy skillet over high heat. Season the duck breasts with a little salt, add skin side down to the skillet, and sear until well colored on the first side, 4 to 5 minutes. Turn the duck, lower the heat to medium, and continue cooking until medium-rare, about 4 minutes more: Check for doneness—the meat should be a rosy pink. Transfer to the rack to rest for 5 minutes.

Swirl the butter into the braising liquid. Taste and adjust the seasoning (you may want to add a drop of vinegar). Add the legs to the sauce and heat through. Slice the duck breasts on an angle and fan the slices on serving plates. Place the legs next to the breasts and spoon the sauce over them. Place the fig relish alongside the breasts and serve.

TO DRINK: Cornas, Thierry Allemand
    Syrah, Qupé

SQUAB WITH GRILLED GRITS
AND REDEYE GRAVY

SERVES 4

The Palmetto Pigeon farm, a family business in Dalzell, South Carolina, raises the fresh birds we prepare at our restaurants. I urge you to try these darkly delicious birds. You'll have extra grits left over to enjoy the next day.

FOR THE SQUAB

Four 14- to 16-ounce squab, washed and patted dry, livers reserved

2 tablespoons plus 1 teaspoon olive oil

4 thyme sprigs

4 juniper berries, toasted (see page 346) and crushed

Kosher salt and freshly ground black pepper

1 shallot, finely minced

4 small slices country ham, trimmed and cut into julienne strips, a little of the fat reserved and chopped

One 3-ounce double espresso

¼ cup bourbon, such as Maker's Mark

1 cup Chicken Broth (page 339) or canned low-sodium broth, boiled to reduce to ½ cup

2 tablespoons unsalted butter

1 teaspoon sherry vinegar

FOR THE GRITS

4 cups water

Kosher salt

1 cup stone-ground organic grits

3 tablespoons unsalted butter

3 tablespoons freshly grated Parmesan cheese

Freshly ground black pepper

1 tablespoon olive oil

In a medium-sized saucepan, bring the water to a boil and add salt to taste. Whisk in the grits, turn the heat to low, and simmer, stirring occasionally with a wooden spoon. Cook the grits for approximately 1 hour, until tender.

Pour the grits into a large mixing bowl. Add the butter, cheese, salt, and pepper and mix thoroughly. Taste for seasoning and adjust.

Pour the grits onto a slightly greased sheet pan, forming a layer that is ½ to 1 inch in thickness. Place in the refrigerator until well chilled, 2 hours to overnight.

Cut the squab in half down the back by cutting down either side of the backbone (using poultry shears or a sharp knife) and discard the backbones. Flatten each squab, pressing down hard with the palm of your hand. Remove the rib cage bones by sliding a boning or other flexible knife under the bones and cutting them away; discard.

Combine 1 tablespoon of the olive oil, the thyme sprigs, and juniper berries in a baking dish and add the squab, turning to coat. Cover and marinate at room temperature for about 2 hours.

Preheat the oven to 425°F.

Heat a large cast-iron or other heavy skillet over medium-high heat. Add the remaining 1 tablespoon olive oil and heat until almost smoking. Season the squab with salt and pepper and sear skin side down until golden, about 5 minutes. Turn and place in the oven. Cook until medium-rare, about 10 minutes; the meat should reach 130°F on an instant-read thermometer (squab is best served rare to medium-rare).

Meanwhile, trim the reserved squab livers. Heat the 1 teaspoon of olive oil in a small sauté pan over medium heat. Add the livers and sauté for 2 minutes, or until golden outside and medium-rare inside. Remove from the heat and let cool, then finely chop.

When the squab are cooked, remove the skillet from the oven and transfer the squab to a rack set over a platter to rest while you prepare the gravy.

To prepare the gravy, pour out the excess oil from the skillet. Add the shallot, ham, and ham fat and sauté for 1 minute. Add the espresso and bourbon and boil over high heat, stirring with a wooden spoon, until reduced by half. Pour in the broth and again reduce by half. Swirl in the squab liver and butter, season with salt and pepper, and finish with the vinegar.

Cut the grits into 3 inch squares, brush with the 1 tablespoon olive oil, and grill or broil until hot.

Place the grits on four plates. Serve the squab on top of the grits, with the redeye gravy ladled over.

TO DRINK: Pinot Noir, Adelsheim Vineyards
Chambolle, Musigny, Bertheau

MEATS

I am primarily a sauté

chef. In the Highlands kitchen, I prepare the roasts, braises, and sautés of seafood and meats, as well as devise their sauces. It's my job to come up with the ideas, the combinations, the what-to-include and what-to-leave-out. Quite often it is this last part that requires the most finesse, for knowing how to develop a dish that is simple yet vibrant, without overdoing it, is an art. My colleagues work the grill, prepare the vegetables, compose the salads, assemble the hot and cold appetizers, and create the desserts. Always exciting, always demanding, our endeavor is to find beauty in a plate of food. The goal is food cooked to perfection with respect to the ingredients and appreciation for the farmer, the fisherman, or the rancher—for God himself—for providing us with these glorious ingredients.

At Highlands, we do our best to uphold the French and southern ideals of frugality and celebration of the feast. We strive to be stewards of tradition. I once helped cook a feast marking the end of the *vendange,* or wine grape harvest, in the South of France. Laborers from North Africa allowed me to pitch in and prepare the lamb; as is the North Africans' custom, the lamb had to be eaten within twenty-four hours of its slaughter. We began preparations late in the afternoon, and the lamb went on the spit sometime before dawn. As we took turns at the spit, tending the fire, I came to understand what should be self-evident when we eat meat—the notion of sacrifice. I'm quite sure my forefathers in the hills of Alabama had a reverence for the pork or the chicken that graced their tables. In our present time, so removed from the farm, it's easy to lose sight of the wonder that is food.

{ **Red Wine–Braised Rabbit with Wild Mushrooms, page 229**

It was well-meaning if misguided nutritionists of the mid-twentieth century who urged that sides of meat be cut into portions and covered in sterile plastic, wet and cold. We'd hurriedly remove the plastic and, as if we were handling poison or playing hot potato, quickly put the meat on to cook. I, however, urge you be more in contact with what you're cooking.

Handling meat is the antidote to the chilled detachment of shrink-wrap, and the process of marinating it is imperative. You must rinse, trim, and pat the meat dry. Add the marinade, then step away and be patient in anticipation of the meal to come. The meat will meld with the flavors of the marinade (always allow meat to come to room temperature before cooking—an important but often-forgotten step) and the combination of these simple ingredients will yield spectacular results.

In respecting our food with proper handling and preparation, we must also pay more attention to where our food comes from. In the past, many of our nation's farms became virtual factories, and mass production created some legitimate health problems for the animals and quite probably for us.

The cheapest and easiest method of production is not always the most desirable. We need to change our habits and support our local farmers who are stewards of the land and care about what they produce. There is an ever-growing network of farmers who work toward sustainability and humane animal husbandry—search them out. We list information on Niman Ranch and Jamison Farm in the back of the book to help you do so (see Sources, page 352). While meat from no-grain-fed, open-air–raised pigs or chickens will not be as cheap as factory-produced versions, you can be almost certain that they'll be better for you, and you will know where they came from. And, as more people support their local farms or demand naturally raised meats from their grocer, the costs will become more competitive.

ROAST LEG OF LAMB WITH SPRING VEGETABLE RAGOUT

SERVES 8 TO 10 • PHOTOGRAPH PAGE 202

This herb-and-garlic-scented leg of lamb should not be reserved for springtime alone. Serve it with eggplant in the summer, sweet potatoes in the fall, or turnips in the winter. Be sure to have your butcher remove the aitch bone, or hip and ball socket, from the lamb. When preparing it, make sure to trim away any excess fat and allow the meat to come to room temperature before roasting. Allow it to rest before carving.

3 garlic cloves, crushed and finely chopped

1 tablespoon chopped fresh thyme or 1 teaspoon dried

1 tablespoon chopped fresh marjoram or 1 teaspoon dried

1 scant tablespoon chopped fresh rosemary or 1 teaspoon dried

1 tablespoon chopped flat-leaf parsley

3 tablespoons extra virgin olive oil

Kosher salt

1 heaping teaspoon cracked black pepper, plus more to taste

One 8- to 10-pound bone-in leg of lamb, trimmed

Spring Vegetable Ragout (page 266)

Preheat the oven to 325°F.

Combine the garlic, thyme, marjoram, rosemary, and parsley in a small bowl and add 1 tablespoon of the olive oil, salt to taste, and the teaspoon of pepper.

With a sharp boning knife, make deep slits all over the leg of lamb at 2- to 3-inch intervals. With your fingertips, gather up the herb mixture a pinch at a time and push it into the slits. Season the lamb with more salt and cracked pepper. Rub another tablespoon of olive oil onto the lamb.

Place the lamb on a roasting rack in a shallow roasting pan. Roast the lamb for about 1½ hours until medium-rare; an instant-read thermometer should register 130°F in the thickest section. Let rest on a rack set over a platter for 15 to 30 minutes before carving.

Carve the lamb and serve with the vegetable ragout. Drizzle the meat with the remaining 1 tablespoon olive oil.

TO DRINK: Saint-Julien, Château Lagrange
Côte-Rôtie, Guigal

Roast Leg of Lamb with Spring Vegetable Ragout, page 201. *Opposite:* Lamb Chops and Leg with French Lentils, page 204.

LAMB CHOPS AND LEG WITH FRENCH LENTILS

SERVES 4 • PHOTOGRAPH PAGE 203

We serve lamb chops with the leg because the high cost of the luxuriously rich chops is offset by the modest price of the lean leg of lamb. Do not hesitate to use just one or the other, but combining the two cuts and textures can be very appealing. French green lentils, *lentilles du Puy*, have superior flavor and maintain their firm texture when cooked. There is a wonderful earthiness about their taste and their green color makes for an attractive presentation. Savory Leek Bread Pudding is a great accompaniment to the lamb.

5 tablespoons plus 1½ teaspoons olive oil

4 garlic cloves, crushed

2 thyme sprigs

2 large rosemary sprigs

4 double-rib lamb chops

1 boneless leg of lamb (about 6 pounds), trimmed

Kosher salt and freshly ground black pepper to taste

1 cup French green lentils (du Puy; or substitute brown lentils),
    rinsed and picked over (see Note)

½ small onion, cut into ¼-inch dice

1 carrot, cut into ¼-inch dice

1 small celery stalk, cut into ¼-inch dice

1 cup Lamb Jus (page 341) or beef broth

1 tablespoon roasted garlic puree (see page 345),
    plus roasted garlic cloves for garnish

2 tablespoons pureed roasted red pepper (see page 345)

1 red bell pepper, roasted (see page 345), peeled, seeded,
    and cut into ½-inch-wide strips for garnish

Marjoram leaves for garnish

Savory Leek Bread Pudding (page 265)

Combine 2 tablespoons of the olive oil, the crushed garlic, thyme, and rosemary in a large glass or ceramic dish. Add the lamb chops and leg and massage the mixture into the meat. Cover and refrigerate for a few hours, or up to 3 days.

Preheat the oven to 450°F. Bring the lamb to room temperature.

Bring 3 cups water to a simmer in a medium saucepan and season with salt. Add the lentils, stir, and return to a low simmer. Cover and cook until just tender, about 20 minutes. Drain, transfer to a saucepan, and set aside.

Meanwhile, heat 1½ teaspoons of the olive oil in a medium sauté pan over medium heat. Add the diced onion, carrot, and celery and cook until crisp-tender, 6 to 8 minutes. Remove this mirepoix from the heat and set aside.

Heat a heavy sauté pan just large enough to hold the lamb leg over medium-high heat and add 1 tablespoon of the olive oil. Season the leg with salt and pepper. Reduce the heat to medium and sear the leg, turning occasionally, until golden on all sides, about 8 minutes total. Transfer the lamb to a rack set in a small roasting pan (set the sauté pan aside) and roast until medium-rare (the internal temperature should be 130°F), about 12 minutes, depending on the thickness of the meat. Transfer the lamb to a rack set over a baking sheet and let rest to allow the juices to settle.

Heat the sauté pan over high heat, then add the remaining 2 tablespoons olive oil to the pan. Season the lamb chops on both sides with salt and pepper. When the oil is hot, add the chops and sear over medium-high heat on both sides, about 6 minutes total. Transfer the chops to the rack to rest; cover loosely to keep warm. Pour off the oil from the pan and add the lamb jus, roasted garlic puree, and red pepper puree. Bring to a boil, taste, and adjust the seasoning.

Meanwhile, add the mirepoix to the lentils, along with about 1 tablespoon water, and heat over medium-high heat until warmed through.

Slice the leg of lamb into thin slices and cut the lamb chops into individual chops. Arrange the lamb over the lentils and sprinkle with the marjoram. Surround with the roasted pepper strips and garlic cloves and serve with savory leek bread pudding and the warm sauce on the side.

NOTE: Always cook extra lentils for other uses. They make a hearty salad when tossed with a simple vinaigrette and herbs such as basil or marjoram; serve with Goat Cheese and Corn Bread Crostini (page 126). Cooked lentils keep for several days in the refrigerator.

TO DRINK: Cornas, A. Clape
        Côte-Rôtie, G. Bernard

LAMB AND BLACK BEAN CHILI WITH SAFFRON RICE

SERVES 8

This isn't your usual three-alarm chili; instead, it is a one-pot meal that is all about the slow development of flavors. The beans get a long simmer with lamb bones, extracting their very essence. Saffron, ginger, allspice, and red wine work in unison with the lamb. We like to serve this chili with fragrant saffron rice and garnish it with avocado, scallions, and sour cream.

FOR THE BEANS

1¾ cups black beans, rinsed, picked over, and soaked
    overnight in water to cover
2 pounds lamb bones (see Note)
4 thyme sprigs, 4 flat-leaf parsley sprigs, and 1 bay leaf,
    tied together to make a bouquet garni
1 garlic clove, crushed

FOR THE CHILI

6 tablespoons olive oil
2 large yellow onions, chopped
2 large garlic cloves, minced
1½ pounds ground lamb shoulder
2 tablespoons chili powder
2 tablespoons minced ginger
2 tablespoons minced thyme
1 tablespoon minced hot red chile
2 to 3 canned chipotle chiles, chopped
1¼ teaspoons dried marjoram
1 scant tablespoon cumin
¾ teaspoon ground allspice
¾ teaspoon *each* freshly ground white and black pepper
¾ teaspoon cayenne pepper
Two 28-ounce cans Italian plum tomatoes, drained,
    juices reserved, and coarsely chopped
¾ cup red wine
Kosher salt

FOR THE RICE

½ teaspoon ground cumin
½ teaspoon ground coriander
½ teaspoon saffron threads, crushed in a mortar or crumbled
2 cups basmati rice

1 avocado, pitted, peeled, and cut into thin slices
¼ cup sour cream
Minced greens from 2 scallions

Drain the beans, transfer them to a large heavy saucepan, and add fresh water to cover by 2 inches. Bring to a boil and add the lamb bones, bouquet garni, and garlic. Reduce the heat and simmer, skimming off the foam occasionally and adding more water as necessary to keep the beans covered, until they are tender but not mushy, about 1 hour. Drain, reserving the liquid.

Meanwhile, heat 3 tablespoons of the olive oil in a large heavy nonreactive saucepan over medium heat. Add the onions and cook, stirring occasionally, until soft, about 10 minutes. Add the garlic and cook until soft, about 2 minutes. With a slotted spoon, transfer the onions to a bowl. Pour off the oil and add the remaining 3 tablespoons of oil to the pan. Increase the heat to medium-high, add the lamb, and cook, breaking it up with a spoon, until it is no longer pink, about 6 minutes. Return the onions to the pan, add the chili powder, ginger, thyme, red chile, chipotles, marjoram, cumin, allspice, and peppers, and stir well. Cook, stirring, until fragrant, about 5 minutes. Add the tomatoes and half of their reserved juices and bring to a boil. Reduce the heat and simmer for 5 minutes. Add ½ cup of the wine and simmer, skimming and stirring occasionally, for 30 minutes.

Add the beans, bones, bouquet garni, remaining ¼ cup wine, and salt to taste to the chili. Taste and adjust the seasoning. Simmer for 30 minutes, skimming and stirring occasionally and adding enough of the reserved bean cooking liquid and tomato juices to keep the chili moist.

While the chili is cooking, prepare the rice: Combine 4 cups of water, the cumin, coriander, and saffron in a medium saucepan and bring to a boil. Stir in the rice and return to a boil. Reduce the heat, cover, and simmer until the rice is tender and most of the liquid has been absorbed, 16 to 18 minutes.

Remove the bones and bouquet garni from the chili. Taste and adjust the seasoning. Spoon the rice into bowls and spoon the chili over it. Garnish with the avocado, sour cream, and greens, and serve.

NOTE: Reserve the bones from lamb whenever possible and freeze to use here or to make Lamb Jus (page 341). Or ask your butcher for any lamb bones that would otherwise be discarded.

TO DRINK: Ice-cold beer

LAMB SHANKS SIMMERED WITH FAVAS AND SPRING VEGETABLES

SERVES 4

Lamb shanks are perfect for a classic braise. Have patience and cook the meat very slowly until it's tender to the touch (the meat will almost fall off the bone), and you will have sensational results. The cooking vessel you choose also plays a key role in the success of the dish. A heavy earthenware casserole with a tight-fitting lid retains heat better at a lower temperature than thin lightweight versions. Wipe the shanks dry before searing and take time browning them. You want the meat to get a dark golden crust, because it's the caramelization that gives the dish its concentrated flavor. Leftovers only get better.

1 tablespoon plus 2 teaspoons olive oil

4 small lamb hind shanks (12 to 14 ounces each), trimmed of fat

Kosher salt and freshly ground black pepper

2 carrots, finely diced

1 small onion, finely diced

1 celery stalk, finely diced

3 garlic cloves, crushed

1 cup white wine

4 thyme sprigs, 4 flat-leaf parsley sprigs, 3 marjoram sprigs, and 2 bay leaves, tied together to make a bouquet garni

3 cups Chicken Broth (page 339) or canned low-sodium broth, or as needed

4 flat-leaf parsley sprigs, leaves removed

2 marjoram sprigs, leaves removed

2 thyme sprigs, leaves removed

12 baby carrots, peeled, blanched in boiling water until tender, and cooled in ice water

8 new potatoes, cooked in boiling salted water until tender, quartered

4 fava beans, shelled, blanched, and peeled (see Note)

2 tablespoons extra virgin olive oil

Preheat the oven to 375°F.

Heat 1 tablespoon of the olive oil in a large heavy sauté pan over high heat. Season the lamb with salt and pepper. Reduce the heat to medium-high, add the meat, and cook, turning occasionally, until nicely browned on all sides; wait until each side is well colored before turning the shanks.

Transfer to a rack set over a baking sheet and pour out the excess oil from the pan. Add the remaining 2 teaspoons olive oil and heat until hot. Add the diced carrots, onion, celery, and garlic and cook until softened, 7 to 8 minutes. Add the wine, bring to a boil, and reduce by half. Add the bouquet garni and chicken broth and bring to a boil.

Place the shanks in a deep heavy casserole just large enough to hold them in a single layer and pour the broth over; it should almost cover the shanks. Cover the meat directly with parchment paper and then cover the pot with a tight-fitting lid or aluminum foil. Place in the oven, reduce the temperature to 325°F, and braise for 20 minutes.

Check to make sure the braising liquid is at the barest suggestion of a simmer—you should just be able to detect an occasional bubble. Adjust the heat accordingly and cook for about 1½ hours more. Check for tenderness with the tip of a knife: The meat should be very tender. Carefully transfer the shanks to a platter.

Strain the braising liquid into a large saucepan, pressing on the vegetables to extract their flavorful essences. Discard the vegetables and bouquet garni. Place the saucepan half on and half off the burner (the fat will accumulate on the cooler side of the pan, allowing for easy removal) and bring the liquid to a simmer. Reduce the braising liquid by half, skimming all the fat from the surface.

Meanwhile, chop the herb leaves together to combine.

Add the shanks, carrots, potatoes, and favas to the reduced braising liquid and heat until hot. Season to taste with salt and pepper, sprinkle with the chopped herbs, and drizzle with the extra virgin olive oil. Serve family style, directly from the pot.

NOTE: Fava beans may seem a little tedious because, once the beans are shelled, there is still a layer of thin membrane that needs to be removed. Simply blanch the beans in boiling water for 2 to 3 minutes, then drain and gently slip the outer skins off with your thumb and index finger. Now these emerald-green jewels are ready for the lamb, or any other dish.

TO DRINK: Châteauneuf-du-Pape rouge, Château de Beaucastel

Gigondas, Château du Trignon

ROAST LEG OF LAMB STUFFED WITH GREENS AND GARLIC

SERVES 6, WITH LEFTOVERS • PHOTOGRAPH PAGE 195

This rosy lamb, with its garlicky green center, is a special-occasion dish, but with the help of your butcher (to butterfly the leg), it becomes quite easy. Jamison Farm in Latrobe, Pennsylvania (see Sources, page 352), is our lamb purveyor, and I think theirs is the best lamb in America. John and Sukey Jamison like to give credit for the quality of their lamb to the grass they grow, but whatever it is, their lamb is very finely flavored and incredibly delicious. Consider serving Old-fashioned Potato Gratin (page 257) to round out the meal.

8 garlic cloves, peeled
Kosher salt and freshly ground black pepper
¼ cup plus 1 teaspoon extra virgin olive oil,
 plus extra for drizzling
1 large bunch mustard greens or Swiss chard,
 washed and stems trimmed
Grated zest of 1 lemon
1 boneless leg of lamb (about 6 pounds)

Preheat the oven to 375°F.

Tear off a sheet of aluminum foil about 10 inches long. Place the garlic in the center, season with a little salt and pepper, and drizzle with the 1 teaspoon of olive oil. Wrap tightly and bake for 20 minutes. Let cool slightly, then finely chop the garlic.

Meanwhile, bring a large pot of salted water to a boil. Prepare an ice bath (see page 346). Toss the mustard greens into the boiling water and blanch for 2 minutes. Drain the greens and plunge them into the ice bath to stop the cooking and to set the color. When they are completely cool, drain and squeeze the greens dry—this takes a bit of effort, so continue diligently until little moisture remains. Wrap the greens in paper towels to extract any remaining moisture, then chop them.

In a medium bowl, combine the chopped garlic, 3 tablespoons of the olive oil, the lemon zest, and mustard greens; mix thoroughly. Set aside.

Prepare the lamb by carefully trimming away any excess fat. To butterfly the lamb, slice through the thickest part almost all the way through and spread out the resulting two flaps. Flatten the meat with the heel of your hand to a relatively even thickness.

Season the lamb with salt and pepper and spread the greens mixture lengthwise down the center. Roll up the lamb and tie securely at 1-inch intervals with kitchen twine to make a compact roast.

Heat the remaining 1 tablespoon olive oil in a large heavy ovenproof skillet over medium-high heat. Add the lamb and sear on all sides until browned. Place in the oven to roast for about 45 minutes, or until medium-rare; the internal temperature should register 130°F on an instant-read thermometer. Transfer to a rack set over a platter and let rest for 10 to 20 minutes.

Slice the lamb and serve with a drizzle of olive oil.

TO DRINK: Pauillac, Château Batailley Bordeaux
 Cabernet Sauvignon, Whitehall Lane

SKIRT STEAK WITH WATERMELON AND RED ONION RELISH

SERVES 4

Incredibly flavorful, juicy, and well marbled, with a satisfying, slightly chewy texture, skirt steak has become one of our favorite cuts of beef. We borrow the marinade idea from South America—think Argentine *chimichurri*—and the relish is a refreshing southern summer garnish. The crunchy sweetness of the watermelon, along with the tangy mint and onions, lends an unexpected flavor. We also serve these steaks with roasted new potatoes or mashed sweet potatoes, or with grilled sourdough bread and a watercress or arugula salad.

FOR THE MARINADE
Juice of 2 limes
4 garlic cloves, crushed
½ bunch flat-leaf parsley, leaves removed and
**   coarsely chopped**
2 tablespoons extra virgin olive oil
Coarsely ground black pepper to taste

2 pounds skirt steaks, trimmed of excess fat
Kosher salt and freshly ground black pepper
Watermelon and Red Onion Relish (page 29)

Combine all the marinade ingredients in a baking dish, add the beef, and massage the marinade into the meat. Cover and refrigerate for at least a few hours, or overnight. Remove from the refrigerator 1 hour before cooking.

Prepare a hot grill or preheat a stove-top griddle over high heat.

Season the steaks with salt and pepper. Place on the grill rack or the griddle and sear over very high heat for 2 to 3 minutes. Turn the steaks, move to a cooler part of the grill, or lower the heat to medium, and cook for 2 to 3 minutes more for medium-rare. Transfer to a rack set over a platter and let rest for 3 minutes. Slice the steaks across the grain and serve with the relish.

TO DRINK: Barbera d'Alba, Scavino
Zinfandel, Neyers

COWBOY FILLET WITH SWEET POTATO HASH BROWNS

SERVES 4

"Cowboy fillet" refers to a bone-in beefsteak. We use tenderloin cut into large steaks two to three inches thick. Tenderloin fillet is the mildest-tasting cut of beef, but when cooked on the bone, it gains an intensity and concentration of flavor that you just can't get from boneless meat. Ask your butcher to prepare the steaks for you. If necessary, you can substitute a bone-in rib eye (also known as cowboy rib eye), a bone-in strip steak or Kansas City strip sirloin, or the more familiar T-bone or porterhouse.

Kosher salt

2 sweet potatoes, peeled and cut into ½-inch dice

1 tablespoon bacon drippings or olive oil

2 medium onions, cut into ½-inch dice

1 garlic clove, minced (optional)

1 marjoram sprig, leaves removed and chopped

Freshly ground black pepper

1½ teaspoons olive oil

Four 10- to 12-ounce bone-in beef tenderloin fillets
    (see headnote)

Coarsely ground black pepper

4 slices Blue Cheese Butter (page 337) or olive oil
    for garnish (optional)

Bring a large pot of water to a boil and add 1½ teaspoons salt. Add the sweet potatoes and cook until tender, 6 to 8 minutes. Drain, pat dry, and set aside.

Meanwhile, heat a large sauté pan over medium heat, then add the bacon drippings and let melt. Add the onions and cook, stirring occasionally, until golden, 10 to 12 minutes. Add the sweet potatoes and garlic and cook over medium-high heat, stirring, until the sweet potatoes take on a little color, 3 to 5 minutes. Season with the marjoram salt, and pepper. Taste and adjust the seasoning.

While the onions and sweet potatoes are cooking, heat a large heavy skillet over high heat. Add the olive oil and heat until almost smoking. Season the steaks with salt and lots of coarse black pepper. Reduce the heat to medium-high and sear the steaks, turning once, until nicely browned on both sides, then cook to desired doneness, 4 to 6 minutes total time for rare, 8 to 10 minutes for medium-rare. Transfer to a rack set over a baking sheet and let rest for 5 minutes.

Scatter the sweet potato hash browns onto individual plates and top each with a cowboy fillet. Garnish with the blue cheese butter (or a drizzle of olive oil), if desired.

TO DRINK: Spring Mountain Red
        Rioja Gran Risérva, Conde de Valdemar

Bill Niman is one of the most important American food purveyors of our generation. Through the development of coalitions who care about the land and the livestock they raise, he has fostered the growth of environmentally conscious ranchers and farmers who follow natural methods and humane practices. Bill started ranching north of San Francisco in the early 1970s, providing his high-quality beef and pork first to Chez Panisse and other noteworthy restaurants before taking it mainstream. Unlike the conventional beef, pork, and chicken industries, which are oftentimes shameful and unhealthy, Bill's ranch is an example of how the raising and processing of livestock can be done in a humane, healthy, and profitable way.

I was fortunate to be invited by Bill to visit a group of proud pig farmers he had organized in Iowa who were raising healthy pigs and farming sustainably, a model that could be replicated in every part of our country if we insisted upon it. And I saw for myself the quality of life of the small farmer who is a steward of the land, who rotates the crops, nurturing the health of the soil and thus the health of the livestock he allows to roam freely and root there. This is a renewed definition of what animal husbandry should be. It depends on the symbiotic relationship between farmer, livestock, and earth.

The Chefs' Collaborative and the Slow Foods movement are two groups I belong to that also support sustainable agriculture. Join these organizations and others like them to become a part of the solution. As chefs and consumers, we must learn more about and support sustainable agriculture, aquaculture (and sustainable fishing), and humanely raised livestock. The bottom line is to patronize your local farmers' markets and choose organically or locally raised poultry, meat, and vegetables whenever possible.

In Europe, locals have a connection to the land, the seasons, and the farmer as they partake in the daily ritual of buying food at the bustling local markets. Become familiar with *your* purveyors, strengthen your bond with the farmer or grocer who brings you your food, and you too can get back in touch with the circle of life that sustains us.

SIRLOIN STRIP
WITH GRILLED RED ONIONS, CORN BREAD, AND SALSA VERDE

SERVES 4

The layering of this dish is quite important. The base is a slab of corn bread cut to a size similar to the steak and positioned to catch all the juices, next the peppery beef and salsa verde, and then grilled onions stacked on top.

Four 12-ounce sirloin strip steaks, trimmed
2 garlic cloves, crushed
2 tablespoons extra virgin olive oil
2 medium red onions, cut into 1-inch-thick slices
Kosher salt and freshly ground black pepper
¼ cup black peppercorns, very coarsely crushed in a mortar or under a heavy skillet
Corn Bread (page 26), cooked in a 10-inch pan
Salsa Verde (page 327)

Rub the steaks with the crushed garlic and drizzle with 1 tablespoon of the olive oil. Put them on a platter, cover, and allow them to sit at room temperature for about 1 hour.

Prepare a hot grill or preheat a cast-iron or other heavy skillet over high heat.

Drizzle the remaining 1 tablespoon olive oil over the onions and season with salt and pepper. Grill or sear the onions until charred and just lightly softened, about 5 minutes on each side. Transfer to a plate, cover to keep warm, and set aside.

Season the steaks with salt and press the crushed peppercorns into both sides of the steaks. Sear on the hot grill or in the skillet until a good crust has formed, about 5 minutes. Turn the steaks, move them to a cooler part of the fire or reduce the heat to moderate, and cook to medium-rare, another 4 to 5 minutes. Transfer to a rack set over a platter to rest, and cover to keep warm.

Meanwhile, cut the corn bread into 4 rectangular strips about 3 inches wide and 7 to 8 inches long, then cut each piece horizontally through the middle in half. Grill the corn bread slices to warm.

Place 2 slices of corn bread on each plate and moisten with 1 tablespoon salsa verde. Top with the steaks, scatter some red onions over each, and garnish each serving with one more spoonful of the salsa verde. Serve the remaining salsa verde on the side for those who want more—or to dunk their corn bread in.

TO DRINK: Cabernet Sauvignon, Paul Hobbs
Cabernet Sauvignon, Livingston-Moffett

Grilled Veal Medallions with Artichoke and Niçoise Olive Relish, page 214 }

GRILLED VEAL MEDALLIONS WITH ARTICHOKE AND NIÇOISE OLIVE RELISH

SERVES 4 • PHOTOGRAPH PAGE 213

We serve the accompanying relish with everything from grilled fish to lamb, pork, beef, and veal. The grilled veal's mild flavor is a great showcase for the relish—full of artichokes, crunchy charred onions, herbs, tangy vinegar, and little olives. The relish may be prepared several hours in advance. We use rosy grass-fed veal from Canada; while not as pale in color as the veal you'll find in most butcher shops, it is much more flavorful. If you don't have a specialty butcher who carries grass-fed veal, D'Artagnan is a good source (see Sources, page 352). Serve the tender veal with Crushed Creamer Potatoes (page 263).

2 pounds boneless veal top round, trimmed and cut into
    12 thin medallions (have the butcher do this if you like)
1 garlic clove, crushed
4 thyme sprigs, leaves removed
1 tablespoon extra virgin olive oil
Kosher salt and freshly ground black pepper
Artichoke and Niçoise Olive Relish (page 327)
A small handful of flat-leaf parsley, thyme, or mint leaves
    for garnish

Place the veal medallions on a platter and rub with the garlic. Sprinkle with the thyme, drizzle with the olive oil, and massage them into the veal. Cover and let rest at room temperature for 30 minutes.

Prepare a hot grill. Rub the grill rack with an oiled paper towel.

Season the medallions with salt and pepper and grill until the edges begin to turn opaque, 2 to 3 minutes. Turn and cook until just done, about 2 minutes more. Transfer the veal to a rack set over a plate and let rest briefly.

Arrange the veal on four plates and spoon the relish over the top. Garnish with the additional herbs.

TO DRINK: Barbera d'Alba, Parusso
    Tocai Friulano, Schiopetto

ROAST VENISON WITH CABBAGE, SPOONBREAD, AND BOURBON

SERVES 6

High-quality venison is readily available fresh from New Zealand. D'Artagnan is a good mail-order source (see Sources, page 352). In New Zealand, the venison is properly processed and aged a minimum of two weeks in a carefully controlled environment. The result is meat that is mild and tender, with a rich flavor that is not at all gamy. Because it is extremely lean, it is best cooked only rare to medium-rare. While New Zealand venison is available year-round, we tend to stick to serving it during our own conventional hunting season of October to February. That's also the perfect time of year to enjoy a side of comforting spoonbread. If you have the butcher trim the venison, be sure to ask for the trimmings, which are necessary for making the sauce.

FOR THE MARINADE

1 tablespoon olive oil
4 juniper berries, toasted (see page 346) and finely ground in
    a mortar or a coffee/spice mill
1 garlic clove, crushed
2 rosemary sprigs, leaves removed and coarsely chopped
1 cup red wine
¼ cup port (we like Warre's Warrior vintage port or
    Warre's Ruby)

2 pounds boneless venison leg, trimmed (reserve the trimmings)

FOR THE CABBAGE

1 tablespoon olive oil
1 medium onion, thinly sliced
1 garlic clove, crushed
1 dried hot chile pepper
½ head savoy cabbage, cored and thinly sliced
Kosher salt and freshly ground black pepper

3 tablespoons olive oil

2 cups Beef Broth (page 340) or canned low-sodium broth

Kosher salt and freshly ground black pepper

2 tablespoons bourbon

4 tablespoons unsalted butter

Spoonbread (page 20)

To prepare the marinade, in a bowl or other nonreactive container, combine the oil, juniper berries, garlic, rosemary, red wine, and port. Add the venison and massage it with the marinade. Cover and refrigerate for at least a few hours, or up to 24 hours.

To prepare the cabbage, heat the oil in a large sauté pan over medium heat. Add the onion and sauté until softened, 6 to 8 minutes. Add the garlic and chile pepper and cook for another 2 minutes, or until fragrant. Add the cabbage and cook for 2 minutes more. Season with salt and pepper and set aside.

Preheat the oven to 375°F.

Remove the venison from the marinade, reserving the marinade; set it aside. In a saucepan, heat 2 tablespoons of the olive oil over medium-high heat. Add the reserved venison trimmings and cook until browned and caramelized, 10 to 15 minutes. Add the reserved marinade, bring to a boil, and reduce by three-quarters, skimming the surface of any fat. Add the broth and bring to a simmer. Skim and simmer until reduced by half. Strain the sauce and set aside.

Pat the venison dry and season with salt and pepper. Heat the remaining 1 tablespoon of oil in a heavy ovenproof skillet over high heat. Add the venison and sear on all sides. Put the skillet in the oven and cook until medium-rare (the internal temperature should be 130°F), about 8 minutes; the meat will be springy to the touch. Transfer the venison to a rack set over a plate and let rest for 10 minutes, covered to keep warm.

Meanwhile, pour off the fat from the skillet and add the bourbon. Carefully flame the bourbon by tilting the skillet close to the flame to ignite it, or light it with a long match. When the flames die down, add the sauce, bring to a hard boil, and reduce slightly. Swirl in the butter bit by bit, stirring until incorporated and silky. Taste and adjust the seasoning.

Just before serving, reheat the cabbage. Remove the chile pepper.

Slice the venison and serve with the cabbage and spoonbread. Ladle the sauce over the meat.

TO DRINK: Barbaresco, Giacosa
Côte-Rôtie, Rostaing

In the South, pork shows up everywhere. Meaty ribs or slow-cooked pork butt are as common as fried chicken. But, aside from the obvious main course fare, pork is a versatile ingredient that, depending on how it has been processed, can lend either a smoky richness to a dish such as long-simmered greens or, as with flaky piecrust, act as a carrier of other flavors much like butter or oil. Yet there is a quality to pork fat that neither butter nor oil can muster. Plus, no other fat comes in so many forms. Typically, it is used only in small amounts for flavoring, so don't pass it over thinking it an unhealthy choice.

At first, the many pork offerings can be daunting, so we've tried to demystify them here. The firm layer of flesh from the belly of the pig is used in many ways and in many cuisines. It is composed of five layers: three layers of mostly pure white fat sandwiched between two leaner, meatier layers. Unlike bacon, *pork belly* is not smoked. It is prepared as both a main dish and, used in small amounts, to enrich a recipe. Salt-cured pork belly is called *salt pork*. If there is a wide band of the leaner layer of the belly present, it may be called *streak o' lean*. Salt pork is often blanched before being used in dishes such as cooked greens, where it provides richness and seasoning. The layer of pure fat along the back of the pig is found fresh and unsalted as *fatback* and used in dishes as one might use *lard*—rendered, clarified fat that comes from many parts of the pig. Readily available supermarket lard is often hydrogenated and full of other fillers, making it virtually indistinguishable from vegetable shortening. The very best is *leaf lard,* which is the fat protecting the kidneys. Lard is a solid fat at room temperature, much like shortening, and it provides an incomparable flakiness to pastries and biscuits. *Slab bacon,* as its name suggests, is sold as a large chunk of bacon with the pork rind attached; like regular bacon it comes from the side of the pig and is smoked. Typically less expensive than presliced bacon, slab bacon may be cut as required for your recipe. The rind should be removed prior to use, but it can be cut into small pieces and fried to make *cracklin's* (see page 26) to garnish dishes or to lend a crunch to corn bread. *Lardons* are narrow strips of pork fat or slab bacon, usually fried or blanched and added to a dish to impart richness and texture that no oil or butter could provide. *Ham hocks* are small cross sections of a pig's hind leg that can be found smoked, cured, or fresh. They are typically used in long, slow cooking or simmering.

The selection of pork products is vast for probably no other reason than it is a staple that has sustained southerners for many generations. In meager times, a meal of corn bread and greens enriched with ham hocks or streak o' lean provided delicious sustenance. Throughout the South, pork is still king—from the whole-hog barbecues of South Carolina to the pickled pig lips of the Mississippi delta—we love our pork in infinite ways.

PORK ON PORK:
SHOULDER AND BELLY
SIMMERED WITH BOURBON
SERVES 8

Pork shoulder is more flavorful than the tenderloin or chop, and with the addition of pork belly—a cut more commonly used to make pancetta or bacon—you get a dish of incomparable succulence and tenderness. The bourbon, which marries well with most pork preparations, adds a mellow sweetness to the braise. Although the Italians and French have prized pork belly for centuries, and our southern forefathers used "side meat," "streak o' lean," and "fatback" to enrich countless dishes, we chefs have only recently come to appreciate its many virtues. Serve this sublime braise with Glazed Autumn Vegetables (page 255) or Autumn Root Vegetable Puree (page 266) and Creamy Grits (page 22).

2 tablespoons olive oil
2 pounds boneless pork shoulder, trimmed and
    cut into 2-inch pieces
2 pounds pork belly (see page 217), trimmed and
    cut into 2-inch pieces
Kosher salt and freshly ground black pepper
2 medium onions, finely chopped
2 medium carrots, peeled and finely chopped
3 bay leaves, 2 thyme sprigs, and 1 leek top tied together
    to make a bouquet garni
2 garlic cloves, crushed
¼ cup plus 2 tablespoons bourbon
¾ cup white wine
4 cups Chicken Broth (page 339) or canned low-sodium broth
4 medium turnips, peeled and quartered
2 tablespoons unsalted butter, cut into small pieces

Preheat the oven to 325°F.

In a large heavy skillet, heat the olive oil over medium-high heat. Season all the pork with salt and pepper. Add the pork, in batches, and brown on all sides, about 12 minutes per batch. Transfer the pork to a rack set over a baking sheet.

Add the onions and carrots to the same skillet and cook until well colored and almost caramelized, about 15 minutes. Add the bouquet garni and 1 of the garlic cloves. Remove the skillet from the flame and carefully—it may ignite—add the bourbon. Return to the heat and simmer until the liquid is reduced by three-quarters. Add the wine and reduce by half.

Transfer the vegetables and braising liquid to a large enameled cast-iron casserole or Dutch oven. Add the pork, the remaining garlic clove, the chicken broth, and turnips. Bring to a simmer over medium heat (be very careful not to boil, which would toughen the meat), then reduce the heat to low. Cover the surface of the braise with a sheet of parchment paper and cover the pot with the lid or aluminum foil. Place in the oven and cook until the pork is tender, about 1½ hours.

With a slotted spoon, transfer the pork to a rack set over a baking sheet. Strain the broth into a saucepan. Place the saucepan half on and half off the burner (this will make skimming off the fat easier) and boil over high heat until reduced by half, skimming the fat frequently.

Return the pork to the sauce and gently heat through. Swirl in the butter. Taste and adjust the seasoning. Serve family style, directly from the pot.

TO DRINK: Syrah, Qupé
    Vacqueyras Domaine le Sang des Cailloux

ROAST FRESH PORK LEG WITH ONION AND BACON GRATIN

SERVES 10, WITH LEFTOVERS

A "fresh ham" is an unsmoked pork hind leg. A roast pork leg makes for a dramatic presentation, and it provides a vast amount of meat, making it perfect for a buffet. Be sure to remove the aitch bone for easy carving; your butcher can do this if you like. Curing the pork in a brine for twenty-four hours adds both flavor and juiciness. The brine recipe I provide comes from my friend Jeremiah Tower's book *Jeremiah Cooks*.

FOR THE BRINE

2 gallons water

1 cup Kosher salt

½ cup sugar

4 garlic cloves, crushed

1 tablespoon juniper berries, toasted (see page 346) and crushed

6 thyme sprigs, leaves removed

6 bay leaves

½ bunch flat-leaf parsley, leaves removed and chopped

4 dried hot chile peppers

2 tablespoons freshly ground black pepper

1 tablespoon dried thyme

1 fresh pork leg (about 14 pounds), skinned, trimmed of fat, and aitch bone removed (have the butcher do this)

Onion and Bacon Gratin (page 257)

Combine all of the brine ingredients in a large pot and bring to a simmer, stirring until the salt and sugar are dissolved, then transfer to a deep pot. Place in the refrigerator to cool thoroughly before using.

Place the pork leg in the chilled brine, cover with plastic wrap, and refrigerate for 12 hours. Turn the pork over in the brine and leave refrigerated for 12 hours more.

Remove the pork leg from the brine, wipe it dry, set it on a platter. Let it come to room temperature, about 1 hour.

Preheat the oven to 325°F.

Place the pork in a large roasting pan. Roast until the internal temperature reaches 145° to 150°F on an instant-read thermometer, about 4 hours. Remove from the oven and let the pork stand on a large rack set over a baking sheet for 30 minutes.

Serve the pork thinly sliced, with the gratin alongside.

TO DRINK: Gigondas, Faraud

Côtes-du-Rhône, Château du Trignon Rasteau

ROAST PORK RACK
WITH CORN PUDDING AND
GRILLED EGGPLANT

SERVES 4, WITH LEFTOVERS

Ask your butcher for a "frenched" (bones trimmed) pork rack with six to eight ribs. This could be cut into chops and then cooked individually, but a roast rack is beautifully golden and festive and is easy to carve, family style, at the table. Lots of garlic, rosemary, thyme, salt, and pepper are essential for the marinade and lend a rich flavor.

Corn pudding and eggplant are luscious supporters, and the aïoli unites with them to make for a wonderful dinner. Sautéed red and golden peppers or wilted greens also make nice pairing options.

FOR THE PORK

One 3½- to 4-pound center-cut pork loin roast,
    chine bone removed (have the butcher do this)
    and trimmed of excess fat
3 garlic cloves, crushed
3 tablespoons extra virgin olive oil
2 thyme sprigs, leaves removed
2 rosemary sprigs, leaves removed
Kosher salt and freshly ground black pepper

FOR THE EGGPLANT

A few thyme sprigs, leaves removed and chopped
A few rosemary sprigs, leaves removed and chopped
2 garlic cloves, finely chopped
3 tablespoons olive oil
Kosher salt and freshly ground black pepper to taste
2 firm medium eggplants, sliced into ¾-inch-thick slices

Corn Pudding (page 27)
About ¼ cup Aïoli (page 337)

Put the pork in a baking dish and rub all over with the crushed garlic. Drizzle with the olive oil and sprinkle with the herb leaves. Set aside to marinate at room temperature for 2 hours, or cover and refrigerate for as long as overnight. Bring the meat to room temperature before cooking.

Preheat the oven to 500°F.

Season the pork loin with salt and pepper. Place in a large heavy roasting pan and roast for 15 minutes. Reduce the heat to 325°F and roast for 30 to 45 minutes more, until the internal temperature reaches 145°F on an instant-read thermometer. Remove from the oven and let the meat rest for 15 minutes.

Meanwhile, prepare the eggplant: Prepare a hot grill or preheat the broiler.

Combine the thyme, rosemary, garlic, olive oil, salt, and pepper in a large bowl. Add the eggplant slices and toss to coat. Place on the grill or in the broiler pan and cook until the eggplant is slightly charred, about 3 minutes. Turn and continue cooking until almost soft, 3 to 4 minutes more. Remove from the heat and set aside.

Slice the pork into chops and arrange on individual plates, with the eggplant slices and corn pudding alongside. Garnish each pork chop with a dollop of aïoli.

TO DRINK: Zinfandel, Ridge
    Regaleali Rosso

ROAST PORK LOIN STUFFED WITH ROSEMARY, BACON, AND ONIONS

SERVES 8

Stuffing a pork loin requires a little patience, but the results can be beautiful and show how a few simple ingredients— onion, rosemary, and bacon—can be sublime when combined. Try to find naturally raised pork such as that from Niman Ranch (see Sources, page 352) for the best flavor. If you're lucky enough to have leftovers, they're a real treat. Wilted Greens (page 265), such as escarole or rapini, tossed with olive oil makes a quick and tasty side dish.

½ pound slab bacon, cut into 1-inch cubes

4 medium onions, cut into 1-inch dice

2 cups 1-inch cubes crustless day-old French bread

2 garlic cloves, crushed and finely chopped

2 rosemary sprigs, leaves removed and finely chopped

1 small bunch flat-leaf parsley, leaves removed and
    finely chopped

Kosher salt and freshly ground black pepper

1 to 2 tablespoons olive oil or chicken broth, if necessary

1 center-cut boneless pork loin roast (about 4 pounds)

Place the bacon and onions in a roasting pan and roast, stirring once or twice, until the onions are slightly golden and the bacon is semi-crisp, about 15 minutes. Transfer the onions and bacon, with all the drippings, to a bowl and set the pan aside. (Leave the oven on.) Add the bread cubes, garlic, rosemary, and parsley to the bowl and season with salt and pepper. You may need to moisten the mixture with a little olive oil or a splash of chicken broth. Let cool.

Meanwhile, prepare the pork: Preheat the oven to 450°F. Insert a sharp boning knife or other long thin knife into the center of one end of the roast and turn it in a circular motion to create a hole. Then insert a clean sharpening steel or the handle of a wooden spoon and push against the meat to create a larger space in the center of the pork loin. Continue until you've created a 1½-inch-diameter tunnel all the way through the pork.

Place the stuffing in a pastry bag without a tip and pipe the stuffing into the pork loin. Tie the pork loin into an even roll with kitchen twine. Season with salt and pepper and place in the roasting pan. Roast for 20 minutes.

Turn the oven down to 325°F and continue roasting for another 30 minutes, or until the internal temperature reaches 145° to 150°F on an instant-read thermometer. Allow the pork to rest on a rack set over a platter for 5 or 10 minutes.

Slice the pork 1 inch thick and arrange a couple of slices on each plate.

TO DRINK: Rioja Gran Reserva, Marqués de Murrieta
    Barbera d'Asti, Coppo

PORK CHOPS AND BROCHETTES WITH CREAMY GRITS AND MAKER'S MARK SAUCE

SERVES 4

We suggest the combination of these two cuts of pork for the great contrast in texture and appearance it provides. Should you care to simplify this dish, just serve the brochette without the chop, or vice versa. Paired with Creamy Grits (page 22) and bourbon, it is deliciously down-home.

FOR THE PORK

4 garlic cloves, crushed
2 shallots, thinly sliced
1 teaspoon coarsely ground black pepper
¼ teaspoon coarsely ground allspice berries
¼ cup olive oil
Four 6-ounce bone-in loin pork chops
One 12-ounce pork tenderloin, trimmed and
    cut into four 3-ounce portions

FOR THE SAUCE

1 tablespoon vegetable oil
1 slice bacon, chopped
1 small onion, roughly chopped
1 carrot, peeled and roughly chopped
2 garlic cloves, crushed
1½ teaspoons tomato paste
1 tablespoon molasses or honey
½ cup Maker's Mark or other good bourbon
4 cups Chicken or Beef Broth (page 339 or 340),
    or canned low-sodium broth
1 thyme sprig, 1 parsley sprig, 1 marjoram sprig, and
    1 bay leaf tied together to make a bouquet garni

Kosher salt and freshly ground black pepper
Four 5-inch wooden skewers, soaked for 30 minutes
1 large Vidalia onion, cut into eighths
8 bay leaves

Combine the garlic, shallots, pepper, allspice, and 2 tablespoons of the olive oil in a large shallow baking dish. Add all the pork and massage the mixture into the meat. Cover and marinate in the refrigerator for at least 4 hours, or overnight.

To prepare the sauce, heat the oil in a saucepan over medium-high heat. Add the bacon and vegetables and cook, stirring occasionally, for 10 minutes. Add the garlic and cook for about 5 minutes longer, until the vegetables are caramelized. Add the tomato paste and molasses, stirring to combine. Add the bourbon and ignite with a long match (or carefully tip the pan near the flame so that the vapors ignite). Reduce until a quarter of the mixture remains and a glaze forms. Add the broth and bouquet garni and bring to a boil. Reduce by half, skimming frequently to remove any fat that accumulates on the surface.

Strain the sauce and return to the saucepan. Boil to reduce further, until the broth is dark, rich, and coats the back of a spoon. Remove from the heat and set aside. (The sauce can be made several hours ahead, covered, and refrigerated.)

Prepare a hot grill. Rub the grates of the grill with olive oil.

Remove the pork chops and medallions from the marinade and season with salt and pepper. Grill, turning once, until medium-rare to medium, about 8 to 10 minutes, or cook to desired doneness. Transfer to a rack to rest.

Meanwhile, assemble the brochettes: Thread a wedge of onion, followed by a bay leaf, pork medallion, another wedge of onion, and a bay leaf onto each skewer. Brush all with the remaining 2 tablespoons olive oil and season with salt and pepper. Grill, turning once, until the pork is medium-rare and the onions are tender, 6 to 8 minutes total.

Just before serving, reheat the sauce over low heat.

Spoon a portion of the grits into the center of each dinner plate and place a grilled chop and brochette in the center. Ladle the sauce around and serve.

TO DRINK: Cabernet Sauvignon, Spottswood
            Cabernet Sauvignon, Joseph Phelps

PORK SCALOPPINE
WITH MINT PESTO

SERVES 4

This is a southern take on an Italian dish. The Genovese veal scaloppine would have a pesto with pine nuts, walnuts, and basil. We show off our fondness for pork, pairing it with mint and pecans in a "deconstructed" pesto that highlights these ingredients both separately and combined in a puree. Thin medallions of pork make for quick and easy cooking. Serve with a fluffy rice pilaf or Crushed Creamer Potatoes (page 263).

One 2-pound boneless pork loin roast, cut into 12 medallions
1 heaping cup loosely packed mint leaves (from about
**   2 bunches), plus a few sprigs for garnish**
2 garlic cloves, crushed
Kosher salt and freshly ground black pepper
½ cup pecan halves, toasted (see page 346)
¼ cup freshly grated Parmigiano-Reggiano or Grana Padano,
**   plus shavings for garnish**
¼ cup freshly grated pecorino Romano
½ cup extra virgin olive oil
2 tablespoons peanut, canola, or olive oil

Place the pork medallions between two sheets of plastic wrap and lightly pound each one to ½ inch thick. Place the pork on a platter and let come to room temperature while you prepare the pesto.

Roughly chop the mint leaves and transfer to a large mortar or a food processor. Add the garlic, season with a pinch each of salt and pepper, and pound with the pestle or pulse in the food processor until reduced to a paste. Add three-quarters of the pecans, reserving the rest for garnish, and crush or pulse a little more. Add the grated cheeses and continue crushing or pulsing. If you're using a mortar, transfer the mixture to a bowl and stir in the olive oil. If using a processor, pulse a few more times to incorporate the oil. The pesto should be a bit coarse. Taste and adjust the seasoning.

Heat two large heavy sauté pans over high heat (if you have only one large pan, cook the pork in batches, keeping the first batch warm on a platter covered with foil). Add the peanut oil to the pans and heat until almost smoking. Season the pork with salt and pepper and place the medallions in the pans, without touching one another. Reduce the heat to medium-high and cook until golden on the first side, 3 to 4 minutes. Turn and cook until medium, 3 to 4 minutes more. The juices will be slightly rosy, not clear.

Arrange the medallions on serving plates. Spoon a little pesto on top and scatter about the reserved pecans, shaved Parmigiano, and mint sprigs.

TO DRINK: Valpolicella, Allegrini
        Vino Nobile de Montepulciano, Poliziano

I realized the importance of ceremony at an early age. I was the one who would encourage my mother to set the table with our best china and the silver. Even when it was not a holiday, the dinner hour was sacrosanct. We all had to be properly washed up and, though we did not necessarily have to be well dressed, we would never have thought of wearing just a T-shirt and jeans to the dinner table. When we sat down to eat, it was "Yes, ma'am" and "Yes, sir" and "Thank you, Mother, for dinner."

The ritual was almost militaristic in its formality. As a somewhat cocky and obnoxious twelve-year-old, I once had the audacity to leave the table without thanking my mother. My father whipped me for the indiscretion. In my house, manners mattered.

Looking back, I think that kind of pomp and ceremony helped me appreciate all the work, the toil, and sacrifices that my parents put into feeding us. It made me realize the value of food in a spiritual kind of way. That nascent awareness also benefited from our family's practice of taking turns saying a blessing over each meal. By the time I was in college, I was likely to be the one who would express an appreciation of the food and of the farmer and of the land, of all things that brought our family together at the table.

As an adult, I came to appreciate the blessing as a time to open our minds to a greater awareness of the beauty of the food we were about to eat. Instead of asking my family to endure a rote blessing, I wanted to pay homage to food as sacrament. I have since refined that idea, incorporating it into the at-table stories I share with friends and family. I want everyone to come to understand the ancient rhythms of life, to know what it felt like to break bread at my mother's table, to understand why upon walking by my maternal grandmother's long-closed smokehouse

I was transported back to the days when our people slaughtered their own hogs. I want them to understand that such acts were honorable, that to harvest a hog with your own hands, by the sweat of your own brow, was to know intimately the consequences and benefits of humanity.

That smokehouse still looms large in my imagination. As a boy, I was curious about its purpose, and my mother told me stories of how, on a cold winter's day, when the winds began howling from the northwest, the men would gather to kill a hog, and to break it down into hocks, bacon, jowls, and hams. And so when I walked by that smokehouse, I conjured up those days: I heard the muffled talk of the men, the scrape of the knife on the stone. I saw it then as I see it today, not as a bacchanal, but as a solemn ceremony whereby one life is sacrificed so that others might be stronger, so that we might prosper and do for others.

RED WINE–BRAISED RABBIT WITH WILD MUSHROOMS

SERVES 6 • PHOTOGRAPH PAGE 198

Rabbit is very versatile, great for sautéing, roasting, braising, or stuffing. Free of fat or skin, it is a healthy alternative to chicken and other more ordinary cuts of meat. Rabbit cooked in a slow braise becomes wonderfully tender, delicate, and sumptuous. Red wine adds a robust quality to the braise, and the wild mushrooms and spoonbread warm the soul.

You could substitute chicken for the rabbit, but rabbit's subtle nuances reward the effort.

2 fresh rabbits, cut into serving pieces (see page 349)

FOR THE MARINADE

1 medium onion, sliced

1 cup red wine, such as Syrah or Côtes-du-Rhône

1 tablespoon olive oil

3 garlic cloves, crushed

4 juniper berries, toasted (see page 346) and coarsely ground

2 rosemary sprigs, coarsely chopped

2 thyme sprigs

Kosher salt and freshly ground black pepper

FOR THE BRAISE

1 tablespoon olive oil, or as needed

1 heaping cup diced carrots

2 garlic cloves, finely minced

3 or 4 slices dried porcini mushrooms, rinsed and soaked for 30 minutes in ½ cup hot chicken broth or water

2 cups red wine, such as Syrah or Côtes-du-Rhône

½ cup port

2 cups Chicken Broth (page 339) or canned low-sodium broth

4 thyme sprigs, 6 flat-leaf parsley sprigs, 1 leek top, and 2 bay leaves, tied together to make a bouquet garni

3 tablespoons unsalted butter

¼ pound fresh porcini, morel, chanterelle, or cremini mushrooms, trimmed

Spoonbread (page 20)

Chopped flat-leaf parsley, basil, or thyme for garnish

Place the rabbit in a shallow ceramic or other nonreactive dish. In a small bowl, combine all the marinade ingredients. Pour the marinade over the rabbit, turning to coat, cover, and marinate in the refrigerator for 6 to 24 hours.

Remove the rabbit from the marinade and set aside. Strain the marinade into a bowl, reserving the vegetables; set the liquid and vegetables aside.

Preheat the oven to 325°F.

Pat the rabbit pieces dry and season them with salt and pepper. In a deep heavy ovenproof skillet or a Dutch oven, heat the oil over medium-high heat. Add the rabbit pieces, in batches, being careful not to crowd the skillet, and sear, turning once until they are golden brown, 10 to 12 minutes; carefully monitor the heat so that the oil does not burn, adding more oil between batches if necessary. Transfer the rabbit to a rack set over a baking sheet.

Add the carrots, garlic, and reserved vegetables from the marinade to the skillet and cook over medium heat until softened, about 10 minutes. Add the dried mushrooms and their liquid, the wine and port, and the reserved liquid from the marinade. Bring to a simmer and skim off any foam. Add the broth, bouquet garni, and the rabbit and bring back to a simmer. Cover tightly with the lid or aluminum foil and place in the oven. Cook for 15 minutes.

Remove the loin pieces and set aside. Continue to braise the remaining rabbit for 30 to 40 minutes, or until tender. Transfer the rabbit pieces to a rack set over a platter.

Place the skillet half on and half off a burner (this will make skimming off the fat easier) and bring to a boil over medium-high heat. Boil to reduce by half, skimming frequently. Then strain the liquid into a saucepan, reserving the vegetables. Discard the bouquet garni and puree the vegetables through a food mill.

Add the pureed vegetables to the skillet, bring to a simmer, and reduce until the sauce is thick enough to coat a spoon. Adjust the seasoning.

Meanwhile, in a small sauté pan, melt the butter over medium-high heat. Add the fresh mushrooms and sauté until some of their juices are released but they are still firm, 3 to 4 minutes. Remove from the heat.

Just before serving, rewarm the rabbit in the sauce.

Place a helping of spoonbread in the center of each plate and surround with the rabbit and mushrooms. Spoon the sauce over the rabbit and garnish with the chopped herbs.

TO DRINK: Saint Joseph, J. L. Chave

Shiraz–Cabernet Franc–Cabernet Sauvignon, Fox Creek JSM

RABBIT STUFFED WITH APPLE DUXELLES

SERVES 4

Although this recipe has a few more steps than the usual braise—boning the leg and preparing the duxelles stuffing—it can be accomplished up to two days in advance. And your efforts will be rewarded with a spectacular dish of incomparable flavor, perfect for special occasions. Instructions are provided here, but you could ask your butcher to bone the rabbit legs. Glazed apple wedges and carrots (see Note) make a delicious rustic accompaniment, or consider Autumn Root Vegetable Puree (page 266).

2 rabbits, legs removed, rinsed, and patted dry (loins reserved for another use, such as Rabbit Loin Salad, page 87)

4 slices apple-smoked bacon, finely chopped

1 shallot, finely minced

1 medium onion, ½ finely minced, ½ finely diced

2 semi-tart apples, such as Braeburn, Fuji, or Granny Smith, finely diced

1 cup mixed fresh trimmed mushrooms, such as cremini and button

1 tablespoon chopped flat-leaf parsley leaves

1 tablespoon chopped thyme leaves

Kosher salt and freshly ground black pepper

½ cup medium-coarse bread crumbs (see page 347)

1 teaspoon unsalted butter

2 carrots, finely diced

1 celery stalk, finely diced

1 tablespoon olive oil

2 thyme sprigs and 2 bay leaves, tied together to make a bouquet garni

¾ cup white wine

2 tablespoons Calvados

1½ cups Chicken Broth (page 339) or canned low-sodium broth

Use a sharp boning knife or other small sharp knife to bone the rabbit. Make an incision along the hip joint of each leg and allow the knife tip to follow the thighbone to the knee joint. Then curve around the knee and follow to the end of the shinbone. Once the bone is exposed, cut along either side to remove it. Flatten the boned leg by lightly pounding it with the heel of your hand (or a meat pounder) to an even thickness, about ½ inch. You may need to "butterfly" the thickest part of the thigh by slicing through it just deep enough to produce two flaps, like a butterfly, without cutting all the way through. Set aside.

Preheat the oven to 325°F.

To prepare the apple duxelles, cook the bacon in a sauté pan over medium heat until semi-crisp. With a slotted spoon, transfer the bacon to paper towels to drain. Return the pan drippings to the stove, add the shallot, minced onion, and half of the apples, and sauté until soft, 5 to 6 minutes. Add the mushrooms and sauté until most of the liquid from the mushrooms has evaporated, about 10 minutes more. Transfer to a bowl, add the bacon, parsley, and thyme, and season with salt and pepper. Add the bread crumbs and mix thoroughly.

To stuff the rabbit, place the legs on a work surface and season with salt and pepper. Spoon 2 to 3 tablespoons of the duxelles onto each rabbit leg, spreading it evenly. Fold over the short ends, then roll up from a long side to form an envelopelike package. Tie each with kitchen twine.

Melt the butter in a medium sauté pan over medium heat. Add the diced carrots, onion, and celery and sauté just until softened, about 5 minutes. Set this mirepoix aside.

Heat a sauté pan just large enough to hold the rabbit over medium-high heat. Add the olive oil, and season the packages with salt and pepper. Sear over medium heat on all sides until golden, 8 to 10 minutes total. Transfer to a casserole and add the bouquet garni, mirepoix, and remaining apples. Pour out any fat from the sauté pan and deglaze with the white wine and Calvados, stirring up the browned bits. Boil to reduce by half, then add the chicken broth and bring to a simmer. Pour the liquid over the rabbit, cover the rabbit with parchment, and then cover tightly with the lid or aluminum foil.

Place the casserole in the oven and braise for about 45 minutes. Check the rabbit for tenderness by testing with the tip of a knife: There should be almost no resistance. Remove the casserole from the oven and allow the rabbit to rest, uncovered, in the braising liquid for 10 minutes.

Transfer the rabbit to a rack set over a platter and cover to keep warm. Strain the braising liquid into a saucepan. Set the pan half on and half off a burner (this will make skimming off the fat easier) and bring to a boil over high heat. Boil to reduce by half, skimming to remove the fat that accumulates on the surface.

Remove the twine from the rabbit and slice each leg on the diagonal into 3 slices. Arrange each portion atop a generous spoonful of root vegetable puree or a helping of roasted apples and carrots. Spoon the sauce around each serving.

NOTE: To glaze apple wedges and carrots, place like-size carrot sections and apple wedges in a sauté pan with a dab of butter, a tablespoon of water, a tiny pinch of sugar, and Kosher salt and freshly ground black pepper to taste and cook over medium heat until glazed, 4 to 5 minutes.

TO DRINK: Pinot Noir, Williams Selyem
Pinot Noir, Ken Wright

VEGETABLES

When I think about the

southern larder of favored ingredients, I first think about vegetables—collard, mustard, and turnip greens cooked with a little smoked pork and a bit of onion, then finished with a splash of hot pepper vinegar. Then there is okra—one of those vegetables that divides people almost as strongly as being an Auburn or Alabama fan. Many will eat only fried okra and would shudder to think of a plate of it boiled. Boiled-okra aficionados are of a gentler breed. They like theirs cooked simply with a bit of butter, but aren't so strident as to turn up their noses at a plate of the fried—especially if prepared the way my grandmother White cooked it. She would toss cornmeal-crusted okra in a half inch of lard in a well-seasoned cast-iron skillet and fry it until it was golden brown and crisp. This crunchy treat was our reward for dangerous work—picking okra. Anyone who has ever spent any time in an okra patch in the hot summertime in short sleeves knows that the okra plant is a formidable opponent: Its leaves are armed with little stinging edges that can make life miserable. But anticipating the treat that would come of our hard labor made it worth the effort.

When a southerner talks about peas and beans, it's a broad subject. There are pink-eyes, black-eyes, crowders, zipper, lady peas, butter peas, baby green butter beans, big Fordhook limas, speckled butter beans, cranberry beans (also called October beans), pinto beans, pole beans, bush beans such as Kentucky Wonder and Blue Lake, and rattlesnake beans, with a reddish stripe down the side. From my north Alabama perspective, small southern farmers developed a big appreciation for the wide variety of peas and beans because, historically, these were crops that could take the place of more expensive proteins such as meat, with two or three types often being served at one meal.

At the beginning of summer, sacks of beans and peas from south Georgia arrive at our Birmingham farmers' market. Eventually, south Alabama produce trickles in, and before long our local farms' harvests appear. To see row after row of mechanical pea shellers in action is quite a sight: These are big ribbed wooden vaults that spin around, separating the peas from the pods. A mountain of pods builds up to the side, destined for the slop pile as hog feed. Paper bags placed underneath the chicken-wire spout catch the shelled peas and beans fresh for cooking. The older pods are filled with the most peas, but the young pods offer up the greenest, smallest, choicest ones—these are what we look for.

Toward the end of the growing season, in late August or September, there is a scramble to "put up" vegetables for the rest of the year. An old-fashioned idea, perhaps, but one I adhere to. We quickly blanch and freeze just-picked vegetables, such as shell peas, beans, corn (off the cob), and okra, on sheet pans and then vacuum-pack them for the freezer. The results are surprisingly good, and in this way I can preserve a little of summer's freshest harvest to enjoy throughout the year.

Pea Cakes with Tomato Salsa, page 254 }

ASPARAGUS SALAD WITH CRAWFISH AÏOLI

SERVES 4 AS AN APPETIZER

Just-dug new potatoes and asparagus are in season at the same time crawfish are at their best, so it's a perfect time to pair them. If crawfish are not available, small chopped cooked shrimp or lump crabmeat makes a delicious variation. Although aïoli is called for here, a simple mayonnaise (homemade if possible) works equally well.

This is actually a springtime composed salad, highlighting favas, little beets, and tender watercress leaves. We boost our standard sherry vinaigrette with mustard, sugar, and tarragon and then dress each vegetable separately so as not to muddle flavors or let the beets color the other vegetables. This salad is a beautiful presentation.

16 to 20 jumbo asparagus spears, tough ends cut off and
    bottom halves peeled
¼ cup plus 2 tablespoons Sherry Vinaigrette (page 330)
1 tablespoon Dijon mustard
1 teaspoon sugar
2 tarragon sprigs, leaves removed and chopped
6 new potatoes, cut into ¼-inch-thick slices, cooked in boiling
    salted water just until tender, drained, and patted dry
Kosher salt and freshly ground black pepper
4 cooked baby beets or 1 large beet (see Note)
1 bunch watercress, trimmed, washed, and dried
¼ pound crawfish tailmeat (see Sources, page 352;
    or substitute chopped boiled shrimp or jumbo lump
    crabmeat), picked free of shells and cartilage
Scant ½ cup Aïoli (page 337)
4 fava beans, shelled, blanched, and outer skin removed
    (see Note, page 207)
A small bunch chives, sliced
A few mint or flat-leaf parsley sprigs, leaves removed and
    torn into little pieces, or a few small chervil sprigs

Bring a medium saucepan of generously salted water to a boil. Prepare an ice bath (see page 346). Add the asparagus to the boiling water and cook until tender, 4 to 5 minutes. Drain and immerse in the ice bath to cool, then drain again and pat dry.

While the asparagus is cooking, in a small bowl, mix the vinaigrette, mustard, sugar, and tarragon until well combined.

In another small bowl, toss the potatoes with 1 tablespoon of the vinaigrette mixture. Season with salt and pepper and set aside.

Toss the beets and watercress with another tablespoon of the vinaigrette mixture in another bowl and season with salt and pepper.

In yet another bowl, season the crawfish with salt and pepper, add 1 tablespoon of the vinaigrette mixture, and toss. Add the aïoli and toss to thoroughly coat. Taste and adjust the seasoning.

To serve, toss the asparagus with 2 tablespoons of the vinaigrette mixture, season with salt and pepper, and arrange on individual plates. Scatter the potatoes, beets, and fava beans about the asparagus. Put a big dollop of the crawfish aïoli in the center of each plate. Drizzle everything with the remaining vinaigrette mixture and sprinkle with the herbs.

NOTE: To bake beets, trim them and wrap in foil. Bake in a 350°F oven for 30 minutes to 1 hour, depending on size. Let cool, then peel.

TO DRINK: Savennières, Domaine des Beaumard
          Pinot blanc, Etude

My favorite green vegetable is asparagus. Out of all my fellow grandchildren, I was the one Grandmother White honored each year with an invitation to the hallowed ground that was her asparagus bed. At the end of every April or early in May, I followed her to the patch situated on a slightly rising hillside next to the vegetable garden on the east side of her house. The beds were rich and dark with old manure from beneath the barn, and the warm spring weather had sent the asparagus shoots upward like little vegetable skyscrapers. Grandmother taught me to break the stalks at their base along the soil line, and we would gather enough for our family to enjoy over the course of several meals: We loved it simply boiled and anointed with melted butter—a taste of heaven on earth. The intense green, almost fruitlike sweetness and earthy aroma of just-snapped asparagus is unforgettable. Grandmother was delighted to see me in such awe of her gardening achievement.

There are so many ways I like to serve asparagus that it's hard to limit myself to just a few, so I offer up some guidelines for preparing my favorite vegetable in addition to providing recipes sure to make you come worship at the asparagus altar. Just-picked asparagus of any size is tasty, but the jumbo spears are the ultimate—meaty, plump, and full of flavor. I hold no fondness for the esteemed white asparagus, with its stringy texture and somewhat anemic taste. Why would anyone go to the trouble of hiding shoots from the sun to keep them from turning their natural vibrant green? Some consider albino asparagus a delicacy, but I have never tasted a pallid stalk that could come close to the springtime flavor of asparagus grown in the sun's full glory, the way nature intended.

{ Asparagus with Farm Eggs and Ham Hock Vinaigrette, page 246

Asparagus with Crawfish Meunière, page 245

One time, at a late spring lunch at Richard Olney's hillside Provençal home, he shared with me the purist's view of asparagus preparation, service, and method of consumption. Peel the bottom half of large fresh asparagus spears. Bring a large pot of salted water to a boil, add the asparagus, and cook over moderately high heat until tender, about 5 minutes, depending on size and freshness. Drain the spears and blot them of excess moisture with a clean kitchen towel. At the table, let each guest create a vinaigrette for the asparagus to suit his or her taste by whisking good red wine vinegar with sea salt, freshly ground black pepper, and the best-quality extra virgin olive oil in a little puddle right on the plate. Those fortunate enough to be seated at your table simply turn the spears in the vinaigrette to be eaten out of hand.

ASPARAGUS
WITH CRAWFISH MEUNIÈRE

SERVES 4 AS AN APPETIZER • PHOTOGRAPH PAGE 244

This is one of those dishes that is so simple, yet so stunningly good. Make sure that all of your ingredients are perfectly fresh, and of the highest possible quality. The crawfish tails are already thoroughly cooked, so be careful to just heat them through to retain their tender plumpness—extended cooking will make them tough. In addition to the shrimp and crab mentioned as alternatives below, you could also substitute steamed mussels or clams for the crawfish.

Kosher salt
16 jumbo asparagus spears, rough ends cut away and
    bottom half peeled
4 tablespoons unsalted butter
2 to 3 spring onions or 2 small sweet white onions,
    such as Vidalia, finely chopped
1 garlic clove, finely chopped
½ pound crawfish tailmeat (see Sources, page 352;
    or substitute chopped boiled shrimp or crabmeat),
    picked over
3 tablespoons white wine
Juice of ½ lemon
Freshly ground black pepper
Dash of hot pepper sauce, such as Tabasco or Cholula
2 tablespoons chopped chives, flat-leaf parsley,
    or mint for garnish

Bring a large saucepan of water to a boil. Add 1 tablespoon salt and the asparagus and cook until tender, 4 to 5 minutes. Drain and pat dry.

Meanwhile, melt a scant tablespoon of the butter in a medium saucepan over medium heat. Add the spring onions and cook until just tender, about 4 minutes. Add the garlic and cook for another minute. Add the crawfish and white wine and simmer until the wine has reduced by half. Add the lemon juice, then whisk in the remaining butter bit by bit. Season with salt, pepper, and hot sauce.

Arrange the asparagus on plates and spoon the crawfish meunière over the top. Garnish with the fresh herbs.

TO DRINK: Pouilly-Fuissé, Domaine Denogent
            Pinot Gris, Pierre Sparr

GRILLED JUMBO ASPARAGUS
WITH EGG AND
HERB VINAIGRETTE

SERVES 4 AS AN APPETIZER • PHOTOGRAPH PAGE 249

This dish embodies the simple, straightforward style of bistro cooking at its best. If you don't have on hand all the herbs listed for the vinaigrette, do try to use at least two of them. Be sure to serve the asparagus sizzling hot from the grill: When the egg and herb vinaigrette hits, the aroma explodes.

16 jumbo asparagus spears, tough ends cut away and
    bottom half peeled
4 hard-boiled large eggs, peeled and pressed through a sieve
    or finely chopped
¼ cup Sherry Vinaigrette (page 330)
⅓ cup coarsely chopped chives, flat-leaf parsley, tarragon,
    and/or chervil
Kosher salt and freshly ground black pepper
Olive oil for brushing

Prepare a hot grill.

Bring a large saucepan of salted water to a boil. Add the asparagus and cook until just tender, about 4 minutes. Drain and blot dry on a kitchen towel.

In a medium bowl, combine the eggs, vinaigrette, and all but 1 tablespoon of the herbs. Season with salt and pepper.

Brush the grill with a little olive oil. Place the asparagus spears on the hot grill and brush with olive oil. Grill, turning occasionally, until lightly charred, about 4 minutes total.

Divide the asparagus among serving plates. Spoon a fat ribbon of the vinaigrette over each plate of asparagus. Garnish with a scattering of the remaining herbs.

TO DRINK: Champagne, Billecart-Salmon Rosé
            Champagne, Pommerey Brut

ASPARAGUS WITH FARM EGGS AND HAM HOCK VINAIGRETTE

SERVES 4 AS AN APPETIZER • PHOTOGRAPH PAGE 242

Oxford is a charming college town that is home to the University of Mississippi. There, not long ago, the first Southern Foodways Symposium was held on a beautiful spring day, and we were honored with an invitation to cook a southern lunch for participants. Underneath the big old oaks on campus, we served a meal of warm asparagus with spring vegetables in an uncommon ham hock vinaigrette and a most unusual main course of pigs' ears blanketed with a crunchy mustard and bread crumb crust. The food was a huge success. That meal was the inspiration for this recipe.

The smoky bits of ham hock add a depth of flavor to this composed salad of spring onions, just-dug potatoes, farm eggs, and asparagus.

2 meaty smoked ham hocks (see page 218)

3 thyme sprigs, 3 flat-leaf parsley sprigs, and 1 bay leaf, tied together to make a bouquet garni

2 small spring onions, quartered

Tiny pinch of sugar

Kosher salt and freshly ground black pepper

2½ tablespoons extra virgin olive oil

4 small creamer potatoes (tiny new potatoes)

16 jumbo asparagus spears, tough ends cut away and bottom half peeled

4 large hard-boiled eggs, organic or "free-range," peeled and quartered

1 heaping cup young lettuces, such as baby arugula or watercress, trimmed, washed, and dried

¼ cup Three-Vinegar Vinaigrette (page 329)

Put the ham hocks in a deep medium saucepan and add water to cover by 3 to 4 inches. Add the bouquet garni, bring to a simmer, and cook slowly until the meat is tender, 2 to 3 hours, adding water if neccessary to keep the hocks well covered. Remove from the heat and let cool in the broth. Remove the ham hocks and pick the meat from the bones; set aside. Reserve the broth for another purpose, if desired.

Place the onions in a small saucepan just large enough to hold them in a single layer and season with the sugar and salt and pepper. Add 1 tablespoon of the olive oil (or ham fat) and bring to a simmer. Cook until the onions are just tender and slightly glazed, about 10 minutes. Set the pan aside.

Prepare a hot grill.

Meanwhile, cook the potatoes in boiling salted water until just tender, 10 to 15 minutes, depending on size. Drain, return to the hot pan, and cover to keep warm.

While the potatoes cook, bring a large saucepan of salted water to a boil, add the asparagus, and cook until just tender, about 4 minutes. Drain and blot dry on a kitchen towel. Spread the asparagus on a platter and drizzle with the remaining 1½ tablespoons olive oil. Season with salt and pepper.

Place the spears on the hot grill, turning to char on all sides, about 4 minutes. Meanwhile, reheat the onions over low heat.

Transfer the asparagus to serving plates and arrange the hard-boiled-egg wedges, potatoes, onions, and lettuces attractively around them. Add the ham hock meat to the vinaigrette, and drizzle it over everything.

TO DRINK: Sancerre, Delaporte

Grüner Veltliner Federspiel, Prager

GRATIN OF ASPARAGUS, SPRING ONIONS, AND MUSHROOMS

SERVES 4 TO 6 • PHOTOGRAPH PAGE 248

Here we combine lots of spring goodness. Yes, it's a little decadent, but this type of big bubbly gratin isn't served every day, and it always brings oohs and aahs at the table. It makes a wonderful accompaniment to grilled quail or a roast pork salad or a simple leg of lamb. For an elegant formal menu, bridge the first course and main course with this rich vegetable gratin.

Eggs boiled and quartered are a provincial French favorite ingredient in gratins. I too love the old-fashioned heartiness they add.

Kosher salt

12 to 14 large or jumbo asparagus spears,
    tough ends cut away and bottom halves peeled

4 tablespoons unsalted butter

2 spring onions, halved or quartered, depending on size,
    green tops included

¼ pound morel or button mushrooms, trimmed and halved
    or quartered, depending on size

Freshly ground black pepper

4 hard-boiled large eggs, peeled and quartered

2 tablespoons freshly grated Parmigiano-Reggiano

2 tablespoons freshly grated Comté or Gruyère

1 cup medium-coarse bread crumbs (see page 347)

½ cup heavy cream

Preheat the oven to 425°F. Butter a 10-inch gratin dish.

Bring a medium to large saucepan of water to a boil. Prepare an ice bath (see page 346). Add 1 tablespoon of salt and the asparagus and cook until just tender, 4 to 5 minutes. Drain and immerse in the ice water to stop the cooking. When they are cold, remove the asparagus and pat dry. Cut into 2-inch lengths; set aside.

In a large sauté pan, melt 1 tablespoon of the butter over medium heat. Add the onions and cook until just softened, about 3 minutes. Add the mushrooms and cook until tender, about 5 minutes. Season with salt and pepper and spread evenly in the buttered gratin dish.

Nestle the asparagus among the onions and mushrooms. Tuck the quartered eggs in and around and season with salt and pepper. Scatter the cheeses over the top, followed by the bread crumbs. Pour the cream along the outside edge so as not to displace the cheese and bread crumbs. Dot the top with the remaining 3 tablespoons butter.

Place the gratin dish on the top rack of the oven and bake until golden and bubbly, about 25 minutes.

TO DRINK: Puligny Montrachet, Domaine Etienne Sauzet
Pinot Gris, Domaine Weinbach

Opposite: Preparations for Gratin of Asparagus, Spring Onions, and Mushrooms, page 247. *Above:* Grilled Jumbo Asparagus with Egg and Herb Vinaigrette, page 245.

Throughout the lean years of Reconstruction, World War I, and the Great Depression, southerners survived on peas and shell beans. Even after World War II, the masses of subsistence farmers lived from their small gardens, and shell beans were a staple alongside corn bread and sorghum syrup. Today, southerners still revere the nuances of a variety of fresh and dried beans. The long summer provides optimum growing conditions, and the beans make ideal candidates for "putting up" for the gray days of winter. Frozen or dried, they hold up very well, but to me, freezing them is the much better choice. Sadly, these days, the majority of black-eyed peas in the marketplace are of inferior quality and come from the least expensive South American sources. They are a far cry from fresh peas that you blanch, shock, and freeze yourself. The frozen ones maintain a green essence not found in dried ones.

Now let's set the record straight: In the South, the words *peas* and *beans* are often confusingly used for the same things. Technically, they all are "shell beans," meaning beans that are shelled for the little beans, or peas, inside—that's where the name can change to peas. Black-eyed peas, pink-eyed peas, crowder peas, zipper peas, and lady peas all look somewhat similar in their pods. Once they are shelled, their differences are more noticeable. Butter peas are similar to crowders but are more oval, while butter beans are flatter. Cranberry beans, pinto beans, cannellini, and borlotti beans have a similar shape and texture but differ in color.

The pea season begins in late spring to early summer, say, June 1, and lasts, theoretically, until the first frost, late October to mid-November—but the growers' production slows down drastically around the first of September.

{ *Left to right:* Green crowder peas (or zippers), butter peas, pink-eyed peas, baby butter beans, and lady peas.

The younger, smaller shell beans yield peas with more "greenness" to them, full of chlorophyll and fresh plumpness. These do not come out of the shell quite as easily (therefore the yield is diminished), but their uncommon savoriness is worth the effort.

In the South, lady peas and butter peas have an almost cultlike following—they are especially delicate with an elegant flavor. These peas are a bit of a rare commodity, but they are certainly worth the search. Pink-eyed peas, butter peas, baby butter beans or limas, Fordhook limas, speckled butter beans, crowder peas, and lady peas are available seasonally at local farmers' markets, or you can buy them frozen by mail order.

McKenzie's brand offers a wide variety of southern peas. Sold in one-pound frozen packages, they generally are "put up" fresh, maintaining lots of pea flavor. This southern company is now owned by a large conglomerate, so its peas should be increasingly available outside the South.

PINK-EYED PEA SALAD

SERVES 8 AS AN APPETIZER

Here we incorporate an Italian influence of roasted peppers and mozzarella for a flavorful summertime salad.

FOR THE PEAS
2 pounds pink-eyed peas, shelled (see page 251)
1 onion, cut in half
2 bay leaves
4 thyme sprigs
2 dried hot chile peppers
1 teaspoon Kosher salt
1 ham hock or a small chunk of slab bacon

FOR THE SALAD
2 red bell peppers, roasted (see page 345),
    peeled, seeded, and cut into 2-inch-wide strips
2 yellow bell peppers, roasted, peeled, seeded,
    and cut into 2-inch-wide strips
½ pound fresh mozzarella, sliced into ¼-inch rounds
    (or substitute goat cheese)
¼ pound slab bacon, cut into ⅛-inch cubes
    and cooked until crisp
Kosher salt and freshly ground black pepper
1 teaspoon red wine vinegar
2 tablespoons extra virgin olive oil
Basil leaves for garnish
Hard-boiled quail eggs, peeled and halved, for garnish

Combine the peas, onion, bay leaves, thyme sprigs, chile peppers, salt, and ham hock in a large pot, add water to cover by 3 inches, and bring to a simmer. Reduce the heat and simmer gently until the peas are tender, 30 to 45 minutes, depending on how fresh and young the peas are. Set the peas aside to cool in the liquid.

Drain the peas and discard the onion, bay leaves, thyme, and chiles; if desired, remove the meat from the ham hock and reserve for another use (discard the bacon if you used it).

Mound the peas in the center of serving plates. Arrange the pepper strips on one side with the cheese along the other side. Scatter the bacon over the peas, peppers, and cheese. Season with salt and pepper and drizzle the vinegar and olive oil over all. Garnish with the basil and quail eggs.

MARINATED FIELD PEAS AND FRESH HERBS

SERVES 4 TO 6

This southern take on a French lentil salad has become a regular staple in summertime, when peas are at their prime. It is a great barbecue side dish, easy to make, and holds up well for several hours. I like to serve it with creamed corn and fried okra as part of a vegetable plate.

2 pounds pink-eyes, black-eyes, crowders, or butter peas,
    or a combination (see page 251), shelled
2 onions, quartered
1 ham hock or a small chunk of slab bacon
2 dried hot chile peppers
2 bay leaves
1 teaspoon Kosher salt
¼ cup extra virgin olive oil
2 garlic cloves, crushed
1 bunch sage, leaves removed and torn into small pieces
1 bunch thyme, leaves removed
Freshly ground black pepper
Hot pepper sauce, such as Tabasco or Cholula

In a large pot, combine the peas, onions, ham hock, hot peppers, bay leaves, and salt and add cold water to cover by 3 inches. Bring to a simmer, then reduce the heat to low and simmer until tender, 30 to 45 minutes, depending upon the freshness of the peas. Set aside to cool in the cooking liquid, then drain, reserving about ½ cup of the liquid. Discard the onions, chile peppers, and bay leaves; if desired, remove the meat from the ham hock and reserve for another use (discard the bacon if you used it).

In a large pan, heat the olive oil with the garlic, sage, and thyme until fragrant. Add the peas with the reserved cooking liquid and toss to mix. Season with salt and pepper and serve with hot pepper sauce.

PEA CAKES

SERVES 4 • PHOTOGRAPH PAGE 239

Pea cakes are a great way to showcase summer shell beans and are a fine accompaniment to grilled meats, served on their own as an hors d'oeuvre. Top with a big spoonful of Tomato Salsa (page 327) and fresh herbs.

2 cups cooked peas, such as pink-eyes, butter peas,
    or crowders (see page 251; see recipe on page 15
    for cooking instructions), cooking broth reserved
1 cup crumbled Corn Bread (page 26), or more as needed
2 tablespoons chopped chives
1 tablespoon minced hot red chile pepper, such as a ripe jalapeño
1 tablespoon extra virgin olive oil
1 tablespoon all-purpose flour, plus extra for dredging
Kosher salt and freshly ground black pepper to taste
1 large egg, beaten
2 tablespoons vegetable oil
1 recipe Tomato Salsa (see page 327)

Puree ¾ cup of the peas with ¼ cup of the reserved broth in a blender until smooth. Pour into a medium bowl, add the remaining whole peas, 1 tablespoon of the reserved broth, the corn bread, chives, hot pepper, olive oil, flour, and salt and pepper, and mix well. Add the egg and mix again. You may need to adjust the "wetness" by adding a little more corn bread or broth to the mixture; it should be just moist enough to hold together.

Form 8 to 10 small cakes by shaping about 3-tablespoon portions of the mixture into 2-inch-wide disks, compressing the mixture with your fingers and patting it together.

Heat the vegetable oil in a heavy skillet over medium-high heat. Dust the cakes with a little flour and gently place them, in batches if necessary, in the hot oil. Lower the heat to medium and cook, turning once, until golden brown, about 4 minutes on each side. Serve hot.

FIELD PEA AND CORN SALAD

SERVES 4

Great for barbecues or picnics, this dish combines the sweet taste of peas with corn, grilled onion, tomatoes, and a variety of fresh herbs.

2 ears corn, shucked
½ medium red onion
1 cup cooked peas, preferably a mixture
    (see page 15 for cooking instructions)
½ cup seeded diced tomato
½ cup seeded diced green tomato (optional)
1 teaspoon finely minced shallot
1 teaspoon chopped basil
1 teaspoon chopped chives
1 teaspoon chopped flat-leaf parsley
1 teaspoon red wine vinegar, such as L'Estornell's Spanish
    garnacha
1 teaspoon sherry vinegar
2 tablespoons extra virgin olive oil
Kosher salt and freshly ground black pepper to taste

Prepare a hot grill.

Meanwhile, cook the corn in unsalted boiling water for 3 minutes; drain.

Place the corn on the grill and cook, turning occasionally, until charred. Let cool, then slice off the kernels. Grill the onion cut side down until charred. Let cool, then chop.

Combine the corn, onion, and all the remaining ingredients in a large bowl and toss to mix well. Let the flavors marry for an hour in the refrigerator. Bring to room temperature before serving.

GLAZED AUTUMN VEGETABLES

SERVES 4

On a recent fall evening at the restaurant, when we were sending out cabbages, rutabagas, sweet potatoes, and turnips, a guest was overheard saying, "They must not be able to find any good vegetables like asparagus or green beans." I must confess that I derive a great deal of pleasure from incorporating these less glamorous, more humble, "poor-man's" vegetables into a dish. And once people try them, they become converts as well.

4 cipollini onions or pearl onions, peeled and trimmed
4 Brussels sprouts, trimmed and halved
2 medium turnips, peeled and cut into quarters
2 small carrots, peeled and cut into 2½-by-½-inch-thick pieces
1 medium parsnip, peeled and cut into 2½-by-½-inch pieces
1 tablespoon unsalted butter
Pinch of sugar
Kosher salt and freshly ground black pepper to taste
4 thin slices country ham or prosciutto, cut into julienne strips

Place the vegetables in a pan large enough to hold them in a single layer and add just enough water to cover them halfway. Add the butter, sugar, and salt and pepper. Bring to a boil over high heat. Reduce the heat to medium-high and cook until the vegetables are glazed and tender; if the water evaporates before the vegetables are tender, add a little more water and continue cooking. When they are done, keep warm until serving time.

Old-fashioned Potato Gratin

OLD-FASHIONED POTATO GRATIN

SERVES 6

There are countless variations on the potato gratin. You can boil the potatoes in water or milk. You can use broth instead of cream. You can even forgo the cheese (but why?). Experiment, and you'll be sure to find your own signature twist. This recipe is a little decadent because we rely on heavy cream, but it's worth the splurge. A mandoline makes child's play out of slicing the potatoes. Beware of those who cannot resist the golden, crispy top layer—my wife has a tendency to nibble off the top before the gratin ever makes it to the table.

4 large russet potatoes, peeled and sliced about ¼ inch thick
1 garlic clove, crushed
1 tablespoon unsalted butter, at room temperature
Kosher salt and freshly ground white pepper
3 tablespoons freshly grated Parmigiano-Reggiano
3 tablespoons freshly grated Comté cheese (or substitute
  Gruyère or Asiago mixed with a little Parmigiano-Reggiano)
1½ cups heavy cream

Preheat the oven to 350°F.

Put the potato slices in a bowl of water to cover so they don't discolor while you prepare the dish. Firmly rub the garlic clove all over the bottom and sides of a 10-inch gratin dish to coat the interior with its juices. Allow to dry for a few minutes, and then rub the bottom with the butter.

Arrange a layer of potatoes, drained and patted dry, in a slightly overlapping fashion, like a splayed deck of cards, in the bottom of the gratin dish. Season with a good dash of salt and white pepper and a little of each of the two cheeses. Continue layering the potatoes and cheese in this fashion, seasoning each layer and finishing with the cheese (you should have at least three layers). Drizzle the cream along the sides of the dish, so as not to displace the cheese.

Place the gratin, uncovered, on the top oven rack and bake for 1 to 1¼ hours, or until the cream has been absorbed and the top is crispy and golden. Let stand for 10 minutes before serving.

ONION AND BACON GRATIN

SERVES 8

Spring bulb onions, often sold as "Vidalia shoots" from December to May, are mild, sweet, and juicy. There are countless other types of bulb onions found in farmers' markets. Combine them all if you like, and include some of the stems. We love serving this alongside Roast Fresh Pork Leg (page 220).

2 tablespoons unsalted butter, plus (optional) ½ tablespoon
3 large yellow onions, quartered and sliced
2 ounces slab bacon, cut into small lardons
  (1-by-¼-inch-thick strips)
Six 1- to 2-inch-diameter spring onions with stems
Kosher salt and freshly ground black pepper
1 garlic clove, crushed
2 tablespoons freshly grated Parmigiano-Reggiano
2 tablespoons freshly grated Comté (or substitute Gruyère or
  Asiago mixed with a little Parmigiano-Reggiano)
½ cup medium-coarse bread crumbs (see page 347)
½ cup heavy cream

Preheat the oven to 425°F.

In a large sauté pan, melt 1 tablespoon of the butter over medium-high heat. Add the sliced yellow onions and bacon and cook until the onions are quite soft, 10 to 15 minutes. Transfer to a colander to drain.

Meanwhile, trim the spring onions, then cut them, stems still attached, into 4 to 6 wedges each. Place the onions in the sauté pan and add a pinch of salt and pepper, the remaining 1 tablespoon butter, and 2 tablespoons water. Bring to a simmer over high heat and cook until glazed, 5 to 7 minutes.

Rub the bottom and sides of a 10-inch gratin dish with the garlic. Scatter the cooked sliced onions and bacon on the bottom and season with salt and pepper. Top with a layer of the spring onion wedges. Scatter the grated cheeses evenly over the onions, then sprinkle the bread crumbs over the top. Pour the cream in along the edges of the gratin and dot the top with a little extra butter, if desired.

Bake until the gratin is golden and the cream is absorbed, about 25 minutes.

WHITE BEAN AND COLLARD GREEN GRATIN

SERVES 8 TO 10

This recipe came about when I was asked to bring the "fixings" for a side dish to accompany grilled quail at a hunting lodge in Georgia. I love all kinds of vegetable gratins—their crusty tops and rustic appearance never fail to please. Consider this recipe a guide. You can always incorporate other ingredients you have on hand when putting together a vegetable gratin like this. We often serve this alongside Grilled Quail with Rosemary and Garlic (page 186), but it would also be great with a simple pork roast or venison.

5 garlic cloves, 1 crushed, 4 chopped

2 tablespoons olive oil

1 medium onion, chopped

1 small red bell pepper, cored, seeded, and
    cut into 1/2-inch dice

1 large bunch (about 1 pound) collard greens, thoroughly
    washed, blanched in boiling salted water until tender,
    drained, and chopped (to make 1 cup)

3 cups cooked white beans, 1/2 cup cooking liquid reserved
    (see page 15 for cooking instructions)

1/4 to 1/2 cup diced or chopped cooked ham hock, sausage,
    chorizo, or bacon

1/4 cup freshly grated Parmigiano-Reggiano

Extra virgin olive oil

1 rosemary sprig, leaves removed and finely chopped

Kosher salt and freshly ground black pepper to taste

1/4 cup medium-coarse bread crumbs (see page 347)

Preheat the oven to 450°F. Vigorously rub a 10- to 12-inch gratin dish with the crushed garlic clove. Set aside.

In a large sauté pan, heat the oil over medium-high heat. Add the onion and bell pepper and sauté until tender, about 10 minutes. Add the chopped garlic and cook for 1 minute. Add the collard greens and sauté for 1 minute more, stirring to coat.

Transfer the sautéed vegetables to a large mixing bowl and add the beans, ham hock, half of the Parmigiano, a splash of olive oil, the rosemary, and salt and pepper. Taste and adjust the seasoning and add a little of the reserved bean broth as needed to moisten.

Spread the bean mixture in the gratin dish. Top with the remaining cheese, bread crumbs, and a drizzle of extra virgin olive oil. Cover with aluminum foil and bake for 30 to 35 minutes. Remove the foil and bake for an additional 10 minutes, or until the top of the gratin is golden and crusty.

HAM AND PUMPKIN PIRLAU

SERVES 4

Pirlaus are rice stews originally from the Lowcountry, a region that runs from near Myrtle Beach, South Carolina, to Brunswick, Georgia, and about forty miles inland. "Carolina Gold" was the preferred rice of the heads of state—European kings and queens—in the eighteenth and nineteenth centuries, and this fragrant rice has become a staple of Lowcountry cuisine. The word *pirlau* was possibly derived from *pilaf*, another rice dish in which all the ingredients are cooked together. Many different ingredients eventually shared the pot with the Carolina Gold. We now substitute basmati rice—our favorite all-purpose rice—because its nutty aroma brings a fine flavor to our seafood, vegetable, chicken, and pork pirlaus. Here is one especially suited to fall.

2 tablespoons unsalted butter

1 cup peeled, seeded, and diced pie pumpkin (see Note) or
   1 cup peeled, seeded, and diced butternut squash

2 carrots, peeled and diced

1 large onion, chopped

1 leek, trimmed, cleaned, and sliced ½ inch thick

1 sweet potato, peeled and cut into ½-inch dice

1 bay leaf

1 cup basmati rice, rinsed

3 cups Chicken Broth (page 339) or canned low-sodium broth

2 medium ripe pears or apples, peeled, cored, and diced

2 thyme sprigs, leaves removed

6 very thin slices country ham or prosciutto,
   cut into julienne strips

In a large sauté pan or a Dutch oven, melt 1 tablespoon of the butter over medium-high heat. Add the pumpkin, carrots, onion, leek, sweet potato, and bay leaf and sauté for 2 minutes, or until the onion and leek just begin to soften. Cover and cook over low heat for 15 minutes, until tender.

Add the rice and stir for 1 minute to coat. Add 2 cups of the broth and bring to a simmer. Cover and cook for 16 minutes more, or until the rice is tender and the broth has been absorbed.

Meanwhile, bring the remaining 1 cup broth to a boil in a small saucepan and boil until reduced to ½ cup. Remove from the heat and cover to keep warm.

Transfer the rice to a serving bowl (discard the bay leaf) and stir in the remaining 1 tablespoon butter, the pears, and reduced broth. Season with thyme and then stir in the ham.

NOTE: Pie pumpkins are best when small, yielding sweet and tender flesh; as pumpkins get larger, their flesh becomes fibrous and watery. Look for pumpkins with blemish-free skin and store at room temperature until ready to use.

All over Alabama, farmers' markets and roadside stands come to life as soon as the first crop is ripe for harvest each season. The small neighborhood markets are in the midst of a renaissance as offerings like live music and cooking demonstrations bring people in. Some stands develop a reputation for the freshest eggs, others for the sweetest corn, or the most delectable, red-ripe tomatoes. Seeing the interests of their customers empowers the farmers to take risks and grow other unique varieties. A zucchini farmer may see that the squash blossoms displayed nearby are selling like hotcakes and suddenly realize that he has a bonus crop that he hadn't even considered. You can now have a conversation with the farmer who grows your food just by visiting with him at his farmers' market booth. You can and should ask questions: "What is this variety of peach?" "Do you use organic methods?" "Any chance you might consider growing Brandywine tomatoes?" With such questions, you're giving valuable information to the grower about what his customers want. If he gets enough feedback, you might find that next season he has started an experimental patch of Brandywines. The long-lost relationship between the farmer and the consumer is being renewed, and it benefits us all.

At the wholesale Alabama Farmers' Market on Finley Avenue in Birmingham, the scene is a bit different. This is where the small farmers arrive at 4:00 A.M. to park their pickups underneath the open-air loggia. The tin roof provides shade as the trucks crowd side by side underneath, tailgates down to showcase their goods. Here you buy by the bushel or crate instead of by the pound. This is where the chef gets enough Chilton County peaches to make cobbler for one hundred hungry diners, the grocer gets fifty-pound bags of Vidalia onions, and the caterer buys tomatoes in bulk for a large dinner party. You see four-axle container trucks straight from the farm backing into the produce brokers' stands to get the best price possible for their fresh-from-the-field crops—commodity trading at work. The farmers hope to bring in that extra cent or two per pound, while the brokers are looking to get the best price they can. They are good old boys making deals on a handshake, with a mutual respect for one another: They rely on each other as much as the land for their livelihood. The trading goes on through the heat of the day, and on through the seasons, as steady and constant as it has for generations.

POTATO CAKES

SERVES 4

These potato cakes make a great accompaniment to steaks, grilled fish, roast pork, or lamb. And since they are baked in a hot oven, there is a little less mess than if panfrying.

2 russet potatoes, peeled and shredded
1 teaspoon Kosher salt
Freshly ground black pepper
1 heaping tablespoon chopped flat-leaf parsley
2 garlic cloves, finely chopped
1 tablespoon extra virgin olive oil
2 tablespoons unsalted butter, melted

Preheat the oven to 400°F. Butter a small baking sheet.

Place the shredded potatoes in a large bowl of cold water to rinse off the starch. Drain and squeeze dry with your hands. Wipe out and dry the bowl and return the potatoes. Add all the remaining ingredients and toss to combine. Divide the mixture into four portions and shape into ½-inch-thick cakes on the prepared baking sheet.

Bake until golden brown, about 15 minutes.

CRUSHED CREAMER POTATOES

SERVES 4

In the early spring, from late March on, tiny new-crop potatoes come to market. Usually the first ones arrive from south Florida. Then, as the season progresses, the harvest moves northward. Alabama potatoes appear first in May in Baldwin County, outside Mobile. Our north Alabama (Cullman) potatoes find their way to the market, weather permitting, by the beginning of June. No matter where they come from, just-dug potatoes have a beautiful, albeit fleeting, earthy aroma that's worth celebrating. "Creamers" refer to the tiniest new potatoes, and this way of serving them shows off their humble splendor.

Kosher salt
2 pounds tiny red creamer (new) potatoes
Freshly ground black pepper
2 tablespoons very fruity olive oil
Chopped flat-leaf parsley, chives, or mint (optional)

Bring a medium saucepan of water to a boil over high heat. Add 1½ teaspoons salt and the potatoes and cook over medium heat until the potatoes are tender, 10 to 12 minutes.

Drain the potatoes thoroughly, return to the pan, and lightly crush with a pastry cutter or potato masher. Season with salt and pepper and the olive oil. Sprinkle with the herbs, if desired, and serve immediately.

RATATOUILLE

SERVES 4

This dish really showcases these summer vegetables. The outcome is only as successful as the freshness and perfection of the vegetables you use. Seek out organic, locally grown produce from your farmers' market or grocer to make the dish shine. Be sure to cook the vegetables separately to control individual cooking times. The deep color of the vegetables will remain brighter as well. You may want to make an extra big batch, because there is nothing better than having leftover ratatouille—the flavors get even better the second and third days. I encourage you to serve this ratatouille alongside Sea Bass in Fig Leaves (page 153). We enjoy it hot, cold, or at room temperature.

About ¼ cup extra virgin olive oil
2 small eggplants, cut into ¼-inch dice
Kosher salt and freshly ground black pepper
3 small zucchini, cut into ¼-inch dice
2 large red bell peppers, cored, seeded,
    and cut into ¼-inch dice
1 large red or yellow onion, cut into ¼-inch dice
3 garlic cloves, crushed
4 tomatoes, peeled (see page 346), seeded,
    and cut into ¼-inch dice, juices reserved
A handful of basil leaves, chopped
1 thyme sprig
1 savory sprig
2 bay leaves
Extra virgin olive oil for drizzling

In a medium cast-iron or other heavy skillet, heat 2 tablespoons of the olive oil over medium-high heat. Add the eggplant and sauté until tender and slightly caramelized, 10 to 15 minutes. Season to taste with salt and pepper, transfer to a bowl, and set aside. Follow the same procedure for the zucchini and peppers, cooking separately and adding more oil to the skillet as necessary, then transfer them to the bowl with the eggplant. Add another drizzle of oil to the skillet, then add the onion and cook until beginning to caramelize. Add the garlic and cook for a minute or two longer, season with salt and pepper, and add to the bowl.

Transfer the vegetables to a large skillet, add the tomatoes and their juices, most of the chopped basil (leaving a little for garnish), thyme, savory, and bay leaves. Toss over medium heat until warmed through. Remove the herb sprigs and bay leaves.

Drizzle the ratatouille with a little fruity extra virgin olive oil and sprinkle with the reserved chopped basil.

TO DRINK: Corbières rosé, Domaine de Fontsainte
Bandol rosé, Domaine Tempier

SAVORY LEEK BREAD PUDDING

SERVES 6

There is something incredibly appealing about the aroma of this buttery leek custard. Serve this comforting dish with roasted meats such as lamb, pork, or beef for a hearty winter supper.

1½ tablespoons unsalted butter
1 leek, trimmed, cleaned, and cut into ½-inch pieces
1 onion, cut into ½-inch dice
2 garlic cloves, finely minced
1½ cups ½-inch cubes day-old bread (crusts removed)
2 large eggs
1 cup heavy cream
1 marjoram sprig, leaves removed and chopped
Tiny pinch of grated nutmeg
Kosher salt and freshly ground white pepper

Preheat the oven to 300°F. Butter six 6-ounce ramekins with ½ tablespoon of the butter.

In a large sauté pan, heat the remaining 1 tablespoon butter over medium heat until the foam subsides. Add the leek and onion and cook until softened, about 10 minutes. Add the garlic and sauté for 2 minutes more. Transfer to a large bowl, add the bread, and toss well.

Break the eggs into a small bowl and beat thoroughly. Whisk in the cream. Add to the bread mixture, stirring to moisten. Season with the marjoram, nutmeg, and salt and white pepper, mixing well.

Fill the ramekins with the bread mixture. Arrange the ramekins in a shallow baking dish lined with a kitchen towel and pour enough hot water into the pan to reach halfway up the sides of the ramekins.

Carefully place the baking dish in the preheated oven and bake until the bread pudding tops are golden, 45 minutes to 1 hour. Remove from the oven and cool for 10 minutes before serving.

WILTED GREENS

SERVES 6

Collard, turnip, and mustard greens are the traditional "greens" of the South. Typically, a big pot of water with ham hocks, or some other flavorful cut of pork, and a sliced onion would be simmered for a couple of hours, and then the greens—triple-washed—would be added (turnip greens, in particular, are notorious for holding on to sandy soil, so that is why washing them three times is essential). Simmered for at least two hours, they break down to a very soft texture and the flavor is old-time good. Served with a big splash of hot pepper–flavored vinegar and some corn bread, this made a meal that the hill farmers of the South survived on during hard times. Now we cut greens into a chiffonade—thin strips—blanch them to help keep their vibrant color, and cook them again briefly with a bit of pork so they remain loaded with flavor.

1 large bunch of collard, mustard, or turnip greens, trimmed
2 to 3 slices bacon, chopped
1 tablespoon olive oil
1 onion, sliced
1 dried hot chile pepper
1 garlic clove, crushed
Kosher salt and freshly ground black pepper

Take several of the leaves at a time and stack them on top of each other, then roll them up tightly like a cigar and slice crosswise with a large sharp knife to produce very thin strips, called chiffonade.

Bring a large pot of salted water to a boil. Prepare an ice bath (see page 346). Blanch the greens in the boiling water for about 2 minutes. Drain and immerse the greens in the ice bath to stop the cooking. Drain and squeeze dry.

Meanwhile, combine the chopped bacon with the olive oil in a large sauté pan and heat until hot. Add the onion and sauté until soft, about 10 minutes. Toss in the dried chile and crushed garlic and toss until fragrant, about 2 minutes more. Add the greens and toss over high heat until wilted and glossy, 3 to 4 minutes. Remove the chile and garlic, season with salt and pepper, and serve.

SPRING VEGETABLE RAGOUT

SERVES 4

This is a welcome addition to roast chicken (page 179) or roast leg of lamb (page 201). If they are available, add a handful of fava beans—from two to three pods—that have been blanched briefly in boiling water and then peeled.

Juice of ½ lemon
8 baby artichokes, trimmed (see page 345) and quartered
1 pound medium asparagus, trimmed, blanched in boiling
 salted water until just tender, and cooled in ice water
3 thyme sprigs
1 teaspoon extra virgin olive oil
2 tablespoons unsalted butter or extra virgin olive oil
1 shallot, finely minced
6 spring onions, halved or quartered and glazed (see page 346)
1 cup fresh or frozen sweet peas, blanched in boiling salted
 water until tender and cooled in ice water if fresh,
 rinsed under hot water if frozen
Kosher salt and freshly ground black pepper
¼ cup coarsely chopped mixed fresh herbs, such as mint and
 flat-leaf parsley

Add the lemon juice to a large pot of water and bring to a boil. Add the artichokes and cook until tender, about 15 minutes; drain.

Slice the asparagus on the diagonal into thirds. Combine the asparagus, artichokes, and thyme in a bowl, add the olive oil, and toss well; set aside.

In a large sauté pan, heat 1 tablespoon of the butter (or olive oil) over medium-low heat. Add the shallot and sauté until softened, about 1 minute. Add the spring onions, artichokes, asparagus, peas, and 2 tablespoons water, bring to a simmer, and cook until the vegetables are heated through. Remove the thyme sprigs, season with salt and pepper, and stir in the chopped herbs. Swirl in the remaining 1 tablespoon butter and serve hot.

AUTUMN ROOT VEGETABLE PUREE

SERVES 4 • PHOTOGRAPH PAGE 233

This puree is one of the components of our Chicken with Autumn Vegetables and Madeira (page 174), and it is also a wonderful vegetable side dish for any cool-weather braise or stew.

2 medium turnips, peeled and cut into 2-inch pieces
2 small carrots, peeled and cut into 2-inch pieces
1 medium parsnip, peeled and cut into 2-inch pieces
1 medium sweet potato, peeled and cut into small chunks
½ medium rutabaga, peeled, trimmed, and cut into small chunks
Kosher salt
1 to 3 tablespoons unsalted butter, at room temperature
Freshly ground black pepper

In a medium saucepan, combine the turnips, carrots, parsnip, sweet potato, and rutabaga, add a good pinch of salt, and cover by 2 inches with water. Bring to a boil, then reduce to a simmer and cook until the vegetables are tender, 30 to 40 minutes.

Drain the vegetables and then return them to the saucepan to dry out over medium heat for 2 minutes. Transfer the vegetables to a food mill and puree. Add the butter and salt and pepper to taste, and reheat if necessary before serving.

Alabama's soil is composed of dense clay that is backbreaking to work and difficult to farm. Some vegetables—corn, okra, tomatoes, and eggplant—thrive in it. But others, such as the tender, young baby lettuces and delicate herbs that we love to use at Highlands, need a little help to grow. That's where our good friend Michael Dean comes in. It all started a while back when Michael worked as a waiter at Bottega Café, one of our sister restaurants. He was a longtime associate who was ready to do something else: work with his hands . . . be outdoors. He came up with the idea of converting a half acre of land outside of Birmingham into an experimental garden, growing produce for our restaurants.

We had always struggled to get naturally farmed organics at reasonable prices. For years we'd ordered from a Midwest farm that supplied many of the East Coast's top restaurants, but a crate of organic potatoes weighed so much that the shipping cost alone made it prohibitive. It wasn't that we couldn't find organically grown ingredients at all, but those that we could find were often varieties that lacked the intensity of flavor we were after. So when Michael hatched his plan, our restaurants agreed to pay his irrigation costs the first year to help him get started. It's been eight years, and his efforts have paid off. He's added another acre and a half, and two people to his payroll. He supplies produce to many area restaurants and a specialty market, and has changed much about the quality of the food in Birmingham.

In many ways, Michael isn't all that different from a chef in a kitchen. Instead of creating recipes for enjoying food, he creates recipes for feeding the soil, so that, in turn, he reaps a bountiful harvest. He doesn't take this job lightly. He has the soil tested regularly, amends it based on his studied understanding of soil chemistry, and uses only naturally occurring fertilizers that break down and feed the soil in a beneficial way. He even brews a great compost tea. We'll share a trusted recipe: Soak 1 cup cornmeal in 1 gallon water and let it sit in the sun to ferment for three to five days, stirring regularly to aerate. Drain, reserving the liquid, and recycle the cornmeal in the compost bin. In a large container, mix a shovel of compost with a shovel of topsoil. Add 1 to 2 tablespoons molasses (the sugar feeds the beneficial microbes in the soil and the sulfur acts as a fungicide) and 2 tablespoons apple cider vinegar (to dechlorinate the water), then pour in the fermented cornmeal water (also a fungicide). Stir well. Sprinkle this "tea" on the leaves and tops of plants and drench the soil from time to time. Your garden will thank you.

Just like a chef who must look for visual cues—a brown crust when searing meat, the set center of a custard, a perfect reduction—for recipes to succeed, Michael must sometimes amend his recipe. In addition to soil tests, he watches for signs from the plants in his gardens. Purple-tinged lettuce leaves are a call for potassium. A sudden proliferation of dandelions suggests a lack of micronutrients. Yellowing leaves signal an iron deficiency. And so forth. He must also be on the lookout for pests, which he controls by handpicking and use of beneficial insects and nematodes. The best time to do this handpicking is after dark, when, he says, you will, without a doubt, see what's eating your garden. Perform this ritual regularly, and your garden will thrive without the need for harmful pesticides.

The success of Michael's garden, through his ability to create a soil that meets the needs of the plants he's planted, allows Highlands to experiment with rare varieties. These are plants that produce fruit with phenomenal flavor, texture, and character. Seeds gathered from trips abroad and dried from vegetables enjoyed often end up in Michael's hands. Once planted, some are successful and some fail—but just like experiments in the kitchen, things don't always work out as planned.

Unique varieties that we have had great success with include a little hot Italian pepper called *celligia* and cavaillon melons from the South of France. We're still trying with my favorite *arugula selvetica,* and we're not giving up. Michael will continue to tinker with the growing method and the soil recipe, and I'll continue dreaming up great dishes that feature unique, always flavorful, varieties of produce.

AUTUMN VEGETABLE RAGOUT

SERVES 4

Alain Ducasse is a hero of mine. On a blustery day not long ago, my wife, Pardis, and I had the pleasure of dining at one of his Paris restaurants. We were served pristine cold-weather vegetables and fruits simmered in their own syrupy juices. The dish was elegant yet rustic and healthy. All the components were beautiful—the tender pink of the glazed radishes with their pale green stems, the bluish turnips, and the most orange of carrots. The surprise of the fruit with root vegetables was a revelation.

My version of the dish came about after a visit to our friend Michael's farm, where the fertile earth yielded a late-fall crop of beautiful little leeks, vibrant beets, small sweet carrots, and a variety of radishes and turnips. Every season inspires its own combination: Spring finds asparagus, young peas, and bulb onions, perhaps with a few morels; summer offers corn, tomatoes, butter beans, and perhaps peaches. The combinations are subtle and endless.

4 baby beets (preferably of different colors), washed and
    stems trimmed to ½ inch
About 4 tablespoons extra virgin olive oil
Sherry vinegar
Kosher salt and freshly ground black pepper
8 cipollini onions, peeled
8 yellow or red pearl onions, blanched in boiling water
    for 1 minute, trimmed, and peeled
4 baby carrots, peeled
3 tablespoons unsalted butter
Pinch of sugar
About 2½ cups water
½ Granny Smith apple, peeled, cored, and cut into 8 wedges
4 fingerling potatoes, scrubbed, quartered lengthwise,
    and cooked in boiling salted water until tender
2 small turnips, quartered, bottom half peeled, and
    cooked in boiling salted water until tender
1 large parsnip, peeled, halved, and cut into 2-inch lengths
Juice of ½ lemon
Handful of arugula, trimmed, washed, and dried
Handful of flat-leaf parsley leaves

Preheat the oven to 375°F.

Place the beets in a small baking pan and season them with about 2 tablespoons olive oil, a dash of sherry vinegar, and salt and pepper. Cover with foil and bake until tender, 25 to 35 minutes. Let cool.

In a large saucepan, combine the cipollini, pearl onions, carrots, 1 tablespoon of the butter, the sugar, and salt to taste. Add enough water to cover by half, bring to a simmer over medium heat, and cook until the vegetables are tender and glazed, about 15 minutes; if necessary, add a splash more water and continue cooking until tender.

Meanwhile, slip the skins off the beets and cut into quarters.

Add the apples to the vegetables and cook for another 3 minutes. Add the potatoes, turnips, parsnip, and beets and warm thoroughly. There should be 3 to 4 tablespoons of the liquid remaining; add a little water if necessary. Drizzle with the remaining 2 tablespoons olive oil, the lemon juice, and 1 tablespoon sherry vinegar. Stir in the remaining 2 tablespoons butter until melted, then taste and adjust the seasoning.

Spoon the ragout, with its juices, into small bowls and garnish with the arugula and parsley.

FIELD PEA AND WILD MUSHROOM RISOTTO

SERVES 6

Like pasta, risotto is a dish of which we never tire. It is essential to use Arborio rice, because it becomes creamy while maintaining its texture. Once you perfect your risotto technique, I guarantee that risotto will become a standard in your repertoire—something you can pull off wonderfully by simply combining seasonal ingredients or even leftovers you have on hand. Remember, less is better when combining flavors. A splash of vermouth here really brightens the taste of the risotto.

¼ cup dried wild mushrooms, such as porcini,
    or a mixture of several types
2 tablespoons olive oil
3 tablespoons unsalted butter
1 onion, halved and sliced
2 cups Chicken Broth (page 339) or canned low-sodium broth
1 garlic clove, crushed
1 bay leaf
4 thyme sprigs, leaves removed, plus a scattering of leaves
    for garnish
1 cup Arborio rice
¼ cup white wine
Kosher salt and freshly ground black pepper
1 cup cooked peas, such as pink-eyes, butter peas
    (see page 251; see page 15 for cooking instructions),
    or favas
½ pound fresh mushrooms, such as cremini, button, or porcini,
    trimmed and sautéed in 2 teaspoons unsalted butter
3 tablespoons freshly grated Parmigiano-Reggiano,
    plus extra for serving
1 tablespoon dry white vermouth

Soak the dried mushrooms in hot water until softened, 20 to 30 minutes. Lift the mushrooms from the liquid and set aside. Strain the liquid and reserve ½ cup.

Heat the olive oil and 1 tablespoon of the butter in a medium nonreactive saucepan over medium heat. Add the onion and sauté until softened, about 10 minutes. Meanwhile, bring the broth to a simmer in a small saucepan; keep warm over very low heat.

Add the garlic, bay leaf, thyme, rice, and the reconstituted mushrooms to the onions and stir until the rice is coated, shiny, and almost translucent. Add the white wine and the reserved mushroom soaking liquid, stirring constantly until the liquid has evaporated. Begin adding the chicken broth, a small ladleful at a time, adding more only after the previous addition has been incorporated. A creamy emulsion will begin to form. Be careful not to add too much liquid at a time or the rice will drown—or too little or the rice will stick. Continue to add the broth until the rice is no longer hard but is still al dente, and the risotto is creamy.

Season with salt and pepper. Add the peas, sautéed mushrooms, the remaining 2 tablespoons butter, and the cheese, then stir in the vermouth. Taste for seasoning and remove the bay leaf. Garnish with thyme leaves and serve with freshly grated Parmigiano.

TO DRINK: Meursault, Domaine Roulot
    Rosso di Montalcino, Tenuta Capar

BUTTERNUT SQUASH AND DRIED FIG RISOTTO

SERVES 4

Cooking risotto requires the use of all your senses. Each step of the process has its signals: the rising aroma of the vegetables sautéed in butter, the sizzle of the rice as it is added to the hot pan, the resistance of the mixture against the spoon, and then, of course, there is the tasting after the last addition of vermouth, butter, and Parmigiano. Risotto can be superb with just a few impeccable ingredients—say, onion, a great homemade broth, and a grating of fresh Parmigiano-Reggiano. It can be subtle, as here, with the creamy butternut and unexpected musky sweetness of figs. The variations are endless. This version is perfect alongside grilled quail (page 186).

2¾ cups Chicken Broth (page 339) or canned low-sodium broth
6 dried figs, stems removed, quartered and diced
3 tablespoons unsalted butter
1 teaspoon olive oil
1 medium onion, halved and thinly sliced
2 medium carrots, peeled and thinly sliced
½ cup finely diced butternut squash
1 medium celery stalk, thinly sliced
1 cup Arborio rice
¼ cup dry white vermouth, plus a splash to finish
¼ cup freshly grated Parmigiano-Reggiano
Kosher salt and freshly ground black pepper
Thyme and rosemary sprigs for garnish (optional)

In a medium saucepan, combine ¾ cup of the chicken broth with the figs and bring to a simmer. Remove the saucepan from the heat and let stand until the figs are plump and tender, about 5 minutes. With a slotted spoon, transfer the figs to a plate and set aside. Add the remaining broth to the pan and bring just to a simmer; keep warm over very low heat.

Meanwhile, in a medium nonreactive saucepan, heat 1 tablespoon of the butter and the oil over medium heat. Add the onion, carrots, squash, and celery and sauté for 5 minutes. Add the rice and cook until it is coated with oil and begins to crackle a little, about 3 minutes; it should be quite aromatic. Add the vermouth and allow it to sizzle until evaporated. Begin adding the remaining chicken broth approximately ½ cup at a time, stirring constantly and allowing each addition to be absorbed before adding another. Continue cooking until the broth is incorporated and the rice is tender, about 15 minutes.

To finish the risotto, stir in the plumped figs, the remaining 2 tablespoons butter, the Parmigiano, and a splash of vermouth. Taste and season with salt and pepper.

Spoon the risotto onto serving plates and garnish with thyme and rosemary, if desired.

TO DRINK: Tempranillo, Ribera del Duero Viña Sastre Pinot Noir, Chalone

EGGPLANT STUFFED
WITH SUMMER VEGETABLES

SERVES 4

This makes a great appetizer or light summer lunch, or it can be a beautiful accompaniment to lamb or fish.

2 eggplants, cut lengthwise in half
Kosher salt and freshly ground black pepper to taste
1½ teaspoons olive oil
1 onion, finely diced
2 garlic cloves, finely chopped
2 zucchini, 1 shredded, 1 finely diced
1 cup cremini or button mushrooms, trimmed and finely diced
1 tomato, seeded and cut into medium dice
½ bunch flat-leaf parsley, leaves removed and chopped
½ bunch basil, leaves removed and chopped
½ cup medium-coarse bread crumbs (see page 347)

With a sturdy spoon, scoop the flesh out of each eggplant half, leaving ¼-inch-thick shells; reserve the shells. Sprinkle the inside of the shells with salt, invert onto a plate, and let stand for 30 minutes. Dice the flesh and set aside.

Preheat the oven to 350°F.

Turn the eggplant shells over, pat dry, and place on a baking sheet. Bake until softened, about 15 minutes. Remove from the oven and set aside. Leave the oven on.

Meanwhile, heat the olive oil in a large sauté pan over medium heat. Add the onion and sauté until tender, 5 to 7 minutes. Add the garlic, diced eggplant, zucchini, and mushrooms and sauté until the mushrooms begin to soften, about 3 minutes. Add the tomato, parsley, basil, and bread crumbs; stir to combine and season with salt and pepper. Remove from the heat.

Fill the baked eggplant shells with the vegetable stuffing, mounding it loosely. Bake for 20 minutes; serve hot.

TO DRINK: Rosé, Bandol Domaine Ott
　　　　　　Vin Gris, Saintsbury Vincent

...AND SOMETHING SWEET TO FINISH

Desserts are the grand

finale, and I adore the more old-fashioned sweets that are jazzed up by careful attention to detail. When we were testing Grandmother White's Fried Apple Pies (made with dried apple butter), almost every staff member had a memory of eating a similar turnover years ago in the family kitchen. Tears welled up in one young woman's eyes as the unbelievably tender, flaky, piping hot fried pie melted in her mouth—memories of a grandmother's kitchen.

Except for the chocolate and perhaps the lemon desserts, most of these are particularly seasonal. Summer brings out peaches, blackberries, and figs. I prefer rustic preparations, such as cobblers, simple tarts, crisps, and the like. If the fruits have never seen the inside of a refrigerator, all the better. Chilling weakens their aromas and flavors. Simply cutting ripe fresh fruit and tossing it with a little sugar and lemon really gets the juices flowing. Bake summer fruits however you choose—whether in a blackberry cobbler or one made with peaches dotted with fresh blueberries—but don't forget to top with a scoop of vanilla ice cream.

Cool weather means apples, pears, pumpkins, and pecans. Or exotic tropical fruits such as pineapple and mango. Even dried fruits can be stars. And then as the weather loses its chill and the sun warms the ground, the first strawberries appear in desserts to herald springtime.

{ Apple and Almond Bread Pudding, page 297. *Page 277*, top shelf: Strawberry Tart with Mascarpone (page 293), Strawberry Milk Shake (page 292); bottom shelf: Brown Butter Almond Financier (page 302), Lemon Buttermilk Chess Tart (page 294), Chocolate Caramel-Nut Tart (page 312).

BOURBON PANNA COTTA

SERVES 8

This is a recipe for those fearful of making desserts, because it is one of the simplest desserts of all and perfect any time of year. As easy as panna cotta is to make, it remains an elegant sight—trembling, delicate, and almost cloudlike. The flavor of this one is cool vanilla with a little kick of sour mash bourbon at the end. Serve a few Pecan Sandies (page 319) alongside.

1 cup plus ½ cup sugar

½ teaspoon fresh lemon juice

2 tablespoons water

4 cups heavy cream

½ cup pecans, toasted (see page 346) and chopped

3 tablespoons bourbon

2 cups whole milk

2 envelopes unflavored gelatin

Set out eight 8-ounce custard cups or ramekins. Combine the ½ cup sugar, lemon juice, and water in a small heavy saucepan and bring to a boil over high heat. Boil until the sugar dissolves. Reduce the heat to medium, brush down the sides of the pan with a wet pastry brush to remove any sugar crystals, and cook, shaking the pan to swirl the caramel (do not stir), until the caramel is mahogany in color, 15 to 20 minutes. (If the caramel is not dark enough, the flavor will be weak, but if it is cooked too long, it will be bitter.) Quickly spoon a little caramel into each custard cup, swirling it around to coat the bottom. Set aside.

In a medium saucepan, combine the cream, the 1 cup sugar, pecans, and bourbon and bring to a simmer over medium-low heat. Simmer for 10 minutes to infuse the cream with the flavor and aroma of the bourbon and pecans. Remove the pan from the heat and let cool for a few moments.

Meanwhile, put the milk in a medium bowl and sprinkle the gelatin over the surface; do not stir. Let the gelatin soften for about 5 minutes, allowing a skin to form on the milk.

Pour the cream over the gelatin mixture, whisking to dissolve all the gelatin. Strain and pour into the caramel-lined cups. Refrigerate for at least 6 hours, or overnight.

To unmold, run a knife around the edge of each cup and carefully flip the panna cotta onto a serving plate.

My mother, Marie, and her mother, Eullalha White, were both very serious cooks. My mother learned the southern basics from her mother before experimenting with more modern international cooking. A natural-born cook, my mother loved nothing more than to spend a day in her kitchen, making cakes, cookies, preserves, stews, roasts—anything. In our Alabama, our kitchen became the neighborhood hangout, and my mother was the happiest when hungry friends and family were gathered there. She introduced many of my high school football buddies to all sorts of delicacies—from roast leg of lamb to asparagus, from caviar to her old standby, New York–style cheesecake.

Grandmother White stayed busy too, keeping our freezer full of her own goodies—strawberries, corn, okra, butter beans, and the like—that she "put up" when they were in season. Mother and Grandmother engaged in a bit of healthy kitchen competition. But, as Grandmother aged, she reluctantly relinquished most of the cooking to Mother. Before she did, however, there was the illustrious Fourth of July at her farm when her washtub cobbler was born.

It was summer and the house was full of relatives, and we all helped gather blackberries. Covered with scratches, we were proud of our booty. When my grandmother realized she did not have a pan big enough to feed the whole clan or to accommodate our grand harvest, she pulled out the old aluminum washtub. As everyone played in the yard and feasted on a boundless summer lunch, my aunt Rosa Faye and I brought out the huge tub—topped with a latticework of pastry bubbling with sugary-sweet blackberry juices. After everyone was served, Aunt Rosa and I elbowed each other as we dug into the dented washtub pan. I haven't been able to turn away a wild berry cobbler since, but it's never tasted quite as good as it did right out of that old tub.

LATTICE-TOPPED BLACKBERRY COBBLER

SERVES 6 TO 8

This is our version of the famed washtub cobbler from my childhood (see page 281), lovingly prepared by my grandmother Eullalha. With blackberries, there is usually a little bitterness in the syrupy purple juice that comes from the smaller, less ripe berries, but this tartness adds character to the finished dessert. At Highlands, we make individual cobblers in ramekins. The lattice top is beautiful, but you could also simply cover the fruit with a single sheet of pastry dough, crimp the edges, and vent the top with a slit or two. Any way you do it, it will be delicious.

2 pints blackberries
¼ cup granulated sugar, or more to taste,
    plus sugar for sprinkling
¼ cup packed light brown sugar
Grated zest of ½ lemon
1 tablespoon fresh lemon juice
Pinch of ground cinnamon
Pinch of freshly ground black pepper
2 tablespoons cold unsalted butter, diced
Galette Dough (page 342)
About 2 tablespoons whole milk for glazing

Preheat the oven to 350°F. Butter a 9-inch glass pie plate.

Place the blackberries in a large bowl and add both sugars, the lemon zest and juice, cinnamon, and pepper, tossing to combine. Let the berries macerate for about 20 minutes. Transfer the fruit to the prepared pie plate and dot with the butter.

Roll out the dough on a lightly floured piece of parchment, or a floured work surface, into a 10-inch circle about ⅛ inch thick. With a fluted pastry wheel or sharp knife, cut the dough into strips about ¾ inch wide. Lay half of the strips evenly spaced over the fruit in the pie plate. Lay the remaining strips of dough across the top at right angles to the first strips. (If the dough is too warm or hard to work with, slide it onto a baking sheet and place in the freezer until it firms up slightly.)

Brush the dough lightly with milk and sprinkle with sugar. Place on a parchment- or foil-lined baking sheet to catch spills and bake for about 35 minutes, or until the fruit is bubbly and the dough has browned nicely. Let the cobbler cool slightly, then serve warm.

PEACH AND BLUEBERRY COBBLER

SERVES 6 TO 8

Rustic cobblers are simple desserts, and they are hard to beat. There is no bottom crust to roll out, blind bake, and fill, but you get equal impact—the aroma of bubbling fruit and spices wafting from the oven and a topping of flaky pastry rounds over the warm filling. A scoop of vanilla ice cream is about the only thing left to ask for.

FOR THE FILLING

8 to 10 large ripe peaches, halved, pitted, and cut into ¼-inch-
     wide wedges (enough to generously fill your baking pan)
½ to 1 pint blueberries, picked over
Grated zest of ½ lemon
¼ cup granulated sugar, or more to taste
¼ cup packed light brown sugar
Pinch of cinnamon
Pinch of Kosher salt
Scant ¼ cup all-purpose flour
2 tablespoons cold unsalted butter

FOR THE DOUGH

1⅓ cups all-purpose flour
¼ cup sugar
1¼ teaspoons baking powder
1 teaspoon baking soda
¼ teaspoon Kosher salt
4 tablespoons cold unsalted butter, diced
½ cup buttermilk, or as needed
About 2 tablespoons whole milk for glazing
1 heaping tablespoon coarse or granulated sugar for topping

Preheat the oven to 375°F. Line a baking sheet with foil or parchment paper.

Put the peaches in a large bowl, add the blueberries, and toss to combine. Add the lemon zest, both sugars, cinnamon, and salt and toss again. Let macerate until juices are released, about 20 minutes.

Taste the fruit mixture; depending on the fruit, you may need to add more sugar to sweeten it or add a little flour to thicken it if a lot of juice has accumulated during maceration. Transfer the fruit to a 10- or 11-inch gratin dish and dot the top with the butter.

To prepare the dough, sift the dry ingredients into a large bowl. Add the butter and, with a fork or a pastry blender, work it into the dry ingredients until the mixture is crumbly and resembles coarse cornmeal. Make a well in the center, pour in the buttermilk, and stir the dough lightly with a rubber spatula until it begins to come together. If the dough looks dry, add a little more buttermilk: The dough should be moist but not wet. Gather it together into a disk.

On a floured surface, roll out the dough to a ½-inch thickness. Dip a 2-inch round biscuit cutter or a juice glass in flour and cut out as many circles as you can. Gather the scraps of dough together, knead gently, and roll out one more time. Cut out as many circles as you can again. (Do not use the scraps again.) Place the dough circles on top of the fruit mixture, brush them with the milk, and sprinkle with the sugar.

Place the baking dish on the prepared baking sheet to catch any spills. Bake until the fruit is bubbly and the biscuit topping is golden brown, about 45 minutes. Let cool slightly before serving.

PEACHES IN BEAUJOLAIS

SERVES 4

This dessert is traditional in the Beaujolais region of central France, where the local wine is soft and very low in tannin. The clear sweet taste of the peaches blends beautifully with the fruity essence of the Beaujolais.

4 teaspoons granulated sugar
4 teaspoons light brown sugar
1 bottle (750 ml) Beaujolais, such as Fleurie from Chignard
4 firm but ripe white peaches, peeled, pitted, and
     cut into 6 to 8 wedges each

Place a teaspoon of each sugar in each wineglass, then add 6 ounces of Beaujolais to each glass and stir to dissolve. Distribute the peaches evenly among the glasses and stir again. Serve immediately.

If luck will have it, by Memorial Day, we begin to see produce from some of the farmers of deep-south Alabama, from down near Dothan. They grow beautiful peppers, beans, peas, tomatoes, cucumbers, and blueberries. By late June, the market begins to hit its stride, with plums and nectarines.

You know that summer has arrived when the first peaches from downstate Chilton County make their debut at the farmers' market. The date varies, but it's usually not until the middle of June. And even if the early ones tend to be a little green, I like to make a green tomato and peach relish with mint, lemon, and lime as a garnish for seafood or meats.

But July is the real heyday. We revel in the most beautiful produce imaginable. For me, the highlight is the arrival of the first Georgia Belle peaches from Mike Burnett in Chilton County. When I think of July, I think of his peaches. I think of sweet White Georgia Belles that are so soft, so ripe, they bruise when you look at them. Those gossamer peaches last just two or three weeks. And then they're gone.

By the first or second week of August, we have become almost complacent, but unless we act quickly, some of those choice lady peas, crowder peas, pink-eye peas, and butter beans will begin to fade away before we've had a chance to put some up in the freezer. Last year, working alongside our pastry chef, I put up pickled peaches and fig preserves, and we canned tomatoes too.

Two or three times a summer, I pull together a group of us on a Sunday or Monday morning. Earlier in the week, we've made arrangements with farmers to get some really outstanding products in on Saturday, so that on Sunday or Monday we can get the big pots of boiling water going as we quickly trim and clean and wash and then blanch the best of the summer produce—peas, beans, okra, and tomatoes. It's nice to work without the pressure of the restaurant being open. Everyone is in a more relaxed mood. For breakfast, we'll usually have leftover cookies from the day before, and eventually we'll get around to fixing a lunch of egg salad sandwiches, or we'll grind some chuck and grill hamburgers.

These end-of-the-season canning sessions feel a bit like a family gathering, in the sense that there's a great deal of coercion involved in most family chores. When we get together, I always straddle the line between asking for volunteers and expecting attendance. But everyone walks out of there with a couple bottles of wine under his or her arm, and a few jars of preserves too.

Peach Crostata, page 290 }

PEACH CROSTATA

SERVES 6 • PHOTOGRAPH PAGE 289

Crostatas are rustic, free-form tarts that usually enclose flavorful fruit. Because of their design, there is lots of crisp buttery pastry. You can prepare the dough well in advance and even freeze it with no loss of quality. Remember to keep the dough thoroughly chilled before baking—this will help ensure flakiness.

FOR THE DOUGH

2 cups unbleached all-purpose flour

¼ cup sugar

1 teaspoon Kosher salt

1¼ sticks unsalted butter, cut into ½-inch cubes and chilled

¼ cup ice water

FOR THE FILLING

¼ cup unbleached all-purpose flour

¼ cup sugar

4 tablespoons cold unsalted butter

2 pounds ripe peaches, pitted, peeled, and sliced into ¾-inch-thick wedges

1 large egg yolk, beaten with 1 teaspoon heavy cream for egg wash

1 tablespoon coarse or granulated sugar for topping

To prepare the dough, combine the flour, sugar, and salt in a food processor and pulse a few times to blend. Add the butter and pulse until it is the size of small peas, about 15 times. With the processor running, add the ice water and process for about 10 seconds; stop the processor before the dough comes together. Turn the dough out onto a sheet of waxed paper, divide the dough in half, and shape it into two disks. Wrap them in plastic wrap and refrigerate for at least 1 hour. (The dough can be refrigerated for 2 days or frozen for up to 2 weeks; if it has been frozen, defrost the dough for 30 minutes at room temperature.)

Preheat the oven to 450°F.

Roll one disk of dough into an 11-inch circle on a lightly floured surface. Transfer to a baking sheet. (Reserve the second disk of dough for another use.)

To prepare the filling, combine the flour and sugar in a small bowl. Blend in the butter with two knives until the mixture resembles coarse meal.

Place the peaches in the center of the dough circle on the baking sheet and top with the butter-sugar mixture. Begin draping the edges up and over, forming about 3 pleats. Crimp the pleats and press down to seal. Brush the pastry with the egg wash and sprinkle with the sugar.

Bake the tart for about 25 minutes, or until golden brown. Let cool on a rack and serve slices with vanilla ice cream or crème anglaise.

VARIATION: Line the dough bottom of the crostata with a heaping tablespoon of pecan frangipane before adding the peaches. To make the frangipane, combine ½ cup toasted pecans and ½ cup sugar in a food processor and process until the nuts are coarsely ground. Add 8 tablespoons (1 stick) of unsalted butter, cut into small pieces, and 1 large egg and pulse until the mixture resembles a coarse paste.

JACK DANIEL'S CHOCOLATE ICE CREAM

MAKES 1 QUART

Whiskey combined with chocolate is an outstanding combination, and this grown-up ice cream definitely has a kick to it. Serve it on its own with cookies or made into milk shakes (see the directions for Strawberry Milk Shake, page 292).

1½ cups whole milk
1 teaspoon pure vanilla extract
¼ pound good-quality bittersweet chocolate, chopped
⅓ cup Jack Daniel's whiskey
5 large egg yolks
½ cup sugar
1 cup cold heavy cream

In a large stainless steel or enameled saucepan, heat the milk until bubbles rise around the edge of the pan. Remove from the heat, add the vanilla, cover, and let steep for 20 minutes.

Meanwhile, melt the chocolate with the Jack Daniel's in a heavy saucepan over low heat, stirring occasionally. Remove from the heat and set aside.

In a large bowl, whisk the egg yolks with the sugar until thoroughly combined. Gradually whisk in the warm milk. Pour this mixture back into the saucepan and heat, stirring constantly, until just slightly thickened; the temperature should be 170°F on an instant-read thermometer. Strain the custard through a fine-mesh strainer into a bowl and let cool.

Stir the melted chocolate mixture and cream into the custard. Cover and refrigerate until chilled.

Freeze the ice cream in an ice cream maker according to the manufacturer's instructions. Transfer to a freezer container and freeze for an hour or two to firm before serving.

STRAWBERRY ICE CREAM

MAKES 1 QUART

For strawberry ice cream, we simply prepare our standard rich vanilla ice cream base and add macerated strawberries. Macerating the berries brings out their sweetness and breaks them down a bit in the ice cream. You'll definitely want two scoops of this flavorful ice cream. Or, try it in our Strawberry Milk Shake (page 292).

1½ cups chopped ripe strawberries
½ cup plus 1 tablespoon sugar
2 cups half-and-half
½ vanilla bean, split
6 large egg yolks
1 cup cold heavy cream

Place the strawberries in a bowl and toss with the 1 tablespoon sugar. Set aside to macerate for 30 minutes.

In a large nonreactive saucepan, combine the half-and-half, the ½ cup sugar, and the vanilla bean and bring to a boil. Immediately remove from the heat, cover, and let steep for 10 minutes.

Meanwhile, whisk the egg yolks in a medium bowl until thick, about 3 minutes.

Temper the egg yolks by gradually adding about ½ cup of the warm half-and-half, whisking constantly. Transfer the yolk mixture back to the saucepan and cook over medium heat, stirring constantly, until the custard begins to thicken. It should register 176°F on an instant-read thermometer or coat the back of a spoon. Immediately strain the custard into the bowl of strawberries and add the cold cream. Cover and refrigerate until thoroughly chilled.

Freeze the ice cream in an ice cream machine according to the manufacturer's instructions. Transfer to a freezer container and freeze for an hour or two to firm before serving.

STRAWBERRY MILK SHAKE

SERVES 4

For a decadent springtime splurge, prepare this glorious pink dessert with the finest, ripest strawberries and richest homemade ice cream. In fact, a good gauge for the perfect berry shake is to keep adding the strawberries until the color is right—a bright shocking pink!

2 cups quartered ripe strawberries,
    plus 4 whole berries for garnish
½ cup sugar
8 scoops Strawberry Ice Cream (page 291)
⅔ cup half-and-half
Lightly sweetened whipped cream

Place the strawberries in a large bowl, add the sugar, and toss to coat. Cover and let the strawberries macerate at room temperature for 2 hours. (The strawberries can be macerated up to 1 day in advance and refrigerated, covered.)

Put the strawberries and their juices into a blender or a food processor and process to a rough puree. Transfer to a bowl.

Make two shakes at a time: Add 4 scoops of the ice cream and half of the strawberry puree to the blender, add half of the half-and-half, and blend until thoroughly combined.

Pour into two chilled tall glasses. Repeat to make the remaining two milk shakes. Garnish each with a whole strawberry and a little spoonful of whipped cream. Serve with straws.

STRAWBERRY TART WITH MASCARPONE

SERVES 8 • PHOTOGRAPH PAGE 277

Dolester Miles, the pastry chef at our Bottega Café, came up with this beautiful dessert—all thanks to a miscommunication. I had asked her to incorporate some strawberries I had just picked into a rustic dessert by making preserves to be sandwiched between a layer of ricotta and sliced fresh strawberries. All this was to be encased, free-form, in a buttery crostata dough and baked. Instead, she baked a perfect tart crust, slathered it with mascarpone instead of ricotta, and topped it off with homemade strawberry preserves and more glazed strawberries. The result was a glorious mistake, far more gorgeous than what I had envisioned.

FOR THE CRUST

1 cup all-purpose flour
2 teaspoons sugar
¼ teaspoon Kosher salt
6 tablespoons unsalted butter, cut into 1-inch cubes and chilled
2 to 4 tablespoons ice water

FOR THE PRESERVES

2 cups quartered ripe strawberries
½ cup sugar, or more to taste
¼ teaspoon fresh lemon juice

1 cup mascarpone cheese
½ cup sugar
Grated zest of 1 small orange
2 cups sliced strawberries, plus a few whole berries, hulled
Lightly sweetened whipped cream (optional)

To prepare the crust, in a medium bowl, whisk together the flour, sugar, and salt. Add the butter and cut in with a pastry blender or two knives until the butter is the size of small peas. Add the ice water 1 tablespoon at a time, mixing until the dough just comes together. Shape the dough into a disk, wrap the disk in plastic wrap, and refrigerate for at least 30 minutes or overnight.

Preheat the oven to 375°F.

To prepare the preserves, combine the strawberries, sugar, and lemon juice in a small saucepan and bring to a simmer, cooking until the juices thicken to a jamlike consistency, 30 to 45 minutes. The mixture will thicken a bit more upon cooling. Transfer to a bowl and let cool.

On a floured surface, roll the dough into a round approximately 11 inches in diameter. Fit it into a 9-inch fluted tart shell with a removable bottom and trim off the excess dough. Line with parchment paper or foil and fill with dried beans or pie weights. Bake for 20 minutes. Remove the parchment and weights and bake until thoroughly golden, 5 to 10 minutes more. Remove from the oven and let cool.

Mix the mascarpone, sugar, and orange zest together in a small bowl. Spread the mascarpone evenly in the cooled tart shell. Spread a thin layer of the cooled strawberry preserves on top.

Arrange the sliced strawberries on top of the preserves, working in concentric circles from the outside in. Place a few whole strawberries in the center.

Pass a generous ¼ cup of the strawberry preserves through a fine strainer. (Cover and refrigerate any remaining preserves for another use.) Combine with 2 teaspoons water in a small saucepan and warm over low heat, stirring, just until smooth. Using a pastry brush, brush the glaze over the strawberries. Serve the tart at room temperature with whipped cream, if desired.

VARIATION: For a flat crust (photograph, page 274), prepare the dough as above and roll it out to ⅛ inch thick. Cut it into an 8- to 10-inch round and place on a parchment-lined baking sheet. Puncture the surface a few times with a fork, cover with parchment or foil, and place pie weights on top of the covering. Bake for 15 minutes, remove the pie weights, and return to the oven. Cook for another 4 to 5 minutes, until golden. Remove from the heat and cool on a cooling rack. When constructing the tart, first place the crust on a perfectly flat surface such as a cake stand.

LEMON BUTTERMILK CHESS TART

SERVES 8 TO 10 • PHOTOGRAPH PAGE 277

Chess pie, the old-time southern standard, is a childhood favorite of mine—buttery, rich, and sweet.

This simple version stands up to the intense sweetness of the traditional recipes with the addition of lemon zest and buttermilk.

FOR THE CRUST

2½ cups all-purpose flour

¼ cup cornmeal

¼ cup sugar

Pinch of Kosher salt

Grated zest of 1 lemon

1 teaspoon grated orange zest

2 large egg yolks

¼ cup ice water

½ pound (2 sticks) cold unsalted butter, diced

FOR THE FILLING

1 cup plus 2 tablespoons sugar

1½ teaspoons cornstarch

¼ vanilla bean, split

Pinch of grated nutmeg

Pinch of Kosher salt

1½ cups buttermilk

3 large eggs

4 tablespoons unsalted butter, melted and cooled

2 tablespoons fresh lemon juice

2 teaspoons grated lemon zest

To prepare the crust, pulse the flour, cornmeal, sugar, salt, and both zests in a food processor. In a bowl, combine the egg yolks and ice water. Add the butter to the flour-cornmeal mixture and pulse until the butter is the size of small peas. With the machine running, drizzle in the egg mixture until the dough just comes together; be careful not to overprocess.

Turn the dough out onto a sheet of plastic wrap, form the dough into a disk, and wrap in the plastic. Chill the dough for at least 3 hours, or overnight. Roll out the dough on a floured surface into an 11-inch round. Fit the dough into a 9-inch fluted tart pan with a removable bottom, gently pressing it into the bottom and up the sides. Trim off the excess dough. Refrigerate the tart shell until firm, 30 to 45 minutes.

Preheat the oven to 325°F.

Line the tart shell with parchment paper or foil and fill with dried beans or pie weights. Bake for 20 minutes. Remove the paper and weights and bake for 5 to 10 minutes longer, until golden brown. If bubbles appear in the crust, prick them with a fork. Let the tart shell cool completely. (The tart shell can be baked a day ahead, wrapped tightly in plastic wrap, and kept at room temperature.)

To prepare the filling, whisk together the sugar and cornstarch in a small bowl. Scrape the seeds from the vanilla bean and add them to the bowl. Add the nutmeg and salt and whisk until the mixture is lump free. Set aside.

In a large bowl, with an electric mixer, beat the buttermilk on low speed until frothy. Beat in the eggs, butter, and lemon juice. Scrape down the sides of the bowl, then add the dry ingredients and lemon zest and beat just to combine. Cover and refrigerate for 2 hours.

Preheat the oven to 300°F.

Whisk the chilled filling until smooth and pour it into the prepared tart shell. Bake for 20 to 25 minutes, until the filling is just set but still jiggly in the center. Let cool on a rack.

Serve the tart warm or refrigerate and serve chilled.

FRIED APPLE PIES

MAKES 6 INDIVIDUAL PIES

Everyone begged Grandmother White to make her fried apple pies even when she was well into her seventies. She would lay out slices of peeled apples—three different old-fashioned varieties—on a screen to dry in the sun of late summer, usually September. Once dried, the apples would be transformed into her famous apple butter, which she put into canning jars so that we could enjoy this throughout the year.

FOR THE DOUGH

1½ cups all-purpose flour

¾ teaspoon salt

1½ teaspoons sugar

3 tablespoons cold unsalted butter, cut into small cubes

3 tablespoons chilled lard (see page 217), cut into small cubes

¼ cup ice water

FOR THE APPLE BUTTER (MAKES ABOUT 1 CUP)

¼ pound dried apples (see Note), preferably organic

3 cups water

1 cinnamon stick

2 cloves

1 cup sugar

Vegetable oil (or lard) for deep frying

To make the dough, sift together the flour, salt, and sugar into a large bowl. Cut in the butter and lard with a pastry cutter or two knives, working quickly; do not overmix. The butter should be the size of small peas. Sprinkle the ice water over and pull the dough together with your fingertips or a fork. Pat into a disk, wrap with plastic wrap, and refrigerate for at least 1 hour, or overnight.

To make the apple butter, combine the dried apples, water, cinnamon, cloves, and sugar in a medium saucepan and cook over medium-low heat, stirring occasionally, until thick and very soft, about 45 minutes. Let cool.

On a floured surface, roll out the pastry into a large rectangle about 16 by 11 inches. Using a pan lid or a plate as a guide, cut out six 5-inch circles. Place 2 tablespoons of apple butter on one side of each circle and fold the dough over to make a half-moon. Press the edges together and crimp with the tines of a fork. (Refrigerate any leftover apple butter—it's great on English muffins.)

Fill a large deep heavy skillet with 2½ inches of oil (or lard) and heat over medium-high heat until the oil reaches 360°F on an instant-read thermometer. Carefully slip the pies into the oil, without crowding, and fry until golden on the bottom, 6 to 8 minutes. Turn and cook the other side until golden, another 6 to 8 minutes. Drain on paper towels and serve hot or at room temperature.

NOTE: Dry your own favorite apple varieties in your oven. Start by washing, peeling, and coring them. Then slice into ¼-inch-thick slices using a mandoline or other vegetable slicer. Place on parchment-lined baking sheets (or use silicone liners if you have them). Bake in a very low oven—250°F—for several hours, checking from time to time. The apples should be golden but pliable. They will firm somewhat upon cooling. Store in an airtight tin at room temperature. Great for snacking too!

APPLE CHARLOTTE

SERVES 6 • PHOTOGRAPH PAGE 298

This charlotte is made from a perfect blend of sweet and tart apples—half slow-roasted to concentrate their distinctive flavor and then blended into a robust sauce, the rest sliced wafer-thin and given a speedy sauté to lend a fine texture to the finished dessert. Slim fingers of buttered brioche stand in for the usual cakey crust.

FOR THE APPLESAUCE

4 tart apples, such as Granny Smith
4 semi-tart apples, such as Braeburn or Fuji
¼ teaspoon cinnamon
¼ teaspoon grated nutmeg
3 tablespoons granulated sugar
2 tablespoons packed light brown sugar

FOR THE FILLING

3 tart apples, such as Granny Smith
3 sweet apples, such as Braeburn or Fuji
¼ teaspoon cinnamon
Pinch of grated nutmeg
2 tablespoons granulated sugar
1 tablespoon light brown sugar
4 tablespoons unsalted butter, or as needed

1 loaf brioche or other egg bread, such as challah,
    crust removed, cut into ½-inch-thick slices
8 tablespoons (1 stick) unsalted butter, at room temperature
½ cup packed light brown sugar
¼ to ½ teaspoon cinnamon
Lightly sweetened whipped cream

Preheat the oven to 350°F. Butter a large baking dish.

For the applesauce, quarter and core the apples, but do not peel them. Cut the quarters crosswise in half. Place the chunks in the buttered baking dish, cover with foil, and bake for 45 minutes to 1 hour, until the apples are soft but not mushy. Remove them from the oven, but leave the oven on.

Transfer the apples to a food mill or strainer set over a bowl (set the baking dish aside) and force the apple pulp through, leaving behind the skins. Add the cinnamon, nutmeg, and sugars and whisk to combine. Return the applesauce to the dish and bake uncovered, stirring every 30 minutes or so, until the juices evaporate and the apples begin to caramelize, about 4 hours total (see Note). The applesauce should be thick with a beautiful pinkish red color. Let cool. (The applesauce can be made up to 2 days ahead, covered, and refrigerated.)

Meanwhile, prepare the filling: Core and halve the apples, but do not peel. With a mandoline, sharp knife, or other vegetable slicer, slice the apples ¼ inch thick. Place in a bowl and then toss the slices with the cinnamon, nutmeg, and sugars. Leave the apples to macerate until they release some of their juices, 20 to 30 minutes.

Heat a large pan over high heat until really hot. Melt about half the butter, then add about one-third of the apples and sauté briefly, about 3 minutes, until barely tender (your goal is to jump-start the cooking process without cooking the apples through). Transfer the apples to a parchment-lined baking sheet to cool and cook the remaining apples in batches, adding more butter to the pan as necessary.

Preheat the oven to 350°F. Butter six 6-ounce ramekins.

Cut the brioche slices into 3-by-1-inch rectangles and set aside. In a large bowl, using an electric mixer, beat the butter on medium-high speed until soft and creamy, 3 to 5 minutes. Add the brown sugar and cinnamon and continue beating until thoroughly combined.

To assemble the charlottes: With a small offset spatula or a butter knife, spread a little of the brown sugar–butter mixture around only the sides of the ramekins to make a layer about ¼ inch thick. (This is the "glue" you will press the brioche slices into—it needs to be thick without being so thick that you end up eating mounds of sugar.) Line the sides of the molds with brioche, standing the rectangles on end and pressing them tightly against the sides of the ramekins. Place 1 tablespoon of the apple filling in the bottom of each ramekin, followed by 1½ tablespoons of the applesauce. Finish by topping off with enough filling to come to the top of the mold. Using a serrated knife, trim away the excess brioche so that the bread is flush with the top edges of the ramekins. With a spatula, gently tamp down the charlottes to compact the ingredients. (Refrigerate the remaining applesauce to enjoy later.)

Place the ramekins on a baking sheet and bake until golden and bubbly, about 30 minutes. While still warm, carefully invert onto individual serving plates. Lift off the molds. Serve with a dollop of lightly sweetened whipped cream.

NOTE: You can make the applesauce on top of the stove, but it's hard to beat the caramelization you get from roasting the apples. Plus, once you've put them in the oven, you can forget about the apples while you are preparing the filling and the molds.

The charlottes can be baked up to 1 day ahead, cooled, and refrigerated. Reheat in a 350°F oven for about 15 minutes.

APPLE AND ALMOND BREAD PUDDING

SERVES 8 • PHOTOGRAPH PAGE 278

Dolester Miles, one of the old-timers of the Highlands kitchen, makes many different bread puddings. This cool-weather version combines some favorite autumn fruit and almonds. Serve the bread pudding warm, by itself, or with whipped cream, or with rum or cinnamon crème anglaise (see pages 308 and 309), or ice cream.

4 semi-tart apples, such as Fuji or Braeburn, peeled, cored, and sliced
1 loaf French bread, crust removed, cut into ½-inch dice (about 4 cups)
1½ cups sliced almonds
3 cups half-and-half
¾ cup sugar
5 large eggs
½ cup almond paste, crumbled
1 teaspoon pure almond extract
½ teaspoon cinnamon
A grating or two of nutmeg
1 tablespoon unsalted butter, at room temperature

In a large bowl, combine the apples, bread, and almonds and mix well. In a medium bowl, whisk the half-and-half, sugar, and eggs to combine. Add the almond paste, almond extract, cinnamon, and nutmeg and whisk until thoroughly combined. Pour this custard mixture over the bread and let soak for about 20 minutes.

Preheat the oven to 350°F. Butter a 10-inch gratin dish with the butter.

Spread the bread and custard mixture evenly in the prepared gratin dish. Bake for about 45 minutes, or until golden on top and the custard is set. Serve warm.

Dessert wines—Sauternes, late-harvest Rieslings, Muscats from the South of France, Australia, and California, or their Italian equivalent, Moscatos—are a delightful way to bring a meal to its close. These wines are exciting because of their balance of fruity sweetness and acidity, which makes for a few basic "rules" for pairing them with desserts. First, desserts should not be overly sweet—definitely not sweeter than the wine. Second, ice creams and sorbets are rarely suited to dessert wines. Lastly, some worthy suggestions to pair with these wines: fruits such as peaches, figs, and nectarines simmered in a wine syrup are ambrosial; apricot, vanilla, and orange flavors work magically with these; subtle cardamom, rose flower water, and pistachio may have Saracen origins, but they are heavenly with the muscats; and the distinctive flavors of almond and pear are ideal companions as well.

Here is a brief list of some of my favorite dessert wines:

Beaumes de Venise from the South of France produces fragrant wines that are an unusually good value; look for Domaine Durban and Guigal.

Quarts de Chaumes produced by Domaine des Baumard from the Loire Valley is a superior late-harvest chenin blanc, sensational and suited to age twenty years or more.

Sauternes and Barsac are some of the most elegant late-harvest wines.

As you'll find, there are not many "great buys" but these are my perennial picks: Climens, Suduiraut, Rieussec, and Coutet. These wines really need some age, at least five to six years, and at around ten years of age they become even more magical.

The Vin de Glaciere from Randall Grahm's Bonny Doon Vineyard is an excellent wine; he freezes the grapes to concentrate them.

Moscato di Asti represents the best value in dessert wines; they are charming and refreshing with low alcohol and a pleasant fizz. Rely on Sirocco, Chiarlo, or La Spinetta.

{ Apple Charlotte, page 296

PEAR AND ALMOND TART

SERVES 6 TO 8

The voluptuous pear, when poached with vanilla bean and baked on a foamy bed of almond cream, is classically delicious. The tender, mellow poached pears in spiced syrup also make a light dessert on their own. Serve the pears simply in the syrup or with a fruit spirit such as poire William or with warm chocolate sauce and crumbled Almond Macaroons (page 318).

FOR THE PEARS

3 cups sugar

6 cups water

½ vanilla bean, split

One 2-inch piece cinnamon stick

6 firm but almost-ripe pears, such as Bartlett, Bosc, or Anjou

8 tablespoons (1 stick) unsalted butter, at room temperature

½ cup sugar

1 large egg

1 cup finely ground blanched almonds

1 tablespoon all-purpose flour

3 tablespoons Calvados or dark rum

1 teaspoon pure almond extract

1 unbaked 10-inch tart shell made with Pâte Brisée
   (page 342), chilled

Combine the sugar, water, vanilla bean, and cinnamon in a large nonreactive saucepan and bring to a simmer, stirring to dissolve the sugar. Simmer gently for 15 minutes.

Meanwhile, peel the pears, cut them lengthwise in half, and remove the cores.

Place the pears in the simmering syrup and cook until tender, 15 to 20 minutes. Test for doneness by piercing one of the pears with a paring knife: It should offer very little resistance. Remove from the heat and allow the pears to cool in the poaching liquid, then discard the cinnamon stick and vanilla bean. (The pears can be stored in the refrigerator in their cooking liquid for up to 3 days.)

Preheat the oven to 425°F.

In a large bowl, using an electric mixer, cream the butter and sugar on medium speed until light and fluffy. Reduce the speed to low, add the egg, almonds, flour, Calvados, and almond extract and mix until smooth, about 2 minutes. Pour this mixture into the chilled tart shell and spread it evenly.

Remove the pears from the poaching liquid, letting excess liquid drain off. Set 1 cup of the poaching liquid aside. Place the pears cut side down close together on the tart with the narrow ends facing in, until the entire surface of the tart is covered. Bake until golden brown, about 45 minutes.

Meanwhile, in a small saucepan over high heat, bring the reserved pear poaching liquid to a boil and reduce to a glaze; there should be 2 to 3 tablespoons remaining. Set aside.

As soon as the tart comes out of the oven, brush the pears with the reduced poaching liquid to give them a sheen.

Serve warm or at room temperature.

BROWN BUTTER ALMOND FINANCIER

MAKES ONE 6-INCH CAKE OR 9 INDIVIDUAL CAKES

Brown butter makes for a very flavorful and rich cake. The financier is an old French classic. Our version combines brown butter with ground almonds, and the result is absolutely fantastic. Diplomat cream—a combination of whipped cream and pastry cream—adds another layer of sophistication, while the strawberries provide a burst of color.

FOR THE BATTER

¼ cup all-purpose flour

1 tablespoon plus 2 teaspoons cake flour

1 teaspoon baking powder

Pinch of Kosher salt

½ cup whole unblanched almonds

1¼ cups confectioners' sugar

1 teaspoon pure vanilla extract

4 large egg whites, at room temperature

9 tablespoons Brown Butter (see page 338), melted and cooled, plus extra for buttering the mold(s)

1 pint strawberries, hulled, rinsed, and quartered

1 to 2 teaspoons sugar

½ to 1 cup whipping cream, whipped with 1 tablespoon sugar

FOR THE PASTRY CREAM (MAKES 2½ CUPS)

2 cups half-and-half

¼ vanilla bean, split

½ cup sugar

¼ cup cornstarch

3 large egg yolks

2½ tablespoons cold unsalted butter, diced

1 teaspoon pure vanilla extract

To make the batter, sift the flours, baking powder, and salt together and set aside.

Pulse the almonds and confectioners' sugar in a food processor until finely ground. Add the dry ingredients and pulse to combine. Transfer to a medium bowl. Add the vanilla to the whites and slowly whisk into the dry ingredients. Whisk in the brown butter in a steady stream, just until well mixed: Do not overmix or the cake will be dry. Cover the bowl with plastic wrap and refrigerate for at least 3 hours or overnight before baking.

Preheat the oven to 325°F. Brush a 6-inch cake pan or nine 6-ounce ramekins with brown butter; set aside.

Give the chilled batter a quick stir with a whisk. Pour into the prepared cake pan, filling it three-quarters full. Or, if using the ramekins, use an ice cream scoop or a large spoon to fill the molds half full. Bake for 18 to 23 minutes (10 to 12 minutes for ramekins) until golden brown and the cake springs back when pressed in the center with a fingertip. Cool on a rack in the pan or molds. Invert to release the cake or molds and then turn the cake upright on a serving plate or individual plates.

Put the strawberries in a medium bowl, sprinkle with 1 teaspoon sugar, and let them macerate for 20 to 30 minutes, until the sugar has dissolved and the strawberries have released some of their juice. Add more sugar, if desired.

While the strawberries are macerating, make the pastry cream by combining the half-and-half and vanilla bean in a medium nonreactive saucepan. Bring to a boil over high heat, then remove from the heat.

Meanwhile, in a stainless steel bowl, combine the sugar and cornstarch, whisking until no lumps remain. Once the half-and-half has come to a boil, quickly whisk the egg yolks into the cornstarch mixture, then gradually add about ½ cup of the hot half-and-half to the eggs, whisking constantly, to temper them. Pour this mixture back into the saucepan and cook over medium heat, whisking constantly, until the mixture is thick, 5 to 7 minutes; it should register 176°F on an instant-read thermometer. Remove from the heat and whisk in the butter and vanilla extract. Transfer to a bowl or other container and place a piece of plastic wrap directly on the surface of the pastry cream to keep a skin from forming. Chill for at least 4 hours, or overnight. (The pastry cream can be refrigerated for up to 3 days.)

Fold the whipped cream into the vanilla pastry cream, starting with ½ cup, taste, then add more cream if desired. This mixture is known as diplomat cream.

To assemble, top the cake or individual cakes with spoonfuls of the cream and, using a slotted spoon, scatter the berries over the top. Spoon the remaining berry juices around the cake to garnish. Serve immediately.

WINTER FRUITS
IN A SPICED SYRUP

SERVES 4

Fruits of the season in a slightly exotic aromatic syrup, flavored with warm spices such as coriander, star anise, and light and dark peppercorns, make a beautiful and flavorful and light dessert. At Highlands we serve this compote with Cornmeal Madeleines (page 318).

FOR THE SYRUP

4 cups water

1 cup sugar

1 vanilla bean, split

One 1-inch piece fresh ginger, peeled and cut into
⅟₄-inch-thick slices

Grated zest of 1 lemon

1 cinnamon stick

3 black peppercorns

3 white peppercorns

2 star anise

6 to 8 coriander seeds

6 to 8 cardamom seeds (not the whole pods,
just the seeds inside)

FOR THE FRUIT

1 banana

1 mango, peeled, pitted, and cut into ½-inch dice
(see page 346)

3 blood oranges, cut into suprêmes (see page 346)

2 oranges, cut into suprêmes (see page 346)

1 pink grapefruit, cut into suprêmes

½ pineapple, peeled, cored, and cut into 1-inch chunks

In a nonreactive saucepan, combine all the ingredients for the syrup and bring to a boil. Immediately remove from the heat, cover, and set aside to infuse and cool for 30 to 45 minutes.

Strain the syrup, reserving the vanilla bean, star anise, and cinnamon stick for garnish, if you wish, and set aside.

While the syrup is cooling, peel and slice the banana. In a large bowl, combine the mango, citrus suprêmes, pineapple, and any juices. Add the sliced banana.

Pour the syrup over the fruit. Cover with plastic wrap pressed directly against the surface of the fruit and refrigerate for at least 4 hours, or overnight.

Spoon the fruit and syrup into individual serving dishes, and serve with madeleines, if desired.

Winter Fruits in a Spiced Syrup, page 304, with Cornmeal Madeleines, page 318.

PUMPKIN CHEESECAKE

SERVES 14

Cheesecake was one of the desserts my mother made throughout my childhood. At every holiday gathering, she presented New York–style cheesecake inspired by the famous Lindy's recipe. I would often sneak downstairs in the middle of the night and trim away piece after little piece, thinking that no one would notice. In retrospect, Mother undoubtedly knew of my forays, but I'm sure she took them as a compliment. With its healthy dose of fresh pumpkin puree—made by simply baking a quartered, seeded pie pumpkin—and a crust of gingersnap cookie crumbs, this rendition is a knockout at Thanksgiving or Christmas.

FOR THE CRUST

30 gingersnaps (to yield 1½ cups crumbs)
½ cup pecans, toasted (see page 346)
¼ cup packed light brown sugar
4 tablespoons unsalted butter, melted

FOR THE FILLING

Four 8-ounce packages cream cheese, at room temperature
4 large eggs
1¼ cups sugar
1½ cups pumpkin puree, homemade (see Note) or
**   canned unsweetened puree**
¼ cup heavy cream
1 teaspoon cinnamon
½ teaspoon allspice

Preheat the oven to 350°F.

To prepare the crust, finely grind the cookies and pecans with the brown sugar in a food processor. Add the melted butter and pulse until incorporated. Press this mixture into the bottom and 2¾ inches up the sides of a 10-inch spring-form pan. Set aside.

To prepare the filling, in the bowl of a stand mixer fitted with the whisk attachment, combine the cream cheese, eggs, and sugar and beat at medium speed until light and smooth, about 8 minutes. Transfer ¾ cup of this mixture to a small bowl, cover, and refrigerate to use for the topping. Add the pumpkin puree, cream, cinnamon, and allspice to the remaining cream cheese mixture and beat until well combined. Pour the filling into the prepared crust.

Bake for about 1 hour and 15 minutes, until the cheesecake puffs, the top browns, and the center moves just a little when jiggled. Transfer the pan to a cooling rack and let cool for 10 minutes. Then run a knife between the sides of the pan and the cheesecake to release it from the sides and let cool completely on the rack.

Remove the sides of the pan and set the cheesecake on a serving plate. Cover and refrigerate for at least several hours, or overnight. Before serving, spoon the reserved cream cheese mixture evenly over the top of the cheesecake. Serve with cups of dark roast coffee.

NOTE: To make your own pumpkin puree, quarter and seed a 3-pound pie pumpkin. Bake in a 350°F oven for 1 hour, or until very tender. Scoop out the seeds, then scoop out the flesh and mash with a fork while it is still warm.

SWEET POTATO TART WITH COCONUT CRUST AND PECAN STREUSEL

SERVES 8 TO 10

This dessert has been the grand finale for every type of fancy dinner at Highlands, from museum balls we've catered to family Thanksgiving meals to nightly desserts. Buttery sweet potato filling, sweet coconut, and crunchy pecans combine with a dark rum crème anglaise to make a minor classic. This also pairs well with a cinnamon crème anglaise (see Variation).

FOR THE CRUST

2½ cups all-purpose flour
2½ teaspoons sugar
1 cup shredded unsweetened coconut
1 teaspoon Kosher salt
12 tablespoons (1½ sticks) cold unsalted butter, diced
½ cup vegetable shortening
2 large egg yolks
¼ cup ice water

FOR THE RUM CRÈME ANGLAISE

4 large egg yolks
¼ cup sugar
1½ cups half-and-half
¼ vanilla bean, split
1 tablespoon dark rum

FOR THE FILLING

2 medium sweet potatoes, scrubbed
2 large eggs
¾ cup sugar
½ teaspoon Kosher salt
½ teaspoon ginger, or to taste
Pinch of cinnamon, or to taste
1 teaspoon pure vanilla extract
1²/₃ cups half-and-half
8 tablespoons (1 stick) unsalted butter, melted
    and cooled slightly

FOR THE STREUSEL

½ cup pecans, toasted (see page 346) and coarsely chopped
½ cup all-purpose flour
½ cup sugar
¼ teaspoon cinnamon
Pinch of salt
4 to 6 tablespoons cold unsalted butter, diced

To make the crust, put the flour, sugar, coconut, and salt in a food processor and pulse a few times to combine. Add the butter and shortening and pulse until the mixture resembles coarse cornmeal. Add the egg yolks to the water and, with the machine running, pour it through the feed tube. Pulse until the dough comes together and forms a ball. Turn it out onto a sheet of plastic wrap, flatten it into a disk, and wrap it tightly. Chill for at least 1 hour, or overnight.

To make the rum crème anglaise, whisk the egg yolks and sugar in a medium bowl until smooth and pale yellow. In a medium saucepan, bring the half-and-half to a boil. Remove from the heat. Gradually add about ½ cup of the half-and-half to the egg yolks, whisking constantly, to temper them. Transfer the egg mixture to the saucepan with the remaining half-and-half and cook, stirring constantly, until the sauce coats the back of a spoon, 2 to 3 minutes; it should register 175°F on an instant-read thermometer. Strain into a bowl and add the vanilla bean and rum. Let cool to room temperature, then refrigerate until chilled. (The crème anglaise can be refrigerated for up to 3 days.)

On a lightly floured surface, roll the dough out to a 12-inch round. Fit the dough into a 10-inch fluted pan with a removable bottom, pressing it gently onto the bottom and up the sides. Trim the excess dough. Prick all over the bottom with a fork. Chill until firm, about 30 minutes.

Preheat the oven to 375°F.

Line the tart shell with parchment paper or foil and fill with dried beans or pie weights. Bake for 20 minutes. Remove the paper and weights and bake for 5 to 10 minutes longer, or until golden brown and crisp on the bottom. Let cool slightly on a rack before filling, about 20 minutes.

To make the filling, prick the sweet potatoes a few times with a fork. Bake for about 45 minutes, until tender. Let cool.

Peel the sweet potatoes and pass through a food mill. (You need 2 cups pureed sweet potatoes for the filling.)

Lower the oven to 350°F.

In a large bowl, combine the sweet potatoes, eggs, sugar, salt, ginger, cinnamon, vanilla extract, half-and-half, and butter and whisk with a sturdy whisk until satiny smooth. (The filling can be made ahead, covered, and refrigerated for up to 2 days.)

To make the streusel, put the pecans, flour, sugar, cinnamon, and salt in a food processor and pulse a few times to combine. Add the butter and pulse a few times until the mixture comes together a bit. Transfer the mixture to a bowl and, working quickly, rub the mixture between your fingers until the streusel is in lumps slightly larger than peas.

Pour the filling into the prebaked crust. Sprinkle the streusel evenly over the top of the tart. Bake for 30 to 40 minutes, or until the filling is slightly puffed and set in the middle. Let cool slightly on a rack. To serve, cut the tart into wedges and drizzle with rum crème anglaise.

VARIATION: Cinnamon crème anglaise is another worthy companion if rum doesn't suit your fancy. Simply omit the rum and add ¼ teaspoon cinnamon along with the vanilla.

SEVEN-LAYER COCONUT CAKE

SERVES 12 TO 14

When you want something truly lavish-looking, this dessert is a sure bet—an awe-inspiring seven-layer tower of fluffy icing and toasted coconut. While there are several components in this recipe, it is quite simple to prepare and impressive to serve. We use unsweetened raw coconut and toast it to bring out its nutty, tropical flavor. Avoid the sweetened grated coconut in the baking aisle of your supermarket—it is much too sweet.

FOR THE PASTRY CREAM (MAKES ABOUT 5 CUPS)

4 cups half-and-half

1 cup shredded unsweetened coconut

1 cup plus 2 tablespoons sugar

½ cup cornstarch

7 large egg yolks

5 tablespoons cold unsalted butter, diced

1 teaspoon pure vanilla extract

FOR THE CAKE

4 cups sifted cake flour

1 teaspoon baking powder

1 teaspoon baking soda

½ teaspoon salt

¾ pound (3 sticks) unsalted butter, at room temperature

2 cups sugar

8 large egg yolks, lightly beaten

1⅓ cups sour cream

2 teaspoons pure vanilla extract

FOR THE FROSTING

5 tablespoons cold water

3 large egg whites

1½ cups sugar

2 teaspoons light corn syrup

¼ teaspoon Kosher salt

¼ vanilla bean, split, or ½ teaspoon pure vanilla extract

¾ to 1 cup shredded unsweetened coconut, lightly toasted (see Note)

To make the the pastry cream, combine the half-and-half and coconut in a large nonreactive saucepan and bring barely to a simmer over medium heat. Turn off the heat, cover, and let infuse for 30 minutes.

In a small bowl, combine the sugar and cornstarch, whisking until no lumps remain. Set aside.

Beat the egg yolks in a medium bowl. Bring the half-and-half back to a boil, then remove from the heat. Whisk the cornstarch-sugar mixture into the beaten yolks a little at a time until the mixture is smooth and thick. Gradually add about 1½ cups of the hot half-and-half to the egg-cornstarch mixture, whisking constantly, to temper the eggs. Add the mixture to the remaining half-and-half and cook over medium heat, whisking constantly, until thick, about 10 minutes; it should register 175°F on an instant-read thermometer. After one or two big bubbles appear at the sides of the pan, remove the pan from the heat before the pastry cream comes to a boil; you don't want it to boil or the cornstarch will break down and liquefy, ruining the pastry cream.

Whisk in the butter and vanilla and transfer the pastry cream to a bowl or other container. Cover with a sheet of plastic wrap placed directly on the surface of the pastry cream to keep a skin from forming. Chill for at least 4 hours, or overnight, before serving. (The pastry cream can be refrigerated for up to 3 days.)

To prepare the cake, preheat the oven to 350°F. Grease and flour two 9-inch cake pans.

Sift the flour, baking powder, baking soda, and salt together. Set aside.

In the bowl of a stand mixer fitted with the paddle attachment, cream the butter and sugar on high speed until light and fluffy. Reduce the speed to medium and add the egg yolks in a steady stream, stopping to scrape down the sides and bottom of the bowl as necessary. Add the sour cream and vanilla and scrape down the bowl again. Reduce the speed to low and add the dry ingredients a little at a time, beating until incorporated after each addition. Scrape down the bowl a final time, making sure no lumps remain and all the flour is incorporated.

continued

Divide the batter evenly between the prepared cake pans. Bake for 35 to 40 minutes, until a tester inserted in the center comes out clean and the cake springs back when pressed lightly in the middle. Let the cake cool completely in the pans on a cooling rack.

Invert the cakes onto a rack. With a long serrated knife, slice each cake horizontally into 4 layers about ½ inch thick. (For easier slicing, chill the cakes in the freezer for a few minutes.) Place one cake layer on a cake stand or plate and spread a ½-inch-thick layer of pastry cream over it. Add another layer and cover with pastry cream. Continue with 5 more layers (you'll have an extra layer, in case of breakage) and the remaining cream. Leave the top layer plain. Chill the cake in the freezer for a few minutes to firm it up while you prepare the frosting.

Combine the water, egg whites, sugar, corn syrup, and salt in a large heatproof bowl. Set it over a saucepan of rapidly boiling water and, with a handheld electric mixer, beat on medium speed for 4 minutes. Turn the mixer up to high and beat for 3 minutes more until the whites have doubled in volume. Transfer the frosting to another bowl (to expedite cooling). Add the vanilla seeds or extract and beat for 3 minutes more to cool the frosting. The frosting must be used immediately.

Frost the top and sides of the cake, working quickly—once the icing is on the cake, it tends to come off the more it is worked (if desired, reserve a little frosting for garnish). Cover the sides of the cake with toasted coconut and sprinkle the top with more toasted coconut or leave the top white and pipe the reserved frosting into rosettes all around the edge.

NOTE: To toast the coconut, preheat the oven to 300°F. Spread out the coconut on a shallow stainless steel baking sheet. Toast in the oven until the coconut turns golden brown, 10 to 15 minutes, stirring every 5 minutes or so, being careful to not let it burn. Let cool completely.

CHOCOLATE CARAMEL-NUT TART

SERVES 8 TO 10 • PHOTOGRAPH PAGE 277

The combination of caramel and salty nuts takes this chocolate tart to an indulgent level that is irresistible.

FOR THE CRUST
2 cups all-purpose flour
¼ cup sugar
¼ teaspoon Kosher salt
10 tablespoons (1¼ sticks) cold unsalted butter, diced
⅓ cup ice water

FOR THE CARAMEL SAUCE
2 cups sugar
2 tablespoons light corn syrup
About ¾ cup cold water
2 tablespoons unsalted butter
Pinch of Kosher salt
⅔ cup heavy cream

FOR THE GANACHE
14 ounces milk chocolate, finely chopped
6 tablespoons unsalted butter, diced, at room temperature
¾ cup heavy cream

½ cup cashews, toasted (see page 346) and roughly chopped
½ cup pecans, toasted (see page 346) and roughly chopped
½ cup walnuts, toasted (see page 346) and roughly chopped
½ cup almonds, toasted (see page 346) and roughly chopped
Pinch of Kosher salt

To make the dough, place the flour, sugar, and salt in a food processor and pulse to combine. Add the butter and pulse 6 to 8 times, until the butter is the size of small peas. With the machine running, drizzle in the ice water and pulse until the dough just comes together. Turn the dough out onto a piece of plastic wrap, shape it into a disk, and wrap it in the plastic. Refrigerate at least 2 hours, or overnight.

Allow the dough to stand at room temperature for 20 minutes or so to make rolling easier. On a lightly floured surface, roll the dough into an 11-inch round. Fit it into a 9-inch fluted tart pan with a removable bottom and trim off the excess dough with a roll of the rolling pin. Chill the tart shell until firm, at least 1 hour.

Preheat the oven to 350°F.

Line the tart shell with parchment or foil and fill with dried beans or pie weights. Bake for 20 minutes. Remove the paper and weights and bake for 5 to 10 minutes longer, until golden brown. (You want a good bit of color on the bottom of the tart shell, since you will not be baking it again.)

To make the caramel sauce, combine the sugar and corn syrup in a shallow nonreactive saucepan and gradually stir in just enough cold water so that the mixture resembles wet sand. Cook over high heat, without stirring (or the sugar will crystallize), until the syrup at the edges of the pan begins to color. Gently tilt the pan to swirl the caramel to distribute the color. Continue cooking until the syrup turns a nice amber color and you begin to smell burned sugar. When the caramel has reached the desired color (lighter amber will be sweeter, darker amber will be more bitter), *very carefully* add the butter, using a long-handled whisk. (Caramel is extremely hot, and the steam can burn you.) Once the butter is incorporated, add the salt and cream, whisking gently until all the bubbles disappear, then set aside to cool completely.

To make the ganache, place the chocolate and butter in a bowl. Bring the cream to a boil in a medium saucepan and pour it over the chocolate. Let sit for 1 minute. Working from the center out, gently whisk the warm cream into the chocolate until incorporated. Let the ganache stand until cooled but still pourable.

In a bowl combine the nuts and salt. Pour a scant ¼ cup of the caramel sauce over the nuts, stirring to coat. Set aside.

To assemble the tart, spread ⅓ cup of the caramel sauce evenly over the bottom of the baked tart shell. Pop this in the freezer for 20 minutes to set.

Pour 1¼ cups of the ganache over the caramel (see Notes). Let the tart stand at room temperature for about 1 hour to set the ganache, or refrigerate for 20 minutes.

When the ganache has firmed up, sprinkle the nuts evenly over the top of the tart, leaving a ¼-inch border of ganache all around. Serve with the remaining caramel sauce.

NOTES: Reserve the remaining ganache for another use—warmed, it makes a great chocolate sauce. It can be refrigerated for up to 5 days.

The tart can be refrigerated for up to 3 days or frozen for up to 2 weeks. Bring to room temperature before serving.

HAZELNUT SEMIFREDDO CAPPUCCINO

SERVES 6

We serve this dessert in coffee cups with clouds of whipped cream to emulate frothy steamed milk. Dig your spoon into the luscious hidden semifreddo and you may swoon. A few of our Cocoa Biscotti (page 315) alongside are a perfect addition to any "cappuccino."

FOR THE HAZELNUTS
8 tablespoons (1 stick) unsalted butter
1 cup hazelnuts, blanched (see page 346) and roughly chopped
1 teaspoon honey
1 teaspoon sugar
1 teaspoon Kosher salt

FOR THE SEMIFREDDO
2 cups heavy cream
¼ vanilla bean, split, or ½ teaspoon pure vanilla extract
1 cup plus 1 teaspoon sugar
½ cup water
6 large egg whites, at room temperature
1 cup crushed Almond Macaroons (page 318; chill first
    to make crushing easier)
Splash of pure vanilla extract (optional)

FOR THE GARNISH (OPTIONAL)
1 cup whipped cream, sweetened with 1 tablespoon sugar
1 heaping tablespoon unsweetened cocoa powder

Preheat the oven to 325°F.

To prepare the hazelnuts, melt the butter in a saucepan over low to medium-low heat and then cook, stirring constantly, until fragrant and brown, 12 to 15 minutes. Strain the brown butter and set aside to cool.

Spread the hazelnuts on a baking sheet. Toast the nuts, stirring occasionally, until they develop a nice brown color and are fragrant, 8 to 10 minutes. Place the hot nuts in a stainless steel bowl, drizzle with about 4 tablespoons of the brown butter (reserve any remaining browned butter for another use), add the honey, and toss to coat. Sprinkle with the sugar and salt, tossing again. Taste and adjust the seasoning if necessary. Pour onto a parchment-lined baking sheet and let cool.

In the bowl of an electric mixer fitted with the whisk attachment, whip the cream with the seeds from the vanilla bean (or the vanilla extract) until soft peaks form. Transfer to a bowl, cover, and refrigerate. Wash and thoroughly dry the mixer bowl and whisk.

To prepare the semifreddo, in a saucepan, bring 1 cup of the sugar and the water to a boil. Attach a candy thermometer to the side of the pan.

Meanwhile, place the egg whites in the bowl of the electric mixer fitted with the whip attachment and begin beating on low speed. When the sugar syrup reaches 210°F, beat the egg whites on medium speed until frothy, about 1 minute. Add the remaining 1 teaspoon sugar, increase the speed to high, and beat until soft peaks form. When the syrup reaches 238°F, reduce the speed of the mixer to medium-high and pour in the hot syrup, pouring it down the side of the bowl so it does not get caught in the whisk and splatter everywhere—especially on you.

Continue to whip on medium speed until the bottom of the bowl feels cool to the touch and the mixture is fluffy and glossy, about 5 to 6 minutes.

When the mixture is cool, transfer it to a large bowl. Fold in the whipped cream, hazelnuts, and crushed macaroons until well combined. Taste and adjust the flavors, if you like, by adding a pinch of salt and/or a splash of vanilla extract.

For the garnish, mix the tablespoon of cocoa powder into the sweetened whipped cream and chill.

Scoop the mixture into coffee cups. Cover and freeze for at least 4 hours, or overnight. Garnish the "cappuccinos" with whipped cream if desired.

COCOA BISCOTTI

MAKES 2 DOZEN COOKIES

If you like to dunk a little something sweet into your coffee, then biscotti are for you. Dark and crunchy with a dose of espresso added to the cocoa and bittersweet chocolate, one of these flavorful biscotti may well send you on a caffeine high even without a cup of the steaming hot stuff.

1⅓ cups all-purpose flour
¼ cup unsweetened cocoa powder
1 tablespoon instant coffee or espresso powder
Pinch of cinnamon
¾ teaspoon baking soda
¼ teaspoon Kosher salt
2 large eggs
¾ cup sugar
¾ teaspoon pure vanilla extract
3 ounces good-quality bittersweet chocolate, chopped
1 cup slivered almonds

Preheat the oven to 325°F. Line a baking sheet with parchment paper.

Sift together the flour, cocoa powder, coffee, cinnamon, baking soda, and salt; set aside.

In the large bowl of an electric mixer, beat the eggs, sugar, and vanilla on medium speed until smooth and pale yellow, about 3 minutes. Reduce the speed to low and slowly add the dry ingredients, mixing until incorporated. Fold in the chocolate and almonds.

Turn the dough out onto a floured surface. Shape the dough into a log approximately 2 inches in diameter and about 6 inches long. Place on the parchment-lined baking sheet. Bake until the surface of the log springs back when pressed with a fingertip, 15 to 20 minutes. Let cool completely, about 30 minutes.

Preheat the oven to 300°F. With a serrated knife, slice the log into ¼-inch-thick slices. Lay the slices on a baking sheet and bake until firm, 6 to 8 minutes. Be careful not to overbake—they will firm up a little more as they cool. Transfer to a rack to cool.

Hazelnut Semifredo Cappuccino with Cocoa Biscotti

CORNMEAL MADELEINES

MAKES 24 MADELEINES • PHOTOGRAPH PAGE 305

Classic madeleines have a tender-soft texture—the cornmeal gives ours a subtle, down-home crunchy quality.

3/4 cup white cornmeal
3/4 cup all-purpose flour plus extra for dusting pans
1/2 teaspoon baking powder
1/2 teaspoon cinnamon
Pinch of grated nutmeg
Pinch of Kosher salt
8 tablespoons (1 stick) unsalted butter, at room temperature
1/2 cup packed light brown sugar
1/4 cup granulated sugar
Grated zest of 1 lemon
4 large eggs
1/4 cup milk
1 tablespoon pure vanilla extract
Confectioners' sugar for dusting (optional)

Preheat the oven to 350°F. Butter and flour two madeleine pans.

Sift together the cornmeal, flour, baking powder, cinnamon, nutmeg, and salt; set aside.

In a large bowl, using an electric mixer, cream the butter and sugars together on high speed until light and fluffy, 3 to 5 minutes. Add the lemon zest and mix to incorporate. Add the eggs one at a time, beating well after each addition and scraping down the bowl frequently.

Combine the milk and vanilla. On low speed, add the flour and milk alternately, starting and ending with flour, beating until incorporated. Continue mixing until no lumps or flecks of butter remain.

Spoon the batter into the prepared molds, filling each mold a little more than half full. Bake until golden brown around the edges, 18 to 20 minutes (the more the butter browns, the tastier the madeleines).

Immediately invert the pan onto a parchment-lined baking sheet and gently tap to release the madeleines from the pans. Let cool, and dust with confectioners' sugar, if you like.

ALMOND MACAROONS

MAKES 2 DOZEN COOKIES • PHOTOGRAPH PAGE 317

These macaroons are great with an espresso or a scoop or two of ice cream, and they also create the wonderful, crunchy layer in our Hazelnut Semifreddo Cappuccino (page 314).

6 ounces unblanched almonds
3/4 cup sugar
1/4 teaspoon pure almond extract
2 large egg whites

Preheat the oven to 300°F. Line a baking sheet with a silicone baking mat or parchment paper.

Pulse the almonds in a food processor until finely ground (but not to a paste), about 2 minutes. Add the sugar and pulse for about a minute more. Pour the almond extract into the egg whites and, with the machine running, pour through the feed tube in a steady stream, and process until thoroughly combined, 1 to 2 minutes.

Transfer the batter to a piping bag fitted with a large plain tip and pipe into 1- to 1½-inch rounds spaced about 1 inch apart on the lined baking sheet (if you don't have a piping bag, use a teaspoon). Bake until light golden brown around the edges but still soft in the middle, 10 to 13 minutes. Let cool completely before removing from the pan. (If not eaten right away, the macaroons will keep in the freezer for up to 1 month.)

PECAN SANDIES

MAKES 3 DOZEN COOKIES • PHOTOGRAPH PAGE 317

These irresistible little cookies are so delicate they dissolve in your mouth like cotton candy, leaving only the lingering nutty pecan flavor. These are sure to become a household standard, so you may want to double the recipe and keep some dough in the freezer so you can bake up a batch when company calls. Serve a few with Bourbon Panna Cotta (page 280).

2 cups all-purpose flour
1/2 teaspoon salt
1/2 pound (2 sticks) unsalted butter, at room temperature
1/4 cup sugar
1 teaspoon pure vanilla extract
1 cup pecans, lightly toasted (see page 346)
    and coarsely chopped
About 1/2 cup confectioners' sugar

Sift together the flour and salt and set aside.

In the bowl of a stand mixer fitted with the paddle attachment, cream the butter and sugar on medium speed until light and fluffy, about 5 minutes. Add the vanilla. On low speed, beat in the flour in two batches. Stir in the chopped pecans. Transfer the dough to a sheet of plastic wrap and form into a log that is about 9 inches long and 2 inches in diameter. Roll up in the plastic, twist the ends to secure, and chill for 30 minutes. (The dough can be frozen for up to 2 months.)

Preheat the oven to 350°F.

Line two baking sheets with parchment paper.

Cut the chilled dough into 1/4-inch-thick slices and place 1 inch apart on the lined baking sheets. Bake for 12 to 15 minutes, until golden around the edges. Let cool on the pans on a rack. Once they are completely cooled, dust the cookies with the confectioners' sugar. (The cookies can be stored in an airtight container for 3 to 4 days.)

PISTACHIO BUTTER COOKIES

MAKES 2 TO 2 1/2 DOZEN COOKIES • PHOTOGRAPH PAGE 317

These delicate pistachio cookies are a welcome tidbit with an afternoon cup of coffee, or enjoy them with a bowl of ice cream.

2 cups all-purpose flour
1/8 teaspoon salt
1/2 pound (2 sticks) unsalted butter
3/4 cup sugar
1/2 teaspoon grated lemon zest
1 teaspoon pure vanilla extract
1 large egg yolk
1 cup shelled raw pistachios, chopped

Sift the flour and salt together and set aside.

In the bowl of a stand mixer fitted with the paddle attachment, cream the butter and sugar on high speed until light and fluffy, about 3 minutes. Add the lemon zest and beat for 1 minute longer. Lower the speed to medium, add the vanilla and egg yolk, and beat until incorporated, about 1 minute more. Scrape down the sides of the bowl with a spatula. With the mixer on low speed, gradually add the dry ingredients. Fold in the pistachios.

Turn the dough out onto a lightly floured work surface and shape the dough into a 2-inch-diameter log. Wrap in plastic wrap and chill until firm, at least 4 hours, or overnight. (The dough can be refrigerated for 2 days or frozen for up to 1 month.)

Preheat the oven to 350°F. Line two baking sheets with parchment paper.

Cut the dough into 1/4-inch-thick slices and place the slices on the prepared baking sheets. Bake until light golden brown on the edges, 12 to 15 minutes. Let cool slightly on the baking sheets, then transfer to a rack to cool. (The cookies can be stored in an airtight container for up to 1 week.)

SHORTBREAD COOKIES

MAKES 3 TO 4 DOZEN COOKIES • PHOTOGRAPH PAGE 317

These cookies are so tender they collapse on your tongue and so buttery a couple seem like just enough—though I usually have to have three. They are the ideal accompaniment to custard-type desserts.

¾ pound (3 sticks) unsalted butter
1 cup confectioners' sugar
½ teaspoon salt
3 cups all-purpose flour

Preheat the oven to 350°F.

Using a stand mixer fitted with the paddle attachment, beat the butter and sugar until smooth, 2 to 3 minutes. Sift the salt and flour, then add to the butter mixture, mixing until just combined.

Form the dough into a log about 2 inches in diameter. Wrap the log with plastic wrap and chill for 3 hours to overnight. Freeze for up to 2 months.

Remove the dough from the refrigerator, remove plastic wrap and slice the dough into ¼-inch disks. Place on an ungreased baking sheet 1 inch apart and bake until the bottoms of the cookies just turn golden, about 10 minutes, turning the sheet 180 degrees after 5 minutes. Remove from the oven and cool completely.

VARIATION: After removing the dough from the refrigerator, slice as above, then roll each disk into a ball. Moisten a thumb and press into the center of each ball. Fill each indentation with high-quality raspberry or other fruit preserves. Place on an ungreased baking sheet. Bake until slightly golden, 10 to 12 minutes. Remove from the oven and allow to cool completely.

OATMEAL COOKIES

MAKES 3 TO 4 DOZEN • PHOTOGRAPH PAGE 317

Even though we serve these with our freshly made sorbets and ice creams, I actually enjoy them most with my mid-morning cappuccino. A cross between crunchy and chewy, they're homey and so easy to make.

1 cup unsalted butter
1 cup light brown sugar
½ cup sugar
2 large eggs
1 teaspoon vanilla extract
2 tablespoons heavy cream
1½ cups all-purpose flour
1 teaspoon baking soda
1 teaspoon cinnamon
½ teaspoon salt
3 cups old-fashioned rolled oats
1 cup raisins (optional)

Preheat the oven to 350°F.

Using a stand mixer fitted with the paddle attachment, beat the butter and sugars until smooth, 2 to 3 minutes. Combine the eggs, vanilla, and heavy cream in a separate bowl. Add the egg mixture to the butter and sugar mixture. Sift together the flour, baking soda, cinnamon and salt, then slowly add to the wet mixture. Add the oats and raisins and combine well.

Drop the dough by heaping tablespoons full on an ungreased baking sheet. Bake until golden, about 10 minutes, turning the sheet 180 degrees after 5 minutes.

BASICS

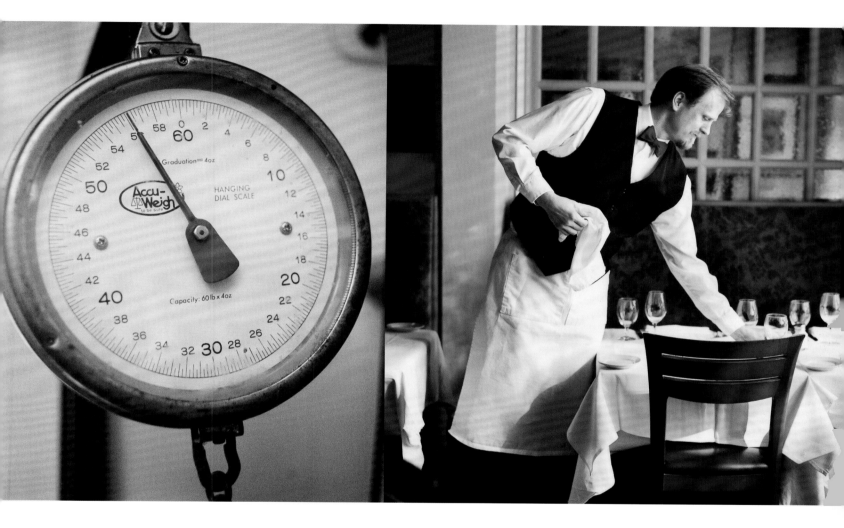

These are the sauces,

vinaigrettes, and relishes that are the workhorses of the Highlands kitchen. As rudimentary as these may seem, they are the building blocks that transform simple cooking into complex dishes with layers of texture and flavor.

For example, note the importance of acidity and the purity of the vinegars used in any vinaigrette. This balances the richness in a dish. Occasionally, we will even combine two different sauces or vinaigrettes in a dish, say, buttermilk dressing and sherry vinaigrette, for a tomato salad. While it may seem excessive at first, once you try it and find your own perfect balance of the two, you'll see it is well worth the effort.

A common mistake is to oversalt a dish. Always begin with a little less than you are inclined to use. Taste and adjust. You'll find this charge in the method for almost every recipe, and it cannot be stressed enough. You can always add a bit more—while the remedy for excess may be starting over.

Finally, always search out the finest and most authentic ingredients possible. You may be surprised that this does not always mean the most expensive choices. Using the best ingredients results in a purity of the flavor in the dishes you create.

{ Ham Hock Vinaigrette, page 246

SAUCE GRIBICHE

MAKES 2 CUPS

One of the Highlands old-time standbys, sauce gribiche is a true classic that just goes to show how some things are best left unchanged. The sauce is really just a pumped-up tartar sauce: The difference lies in the freshness of a homemade mayonnaise, laden with capers, cornichons, shallots, hard-boiled eggs, potato, and a medley of herbs. Serve with grilled, poached, broiled, or sautéed fish and be generous with the sauce. I confess to snacking with unabashed pleasure on a crostini or roasted potato laden with gribiche.

1 heaping cup Homemade Mayonnaise (page 336)
1 heaping tablespoon capers, rinsed
1 heaping tablespoon chopped cornichons
1½ teaspoons finely minced shallots, rinsed
    (rinsing them tones down their bite)
2 hard-boiled large eggs, passed through a fine sieve
    or finely chopped
1 large Yukon Gold potato, peeled, diced, and cooked
    in boiling salted water until tender
1½ teaspoons chopped flat-leaf parsley
1½ teaspoons finely sliced chives
1½ teaspoons coarsely chopped chervil or dill
Juice of ½ lemon
1 teaspoon Dijon mustard

Put the mayonnaise in a bowl and add all of the other ingredients, stirring to combine thoroughly. Taste and adjust the seasoning.

NOTE: You might want to add a splash of tarragon vinegar for a bit of tang, or a chopped anchovy or a dash of hot sauce for a stronger flavor.

MIGNONETTE

MAKES 1 CUP

This classic French sauce for raw oysters delivers a vibrant, racy punch that is worlds apart from the American ketchup-and-horseradish standard. My first encounter with sauce mignonette was in Paris—a platter of cold, salty oysters was moistened with this tart liquid. There is no better way to appreciate a just-shucked oyster.

2 shallots, very finely and evenly diced
1 tablespoon cracked black peppercorns
1 teaspoon crushed pink peppercorns (optional)
½ cup champagne vinegar
1 tablespoon apple cider vinegar or raspberry vinegar
½ cup sparkling wine, such as prosecco

Combine the shallots, peppercorns, vinegars, and sparkling wine in a bowl and stir to mix. Serve in little cruets or ramekins with raw shellfish.

HORSERADISH SAUCE

MAKES ABOUT 2 CUPS

The one appetizer that has appeared every night on our menu since 1982 (even before our famous baked grits) is a carpaccio of thinly sliced beef served with this sauce. It's also good with smoked trout or roast beef.

1 cup grated fresh horseradish, or more to taste
1 cup sour cream, or to taste
2 tablespoons Homemade Mayonnaise (page 336) or
    Hellmann's or Best Foods or to taste
1 tablespoon fresh lemon juice, or to taste
Kosher salt and freshly ground black pepper to taste

Combine all the ingredients in a bowl and mix until thoroughly blended. Taste and adjust the intensity by adding more grated horseradish or more mayonnaise and/or sour cream. Taste and adjust the seasoning.

SALSA VERDE

MAKES 1½ CUPS

You won't find a tomato in this salsa—think vinaigrette meets capers and tons of herbs. This all-purpose Mediterranean sauce, which has many variations, is a wonderful embellishment for full-flavored fish or any grilled meat.

2 garlic cloves, crushed and finely chopped

3 tablespoons capers, rinsed

2 tablespoons chopped cornichons

1 shallot, finely minced

1 or 2 anchovies, rinsed and chopped, if serving with seafood (optional)

½ cup chopped flat-leaf parsley

½ cup chopped basil

¼ cup chopped chives

¼ cup chopped cilantro

¼ cup red wine vinegar

¾ cup extra virgin olive oil

Grated zest of ½ lemon

Kosher salt and freshly ground black pepper to taste

Combine the garlic, capers, cornichons, shallot, anchovies, if using, and herbs in a food processor and pulse to roughly chop. (Alternatively, you can leave the herbs unprocessed—add them whole or roughly torn to the finished sauce.) Add the vinegar, olive oil, lemon zest, and salt and pepper. Pulse a few times to combine. Taste and adjust the seasoning Transfer to a bowl. (This will keep for 1 to 2 days, covered and refrigerated; bring to room temperature before serving.)

TOMATO SALSA

SERVES 4 • PHOTOGRAPH PAGE 239

4 firm, ripe roma tomatoes

½ shallot or 2 scallions, finely minced

1 teaspoon red wine vinegar

1 teaspoon freshly squeezed lime juice

Kosher salt

Freshly ground black pepper

Small handful fresh cilantro (or basil), coarsely chopped

½ teaspoon finely chopped jalapeño pepper

1 tablespoon extra vigin olive oil

In a medium-sized mixing bowl, add the tomatoes, shallot (or scallions), vinegar, lime juice, salt, pepper, cilantro (or basil), Jalapeño, and olive oil. Toss gently to combine. May be served immediately. Will keep 3 to 4 hours at room temperature. Do not refrigerate.

ARTICHOKE AND NIÇOISE OLIVE RELISH

SERVES 6

This relish/vinaigrette/sauce is fantastic with practically everything. The charred red onions provide a sweet crunch, the artichokes add a meaty suave and subtle earthiness, and the salty tang of the olives provides a balance that makes you want to come back for more. This is certainly the time for the fruitiest and freshest extra virgin olive oil, and especially good is sherry vinegar combined with L'Estornell's garnacha.

1 large red onion, cut into ½-inch-thick slices

6 baby artichokes, trimmed (see page 345), quartered, and blanched in boiling water until tender (about 12 minutes)

¼ cup Niçoise olives (or Picholine or other good-quality olives), pitted and coarsely chopped

1 shallot, finely minced

2 tablespoons sherry vinegar

2 tablespoons red wine vinegar (see headnote)

½ cup best-quality extra virgin olive oil

6 sprigs basil, leaves removed and torn

5 sprigs flat-leaf parsley, leaves removed and torn

5 sprigs mint, leaves removed and torn

Kosher salt and freshly ground black pepper to taste

Grated zest of ½ lemon

Prepare a hot grill or preheat the broiler.

Grill or broil the onion slices, turning once, until charred on both sides, about 4 minutes per side. Allow them to cool, then cut into ¼-inch cubes.

In a ceramic or other nonreactive bowl, combine the onions, artichokes, olives, shallot, vinegars, olive oil, and herbs and toss well to combine. Add the salt and pepper, along with the lemon zest. Taste and adjust the seasoning. The relish should taste bright with acidity and herbs.

The vinaigrette is one of the most useful of all sauces. If there is such a thing as "modern" cooking, my guess is that the use of vinaigrette as a sauce for savory dishes exemplifies it. Nowadays superior-quality oils and vinegars are available in almost every supermarket, so there is really no reason not to add a few to your pantry. And you do not have to buy the most expensive Tuscan olive oils, for example, as there are many others available at a fraction of the price. Invest in a good fruity olive oil for finishing a dish and use a less expensive one for everyday cooking. When you realize the countless ways aged vinegar and cold-pressed olive oil can be used, you'll find you can't live without them.

I strongly urge you to seek out sherry vinegar from Jerez, Spain, the town where authentic sherry is made. We often combine two vinegars, such as sherry and balsamic, in our vinaigrettes. The sherry vinegar brings balance by cutting some of the sweetness of the balsamic. Other times we use half cider, red wine, or tarragon vinegar.

When dressing salads, have the lettuces cleaned, thoroughly dried, and chilled. Place them in a large bowl, season with salt and pepper, and spoon enough of the vinaigrette over the lettuces, tossing gently, just to lightly coat—toss with your hands for the best control.

BASIC VINAIGRETTE

MAKES ABOUT 2½ CUPS

The perfect vinaigrette is all about finding the ideal ratio of oil to acidity. You must always taste with a bite of lettuce to determine the right proportions. Once you've mastered the basic vinaigrette, you've got the basis for building many different dressings. This recipe is a good guideline, but again, depending on the fruitiness of the olive oil you use or the acidity of the vinegar, you may need to make adjustments to suit your palate.

In addition to salads, this vinaigrette is great for grilled or roasted meats, fish, or vegetables. You could substitute red wine, cider, champagne, or balsamic vinegar for the sherry vinegar.

1 garlic clove
Kosher salt
½ cup sherry vinegar
Freshly ground black pepper
2 small shallots, finely minced
2 cups extra virgin olive oil (or walnut or hazelnut oil)
Chopped herbs, such as flat-leaf parsley, chives, dill,
    and tarragon

Using a mortar and a pestle, crush the garlic with a pinch of salt, or chop and mash the crushed garlic with the salt using the edge of a chef's knife. In a medium bowl, combine the crushed garlic, vinegar, and salt and pepper to taste. Add the shallots and macerate for 10 to 15 minutes to allow the flavors to come together. Gradually whisk in the olive oil until the dressing is emulsified. Taste and adjust the seasoning. Add the fresh herbs to the dressing just before tossing with your salad. (The vinaigrette can be refrigerated for up to 5 days.)

THREE-VINEGAR VINAIGRETTE

MAKES 1 CUP

This is my dressing of choice when I'm cooking at home. Sometimes I skip the mustard or substitute fresh herbs for the dried.

1 tablespoon finely minced shallots
1 tablespoon red wine vinegar
1 tablespoon sherry vinegar
1 tablespoon balsamic vinegar
1 small garlic clove, crushed and finely chopped
1½ teaspoons Dijon mustard
¼ teaspoon dried thyme
¼ teaspoon dried marjoram
½ teaspoon sugar
Kosher salt and freshly ground black pepper to taste
¾ cup extra virgin olive oil

Combine the shallots, vinegars, garlic, mustard, herbs, sugar, and salt and pepper in a medium bowl. Let macerate for 10 minutes.

Slowly whisk in the olive oil until incorporated. Taste and adjust the seasoning. (The vinaigrette can be refrigerated for up to 5 days.)

SHERRY VINAIGRETTE

MAKES ½ CUP

Spanish sherry vinegar has a superb complex flavor—similar to a great aged wine. The best-quality sherry vinegars come from the Andalusia region of Spain, where world-class sherry is produced. A bacteria is introduced into this fortified wine to turn it into a weak solution of acetic acid, which makes it sour. For a sure bet, look for vinegars produced in the town of Jerez.

If time allows, let the shallot macerate with the vinegar, salt, and pepper for 10 minutes before adding the oil. This tames the bite of the shallot while infusing the vinaigrette with its flavor. And after you whisk in the oil, always taste and adjust the seasoning and acidity. As well as on salads, try using this vinaigrette as a sauce for shellfish, fish, poultry, or beef.

½ shallot, finely minced
4 thyme sprigs, leaves removed
Kosher salt and freshly ground black pepper to taste
2 tablespoons sherry vinegar
6 tablespoons extra virgin olive oil

In a small bowl, combine the shallot, thyme, and a good pinch each of salt and pepper. Add the sherry vinegar and let macerate for 10 minutes.

Whisk in the olive oil in a slow, steady stream. Taste and adjust the seasoning. (The vinaigrette can be refrigerated for up to 5 days.)

SHERRY-HONEY VINAIGRETTE

MAKES 1 CUP

Honey is a great sweetener for vinaigrettes, lending both its distinctive sweet flavor and body to the dressing. We like to use this vinaigrette in our Watercress Salad with Shaved Mushrooms and Radishes (page 108).

2 tablespoons sherry vinegar
1½ teaspoons fresh lemon juice
1½ teaspoons Dijon mustard
1 tablespoon honey
½ teaspoon chopped flat-leaf parsley
2 chives, finely sliced
Kosher salt and freshly ground black pepper to taste
¾ cup olive or canola oil

In a medium bowl, combine the vinegar, lemon juice, mustard, honey, herbs, and salt and pepper. Slowly whisk in the oil. Taste and adjust the seasoning. (The vinaigrette can be refrigerated for up to 5 days.)

BALSAMIC VINAIGRETTE

MAKES ABOUT ¾ CUP

Make sure to use a good-quality balsamic vinegar. At the restaurant we use Il Buon Ansalo, a wonderful artisanal vinegar.

1 shallot, finely minced
2 tablespoons balsamic vinegar
1 tablespoon red wine vinegar
Kosher salt and freshly ground black pepper to taste
½ cup extra virgin olive oil

Combine the shallot, balsamic and red wine vinegars, and salt and pepper in a small bowl and let macerate for 10 minutes. Slowly whisk in the olive oil until emulsified. Taste and adjust the seasoning. (The vinaigrette can be refrigerated for up to 5 days.)

BUTTERMILK VINAIGRETTE

MAKES ABOUT 1 CUP

This tasty vinaigrette is a wonderful dressing for crisp lettuces like romaine, Bibb, iceberg, or a mix of lettuces.

2 tablespoons white wine vinegar or cider vinegar
2 tablespoons fresh lemon juice
½ small shallot, finely minced
Kosher salt and freshly ground black pepper to taste
½ cup buttermilk
⅓ cup Homemade Mayonnaise (page 336) or Hellmann's or Best Foods
2 tablespoons sour cream
2 tablespoons extra virgin olive oil

In a small bowl, combine the vinegar, lemon juice, shallot, and salt and pepper. Slowly whisk in the buttermilk, mayonnaise, and sour cream. Slowly whisk in the olive oil. Taste and adjust the seasoning. (The vinaigrette can be refrigerated for up to 5 days.)

MUSTARD AND HERB VINAIGRETTE

MAKES 1½ CUPS

Not long after we opened Highlands in 1982, we came up with this creamy-style—thanks to the egg yolks and mustard —vinaigrette filled with a great herb flavor. It's subtle yet very satisfying.

2 large egg yolks
½ teaspoon Kosher salt
½ teaspoon sugar
1 tablespoon chopped fresh flat-leaf parsley
1 teaspoon dried thyme
1 teaspoon dried rosemary
1 teaspoon dried oregano
1 teaspoon freshly ground black pepper
1 tablespoon Dijon mustard
¼ cup red wine vinegar
½ cup extra virgin olive oil
½ cup vegetable oil, such as canola or grapeseed

Whisk the egg yolks in a medium bowl. Add the salt, sugar, parsley, dried herbs, pepper, mustard, and vinegar and whisk well to incorporate. Slowly add the olive and vegetable oils, whisking constantly to emulsify. (Refrigerate any leftover vinaigrette and use within 3 days.)

TOMATO VINAIGRETTE

MAKES 2 CUPS

I love the flavor of charred foods, and here is a recipe for the middle of summer, when you're grilling outdoors (or you can use your broiler). Rub the tomatoes with a little olive oil before you toss them on the grill to cook until blackened and blistered. Serve with grilled fish or chicken, or with grilled vegetables such as eggplant and zucchini.

2 pounds ripe tomatoes, cored, halved, and seeded
Olive oil for brushing
1 shallot, finely minced
1 tablespoon cider vinegar
1 tablespoon balsamic vinegar
Kosher salt and freshly ground black pepper to taste
5 tablespoons extra virgin olive oil
1/4 cup basil leaves, thinly slivered

Prepare a hot grill or preheat the broiler.

Lightly brush the tomato skins with olive oil. Place the tomatoes skin side down on the grill rack or skin side up on the broiler pan and grill or broil until the skin is charred. Transfer the tomatoes to a food processor and process until smooth. Transfer the puree to a medium bowl. Add the shallot, vinegars, and salt and pepper to the bowl and whisk until incorporated. Slowly add the olive oil in a thin stream, whisking until emulsified. Add the basil just before using. (Refrigerate any leftover vinaigrette and use within 3 days.)

RASPBERRY VINAIGRETTE

MAKES 1 1/3 CUPS

Fruit vinegars bring a refreshingly bright flavor to salads. Raspberries lend their distinctive essence to this vinaigrette made with both raspberry-infused vinegar and crushed fresh berries.

1 shallot, finely minced
1/3 cup raspberry vinegar
Juice of 1 lemon
Kosher salt and freshly ground black pepper to taste
1 heaping tablespoon crushed ripe raspberries
    (the riper the better)
1 cup extra virgin olive oil

Combine the shallot, vinegar, lemon juice, and salt and pepper in a small bowl and let macerate for 10 minutes.

Add the raspberries, then slowly whisk in the olive oil until emulsified. Taste and adjust the seasoning. (Refrigerate any leftover vinaigrette and use within 3 days.)

FIG VINAIGRETTE

MAKES ABOUT 3/4 CUP

In late summer, when you have figs on hand, use this sauce for grilled fish or shellfish, or even grilled quail, then garnish with fresh figs, halved and grilled.

1/4 cup Ruby port or Madeira
6 dried figs, stems removed and chopped
1 shallot, finely minced
2 tablespoons sherry vinegar
Kosher salt and freshly ground black pepper to taste
6 tablespoons extra virgin olive oil

Combine the port with the chopped figs in a small saucepan and bring to a simmer over medium-low heat. Simmer for 10 minutes; drain.

Transfer the figs to a small bowl and add the shallot, vinegar, and salt and pepper. Let macerate for 1 hour.

Whisk the olive oil into the fig mixture, then taste and adjust the seasoning. (Refrigerate any leftover vinaigrette and use within 3 days.)

MINT-PEPPERCORN DRESSING

MAKES 2 ¾ CUPS

I find this sauce, which borrows an eastern Mediterranean taste with orange flower water and yogurt and combines it with fresh mint, to be very versatile and quite delicious. Serve it with a romaine lettuce salad, grilled vegetables, and lamb or roast fish.

1 bunch mint, leaves removed and finely chopped
1 cup plain yogurt
½ cup heavy cream
1 tablespoon fresh lemon juice
2 drops orange flower water
Kosher salt
1 teaspoon freshly ground black pepper
1 cup olive oil

Combine the mint, yogurt, cream, lemon juice, orange flower water, salt, and pepper in a medium bowl and whisk thoroughly to blend. Slowly whisk in the olive oil until incorporated. Taste and adjust the seasoning. (The vinaigrette can be refrigerated for up to 5 days.)

HAZELNUT OR WALNUT VINAIGRETTE

MAKES 1 ¼ CUPS

Artisanal nut oils—walnut, hazelnut, pecan, and pistachio—are incredibly unctuous and deeply flavorful. Walnut oil has long been used in the cuisine of southwestern France, and small producers now capture the intense flavor of other nuts in their tiny mills. These oils are expensive but their flavors are incomparable. They are quite perishable, so be sure to keep them refrigerated.

¼ cup champagne vinegar
Juice of 1 lemon
1 shallot, finely minced
1 garlic clove, crushed and finely chopped
Kosher salt and freshly ground black pepper to taste
¾ cup hazelnut or walnut oil
¼ cup olive oil

Combine the vinegar, lemon juice, shallot, garlic, and salt and pepper in a small bowl and let macerate for 10 minutes.

Slowly whisk in the oils until emulsified. Taste and adjust the seasoning. (The vinaigrette can be refrigerated for up to 5 days.)

My first wife, Frances, introduced me to a variation on a Christmas tradition that we called the Great Pickle Swap. Among her family and friends in and around Columbia and Charleston, South Carolina, it became very much the thing to give, as Christmas presents, homemade preserves or pickles that had been put up earlier in the year. The idea was that instead of worrying about an unwanted or inappropriate gift, etiquette demanded you give a present made with your own hands, something that anyone would appreciate.

Though people started cheating in later years, no longer making their own, that's how the tradition was born. We would sometimes make cucumber pickles. Or bread-and-butter pickles. Even canned tomatoes—they still qualified as a pickle swap. Our Jerusalem artichokes were the most prized because they were a bit more exotic, spiced as they were with mustard seed and coriander. And they had the most wonderful crunch.

My mother was a pickler too, and the Great Pickle Swap fueled memories of how she put up apple butter, and cooked strawberries down in a big copper pot, and preserved figs with a bit of lemon rind—all in an effort to stow away those fruits of summer for the winter ahead.

But more than anything else, the Great Pickle Swap opened my eyes to how preservation in all its guises—pickling, salting, smoking—functions as a means of conserving memories of summer harvests long after the first frost settles over the South, long after the dogwoods lose their leaves. For whether the locale is the Lowcountry of South Carolina or the hill country of Alabama, the impulse to put up fruits and vegetables bespeaks a commitment to making the most of the bounty of the season, to wresting from life the time to provision your family for the winter ahead. The idea is primal, but the application—both in my home state of Alabama and in my adopted South Carolina—speaks volumes about whom you love and how you care for them.

HOMEMADE MAYONNAISE

MAKES 1 HEAPING CUP

While quality commercial mayonnaise is readily available, nothing compares with mayonnaise made from scratch. There is a liveliness to homemade mayonnaise that is due in large part to the freshness of just-combined ingredients—the zip of the mustard, tang of the freshly squeezed lemon juices, and the option of seasoning to taste. Embellish the mayonnaise to your liking with a few chopped herbs, minced garlic, or even Spanish smoked paprika.

1 teaspoon Dijon mustard
1 large egg yolk
Pinch of cayenne pepper
1 teaspoon Kosher salt
1 cup vegetable oil, such as canola, peanut, or grapeseed
1 to 2 tablespoons tepid water (optional)
Juice of ½ lemon

Combine the mustard, egg yolk, cayenne, and salt in a medium bowl and whisk vigorously for 30 seconds. Slowly add the oil drop by drop, adding more only after the previous addition has been incorporated: Be careful not to add the oil too quickly or the mayonnaise will "break," or curdle. Thin with a little water if needed. Add the lemon juice, then taste and adjust the seasoning. (This will keep for up to 5 days, covered and refrigerated.)

LEMON MAYONNAISE

MAKES 1 HEAPING CUP

Often overlooked as less than glamorous, homemade mayonnaise can star on its own or it can be adapted in infinite ways to embellish meat or fish, to add richness to a vinaigrette, or to carry other flavors. Here lemon juice and lemon zest give it a little punch.

2 large egg yolks
Juice of ½ lemon, or to taste
Zest of 1 lemon
1 heaping teaspoon Dijon mustard
Kosher salt and freshly ground white pepper to taste
1¼ cups vegetable oil, such as canola, peanut, or grapeseed
1 to 2 tablespoons tepid water (optional)
Tabasco (optional)

Combine the egg yolks, lemon juice and zest, mustard, and salt and white pepper in a medium bowl and whisk vigorously for 1 minute. Slowly add the oil drop by drop, whisking constantly. As the mayonnaise thickens, the oil can be added a bit faster. If it becomes too thick, add a bit of water to thin it. When the oil is completely incorporated, taste and adjust the seasoning, adding a splash of Tabasco, if desired. (This will keep for up to 5 days, covered and refrigerated.)

VARIATION: For a Creamy Tomato Chutney that is delicious on grilled or roasted pork or hamburgers, add 2 tablespoons Alecia's Tomato Chutney (see Sources, page 352) to the mayonnaise.

AÏOLI

MAKES ABOUT 2 CUPS

This Provençal garlic mayonnaise is a wonderful, robust sauce for fish and grilled meats such as lamb or pork, and, like ordinary mayonnaise, a flavorful spread on sandwiches. Use it wherever you would use mayonnaise.

2 large garlic cloves, peeled
Pinch of Kosher salt
2 large egg yolks
1½ cups extra virgin olive oil
1 to 2 tablespoons tepid water
Juice of ½ lemon, or to taste
Small pinch of cayenne pepper

In a mortar, using a pestle, grind the garlic with the salt to a paste. Add the egg yolks and stir with a wooden spoon until blended. (Alternatively, using a sharp heavy knife, chop and mash the garlic with the salt to a paste. Transfer to a bowl and stir in the egg yolks.) Transfer to a larger bowl if necessary and whisk in ¼ cup olive oil drop by drop. Add the remaining olive oil in a slow, steady stream, whisking constantly. If necessary, thin with a little water to the desired consistency. Season with the lemon juice and cayenne and taste to adjust the seasoning. (This will keep for up to 5 days, covered and refrigerated.)

VARIATION: For Tomato Chutney Aïoli, add 1 heaping tablespoon Alecia's Tomato Chutney (see Sources, page 352) to ½ cup aïoli to make a fantastic sauce for roasted or grilled pork. Or substitute Pickapeppa sauce or harissa, or even finely chopped Major Grey's Mango Chutney.

BLUE CHEESE BUTTER

MAKES ONE 6-OUNCE LOG

We use this butter to garnish our Cowboy Fillet with Sweet Potato Hash Browns (page 210), but it's also excellent on baked potatoes, lamb chops, or crusty bread.

8 tablespoons (1 stick) unsalted butter, at room temperature
1 shallot, finely minced
1 garlic clove, finely minced
2 ounces blue cheese, such as Bleu d'Auvergne,
      Fourme d'Ambert, or Roquefort, crumbled
½ teaspoon finely chopped lemon zest strips
Juice of ½ lemon
Kosher salt to taste
1 teaspoon coarsely ground black pepper
1 scant tablespoon chopped flat-leaf parsley

Melt 1 teaspoon of the butter in a small sauté pan over medium-low heat. Add the shallot and garlic and cook until just tender and fragrant, about 2 minutes.

Transfer to a bowl and add the remaining butter, the blue cheese, lemon zest and juice, salt, pepper, and parsley. Mix well, then taste and adjust the seasoning. Turn out onto a sheet of waxed paper, shape into a log, and roll up in the waxed paper. Refrigerate until needed. (The butter can be kept for several days in the refrigerator, wrapped in plastic wrap, or freeze it in smaller batches for use as needed, for up to 3 weeks.)

BEURRE BLANC

MAKES ABOUT 2¼ CUPS

Thirty years or so ago, beurre blanc was almost exclusive to the kitchens of French chefs or those who had spent time in France. Then it became so overused as to be almost cliché. However, there is still a place and time for this traditional sauce—with nearly any grilled fish—especially when made with care and delicacy. Don't make the mistake of "stabilizing" the sauce by adding lots of cream, as some chefs do. Rather, regulate the temperature as you incorporate the butter so that the sauce is just warm to the touch: The key is to add the butter little by little to create a stable emulsion. Adding too much butter at once will cause the sauce to cool down excessively, but if the sauce becomes too hot, it may "break," or curdle. Whisk vigorously while carefully monitoring the heat. The acidity of the finished sauce should be lively—be sure to add enough vinegar and/or lemon juice to give it a bright finish.

¾ cup white wine
¾ cup white wine vinegar (or 6 tablespoons *each* sherry
　　vinegar and white wine vinegar), plus a little to finish
1 shallot, finely minced
1 thyme sprig
1½ teaspoons heavy cream
½ pound (2 sticks) unsalted butter, at room temperature
Kosher salt and freshly ground white pepper to taste
Fresh lemon juice to taste
Hot sauce, such as Tabasco or Cholula

In a small heavy nonreactive saucepan, combine the wine, vinegar, shallot, and thyme. Bring to a boil over high heat and reduce to a syrupy glaze, about 12 minutes. Remove the saucepan from the heat and stir in the cream, then reduce just a little bit more, about 1 minute. Reduce the heat to low and whisk in the butter bit by bit, adding more only after the previous addition has been incorporated. Regulate the heat so the sauce is warm, not too hot or too cool. Add the salt and pepper, lemon juice, and hot sauce. Taste and add a little more vinegar and/or lemon juice as needed. Strain and cover to keep warm until ready to use.

TRUFFLED MADEIRA SAUCE

MAKES ABOUT ¾ CUP

This classic sauce takes simple roasts, sautéed or grilled chicken, veal, or braised rabbit to phenomenal heights.

2 tablespoons unsalted butter
2 shallots, finely minced
2 thyme sprigs, leaves removed
½ small black truffle, thinly sliced (about ½ ounce)
　　(see Sources, page 352)
3 tablespoons Madeira
1½ cups Chicken Broth (page 339) or canned low-sodium broth
Kosher salt and freshly ground black pepper to taste

Melt 1 teaspoon of the butter in a small saucepan over medium heat. Add the shallots, thyme, and truffle and cook, stirring, until the shallots are soft, about 3 minutes. Add the Madeira and stir to deglaze the pan, then reduce the liquid to a syrupy glaze. Add the chicken broth and reduce by half. Whisk in the remaining butter bit by bit and season with salt and pepper.

BROWN BUTTER

MAKES A GENEROUS ½ CUP

In both sweet and savory dishes, the addition of butter that has been browned over heat until it takes on a hazelnut hue provides a bigger, richer, nuttier butter flavor. We use it in cookies and cakes, in vinaigrettes, and for sautéed vegetables.

12 tablespoons (1½ sticks) unsalted butter

In a small saucepan, melt the butter over low heat. Continue to cook, whisking occasionally, until the butter turns brown and smells nutty, 15 to 20 minutes. Immediately strain the butter through a fine-mesh sieve into a bowl, leaving the milk solids in the pan.

CHICKEN BROTH

MAKES ABOUT 1 3/4 GALLONS

When you are short on time, the ready availability of high-quality low-sodium canned chicken broth often makes it more practical to go to the store than to spend a day in the kitchen coddling a homemade stock. Such constraints aside, however, there are times when the cook may feel like undertaking an endeavor with such a definite payoff. Making homemade broth enables you to create something to suit your own palate—selecting the aromatics you prefer, for example, or substituting different herb combinations. Do give it a try. That said, homemade and good-quality canned versions can be used interchangeably in the recipes throughout this book.

4 pounds chicken bones (such as backs, wings, and necks),
    excess fat removed and rinsed
1 tablespoon vegetable oil, such as canola or grapeseed
2 onions, quartered
2 carrots, peeled and quartered
1 celery stalk, cut into 2-inch pieces
1 leek, trimmed, cleaned, and cut into 2-inch pieces
4 garlic cloves, crushed
About 10 quarts cold water
Several thyme sprigs, 5 flat-leaf parsley sprigs, and 3 bay leaves,
    tied together to make a bouquet garni
Pinch of Kosher salt
A few peppercorns

Preheat the oven to 475°F.

Place the chicken parts in a roasting pan, drizzle with the oil, and toss to coat (the oil helps the chicken brown). Roast for 15 minutes. Add the onions, carrots, celery, leek, and garlic and continue roasting, turning the chicken and vegetables occasionally, until the chicken bones are golden brown, about 30 minutes longer.

Transfer the bones and vegetables to a tall stockpot and add the water. Pour off any excess fat from the roasting pan, then add a splash of water, scrape up the browned particles from the bottom of the pan, and add to the stockpot. Bring the broth just to a simmer. Skim the fat, reduce the heat to a slow simmer, and add the bouquet garni, salt, and peppercorns. Simmer gently for 3 to 4 hours (monitor the heat so that the broth does not boil), skimming from time to time and adding more water as necessary to keep the bones covered.

Strain the broth through a colander into a large container; allow to drain thoroughly before discarding the bones and vegetables. Strain the broth again through a fine-mesh strainer or a cheesecloth-lined strainer into a large container and place in the refrigerator to cool.

When it's cool, cover and refrigerate; remove the fat once chilled. (The broth will keep for 3 to 4 days in the refrigerator; if not ready to use it then, bring it to a boil and boil for 3 minutes. Then refrigerate for up to 5 days. Or freeze the broth in small batches for future use.)

BEEF BROTH

MAKES ABOUT 4 QUARTS

If you are willing to take the time and make the effort to prepare a homemade beef stock, the results are fantastic. Not only will you have plenty to freeze for future use, but the dishes you make using the homemade broth will have all the more character and flavor. However, good-quality canned low-sodium broth can be substituted in any of the recipes in this book.

4 pounds beef shank bones, cut into 2-inch-thick pieces (have the butcher do this), or beef chuck, cut into 2-inch chunks, excess fat removed
1½ teaspoons vegetable oil, such as canola or grapeseed
2 onions, coarsely chopped
2 to 3 carrots, peeled and coarsely chopped
2 tablespoons tomato paste
1 head garlic, halved crosswise
2 leeks, trimmed, cleaned, and quartered
1 celery stalk
5 thyme sprigs, 5 flat-leaf parsley sprigs, and 2 bay leaves, tied together to make a bouquet garni
1 teaspoon Kosher salt
1 teaspoon peppercorns

Place the beef bones (or chuck) in a large heavy Dutch oven, add the oil, and toss to coat. Cook over high heat, turning occasionally, until caramelized and browned on all sides, about 15 minutes. Add the onions and carrots, lower the heat to medium, and cook until colored and softened, 15 to 20 minutes. Add the tomato paste and garlic and cook, stirring, for 5 minutes more.

Add 1 cup cold water to the pan to deglaze. Stir with a wooden spoon to loosen all the caramelized bits of meat and vegetables. Pour in cold water to cover the meat by 2 inches. Bring to a simmer over medium-high heat, skimming the foam and fat as it rises to the top. When the liquid reaches a simmer, add 2 more cups of cold water, bring back to a simmer, and skim again. Add the leeks, celery, bouquet garni, salt, and peppercorns and simmer, partially covered, for 4 to 6 hours. If necessary, add more cold water to keep the bones (or meat) covered by 2 inches.

Place a colander or strainer, lined with dampened cheesecloth, over a large container and strain the stock; discard the solids. Refrigerate until completely cool, then cover; remove the fat once chilled. (The stock will keep for 3 to 4 days in the refrigerator, or you can freeze the stock in small batches for future use. To reheat, bring to a boil and boil for 3 minutes before using.)

SEAFOOD BROTH

MAKES ABOUT 3 CUPS

Seafood broth is quite easy to make and just like home-made chicken or beef stock, you can make it in advance when you have ingredients on hand and then freeze the broth in batches to use as needed. Fill freezer bags and lay them flat on a sheet pan in the freezer until frozen. They stack well this way and the thin frozen batches will thaw quickly when pulled out for use.

Scant 1 tablespoon olive oil
1 onion, coarsely chopped
1 leek, trimmed, cleaned, and coarsely chopped
1 celery stalk, coarsely chopped
2 shallots, finely chopped
1 garlic clove, finely chopped
½ cup (about ¼ pound) crawfish or shrimp in the shells
1 cup crawfish or shrimp shells
A few thyme sprigs, a few basil stems, and 1 bay leaf,
    tied together to make a bouquet garni
2 allspice berries
1 cup white wine
4 cups water

Heat the oil in a small pot over medium-high heat. Add the onion, leek, celery, shallots, and garlic and sauté, stirring occasionally, until the vegetables are softened, about 10 minutes. Add the crawfish, crawfish shells, bouquet garni, and allspice and cook over medium heat, stirring frequently, for 10 minutes until the shells are brightly colored.

Add the wine and bring to a boil. Reduce the heat and simmer for 5 minutes, until reduced by one-quarter. Add the water and bring to a boil, then reduce the heat and simmer for 20 to 30 minutes until flavorful. Strain the broth, pressing hard on the solids to extract all their essence. Cover and refrigerate until ready to use. (The seafood broth will keep for 3 to 5 days refrigerated or up to 2 months in the freezer.)

LAMB JUS

MAKES ABOUT 1 QUART

For this we use Jamison Farm's lamb (see Sources, page 352), which I think is some of America's finest. Always be sure to trim away any excess fat from the lamb trimmings before using them in stock. You can substitute game, birds, or other trimmings to suit your dish.

1 tablespoon olive oil
3 to 5 pounds lamb bones and trimmings
1 onion, chopped
2 carrots, peeled and chopped
6 garlic cloves, crushed
1 tablespoon tomato paste
1 cup red wine
Several thyme sprigs, a few savory or marjoram sprigs,
    several flat-leaf parsley sprigs, and 3 bay leaves,
    tied together to make a bouquet garni
2 cups Chicken Broth (page 339) or canned low-sodium broth
Kosher salt and freshly ground black pepper

In a large Dutch oven or heavy stockpot, heat the olive oil over medium-high heat. Add the lamb and bones trimmings and brown for about 20 minutes.

Add the onion and carrots and cook, stirring occasionally, until caramelized, about 15 minutes. Add the garlic and cook for 2 minutes, stirring to release all the browned bits in the bottom of the pot. Pour off any excess oil, add the tomato paste and red wine, and bring to a boil. Reduce to a syrupy glaze. Add the bouquet garni, chicken broth, salt and pepper, and enough cold water to cover by 2 to 3 inches and bring to a simmer. Skim the fat or foam from the surface, reduce the heat, and cook very gently for about 4 hours. Taste and adjust the seasoning.

Strain the sauce, pressing hard to extract all of the jus. If desired, pour into a saucepan and reduce the strained juices to concentrate. (The lamb jus will keep for 3 to 5 days refrigerated or up to 2 months in the freezer.)

VARIATION: Adding a few tablespoons each of chopped roasted red bell pepper and roasted garlic puree lends a great sweetness in flavor and silkier body to the lamb sauce.

PÂTE BRISÉE

MAKES ONE 9- TO 10-INCH TART

This is a basic pastry dough, ideal for quiches and other main-dish tarts as well as for sweet tarts.

1 cup plus 3 tablespoons all-purpose flour
6 tablespoons cold unsalted butter, diced
⅛ teaspoon Kosher salt
1 large egg, lightly beaten

Combine the flour, butter, and salt in a food processor and pulse a few times, just until the mixture becomes crumbly. Add the egg and pulse a few more times, until the mixture resembles small peas; do not overprocess. Transfer the dough to a work surface and shape into a disk. Wrap the dough in the plastic wrap and refrigerate for at least 1 hour, or overnight.

Lightly grease a 9- or 10-inch fluted tart pan with a removable bottom. Dust a work surface and the disk of dough with flour and roll out the dough into a round 11 inches in diameter for a 9-inch tart, or 12 inches in diameter for a 10-inch tart. Fit into the tart pan, gently pressing the dough into the bottom and up the sides of the pan. Remove any excess dough with a roll of the rolling pin. Prick the bottom all over with a fork. Refrigerate for 30 minutes before baking.

Preheat the oven to 350°F.

To bake the tart shell, line the tart shell with parchment paper or foil and fill it with dried beans or pie weights. Bake the tart for 20 minutes. Remove the parchment and weights and bake until thoroughly dry and golden, 5 to 8 minutes more. Let cool in the pan on a rack.

GALETTE DOUGH

MAKES ENOUGH FOR ONE 10-INCH CRUST
OR SIX 4-INCH INDIVIDUAL TART SHELLS

This is our primary "workhorse" dough. With its buttery taste and strong texture, it is ideal for free-form crusts. It can be frozen for up to one month.

2 cups all-purpose flour
¼ cup sugar
¼ teaspoon Kosher salt
1 tablespoon grated lemon zest
10 tablespoons (1¼ sticks) cold unsalted butter, diced
⅓ cup cold water

Combine the flour, sugar, salt, and lemon zest in a food processor and pulse to blend. Add the cold butter and pulse the mixture until the butter is the size of small peas. Gradually drizzle the cold water through the feed tube, while pulsing, just until the dough starts to come together. Turn the dough out onto a piece of plastic wrap and gently knead into a disk, being careful not to overwork the dough. Wrap the dough in the plastic wrap and refrigerate for at least 3 hours before rolling out.

SIMPLE SYRUP

MAKES ABOUT 3 CUPS

Simple syrup can be used both at the bar to sweeten a drink or tea and as a component in a range of desserts.

1 cup sugar
2 cups water

In a small heavy saucepan, combine the sugar and water and bring to a simmer over medium heat, stirring and swirling the pan to dissolve the sugar. Dip a pastry brush in hot water and wipe down the sides of the pan to dissolve any sugar crystals clinging to the sides. Simmer for 2 minutes without stirring, remove from the heat, and let cool. (The syrup keeps for weeks in the refrigerator.)

VARIATION: For Mint Simple Syrup, add a large bunch of mint to the hot syrup. Once cool, cover and let the syrup infuse for at least 2 hours in the refrigerator, then strain the mint from the syrup.

TECHNIQUES & TOOLS

Over the years we have developed certain methods for ensuring that our food is prepared in ways to best present its inherent qualities. From cooling racks that prevent any precious meat juices from escaping to the best type of dish for cooking a crusty gratin (enameled cast iron), these notes give further insight into our kitchen.

Techniques

Trimming Artichokes I recommend wearing rubber gloves when working with artichokes, so the strong tannins don't stain your hands. Fill a bowl with cool water and add a generous squeeze of lemon (the acidulated water will keep the trimmed artichokes from turning brown). Peel away the tough outer leaves of one artichoke and then cut off the top half. Cut off the stem so the bottom is flat. Using a paring knife and beginning from the top, trim away all the green outer skin until you reach the pale white meat of the artichoke bottom, working around the artichoke from top to bottom. Drop the trimmed artichoke bottom into the acidulated water and continue with your remaining artichokes.

Preparing Asparagus If advance preparations are required or you're feeding a crowd, cook asparagus ahead of time in boiling water for 2 or 3 minutes and immerse the spears in a bowl of ice water to stop the cooking and lock in the vibrant green color. Once they are cool, remove and blot dry (do not allow the asparagus to get waterlogged). You can then reheat the precooked spears as required for your recipe or serve them at room temperature.

Roasting Garlic Roasted garlic has a sweet, caramelized flavor that is all the goodness of garlic without the pungency. To prepare **roasted garlic cloves,** cut off ¼ inch of the top of one or more bulbs of garlic and place each one on a sheet of aluminum foil. Season with salt and pepper, a few fresh thyme sprigs, and a teaspoon of extra virgin olive oil. Wrap tightly and roast in a 325°F oven for about 45 minutes, or until soft but not mushy. Let cool, then squeeze out the soft pulp. Use the garlic cloves whole, or make **roasted garlic puree:** Squeeze the pulp from a whole head of garlic through a strainer and season the puree with a bit of salt and pepper. The roasted garlic and the puree will keep for 2 to 3 days, covered and refrigerated.

Roasting Peppers Roasting peppers—whether bell peppers or chiles—gives them a versatility that they just don't have in their raw state. Simply place them on a grill over a hot fire or under a hot broiler and turn occasionally until the skin is black and charred all over. Transfer to a bowl, cover with plastic wrap, and let steam for 10 minutes. Remove the blackened skin with your fingertips (use gloves if working with chiles, if you wish), then remove the stem and seeds. It's fine if a bit of skin remains—don't be tempted to rinse the peppers, or you will wash away their flavorful oils. For **red pepper puree,** place the peeled and seeded roasted peppers in a food processor and process until smooth, about 2 minutes, then season with Kosher salt and freshly ground black pepper to taste.

Peeling and Seeding Tomatoes I confess that I do not always peel tomatoes, because I like the skin. There are times, however, when I want just the pulp. To peel tomatoes, simply blanch them for 1 minute in boiling water. Remove them to an ice bath to "shock" them, or cool quickly, and slip off the skins (see Blanching and Shocking Vegetables below). Typically, we then halve the tomatoes and scoop out the seeds with a little spoon or a finger, or hold each tomato half cut side down and give it a little squeeze so the seeds fall out.

Peeling Vegetables Vegetables oxidize once peeled and cut, so we peel shallots and garlic just before use. And we chop or crush garlic only moments before cooking. Do *not* buy packaged peeled garlic. It leaves an aftertaste as a result of the oxidation.

Blanching and Shocking Vegetables Blanching, or briefly cooking, vegetables in boiling water and then **shocking** them in ice water locks in their vibrant color, removes the bitterness of certain greens, and gets a bit of a jump on the cooking process. Bring a large pot of generously salted water to a boil. Meanwhile, prepare an **ice bath** by filling a large bowl with ice and cold water. Add the vegetables to the boiling water and cook for 2 to 3 minutes, or until they are bright but still crisp. Drain the vegetables and shock in the ice bath to stop the cooking. Remove the vegetables as soon as they are cool to the touch (don't let them get waterlogged) and drain or pat dry.

Glazing Vegetables We often glaze vegetables, such as spring onions. To glaze vegetables, place them in a pan large enough to hold them snugly in a single layer, then cover by a third to a half with water, season with Kosher salt, freshly ground black pepper, and a pinch of sugar, and dot with a tablespoon or so of butter. Cook over medium heat until the vegetables are tender and lightly colored and the liquid is reduced to a syrupy glaze.

Preparing Mirepoix Mirepoix is the classic aromatic vegetable combination used as the base of, or added to, a myriad of sauces, soups, and braises. To make about 1 cup mirepoix, cut ½ onion, 1 carrot, and 1 celery stalk into ½-inch dice. Sauté in a teaspoon or so of olive oil over medium-high heat until softened but not colored, 4 to 5 minutes.

Preparing a Bouquet Garni A classic bouquet is composed of thyme sprigs, parsley sprigs, and bay leaf, but any combination you like can be used. Simply tie a few herb sprigs and a bay leaf together with kitchen twine, for easy removal from the finished soup or stew, braise, or other dish. If using whole spices too, such as peppercorns, wrap the herbs and spices in a square of cheesecloth and tie with kitchen twine to form a sachet for easy removal.

Toasting Nuts Toasting nuts brings out their flavor and gives them added crunch. Spread the nuts on a baking sheet and bake in a preheated 350°F oven, shaking the pan from time to time, until aromatic and lightly browned, 10 to 15 minutes. Be careful to monitor the nuts carefully, as they can burn quickly. **Blanching** hazelnuts or other nuts means removing their skins. To toast and blanch hazelnuts, walnuts, or almonds, toast as above, then wrap the warm nuts in a kitchen towel and rub together to remove the skins (don't worry about removing every last bit of skin).

Toasting Spices Toasting spices, such as coriander or cumin seeds, draws out their flavorful oils and fills the air with their aromas. Toast whole spices in a small dry heavy skillet over medium heat, shaking the skillet from time to time, until they are fragrant, usually a few minutes. Remove from the skillet and let cool.

Preparing Citrus Suprêmes (photograph opposite) Suprêmes are cleaned citrus segments, free of any skin, pith, or membrane. Using a sharp knife (or a serrated knife), cut a ½-inch slice off the top and bottom of the citrus fruit. Stand the fruit on a cutting board and cut away the skin and pith in strips by slicing from top to bottom, working your way around the fruit. Then gently pick up the fruit and slice along each membrane to separate the segments and release each beautiful suprême. Remove any seeds.

Dicing a Mango First cut the fruit away from both sides of the large fibrous pit that runs through the mango's center, so you have two large slices. Place each one skin side down on a cutting board and score the flesh, without going all the way through the skin, in a crosshatch fashion. Turn the fruit "inside out" and slice the cubes away from the skin. If desired, slice off the flesh remaining on the narrow sides of the pit.

Preparing Citrus Suprêmes, opposite.

Clarifying Butter Clarified butter is whole butter that has been melted over low heat so that the water it contains evaporates and the milk solids settle to the bottom of the pan; the pure butter is then carefully poured out, leaving the solids behind. Without the milk solids, the butter has a much higher smoke point and is more stable, making it ideal for cooking at higher temperatures and for storing for longer periods.

When clarifying butter, start with at least ½ pound (2 sticks) to 1 pound butter; it is more difficult to clarify a smaller amount, and the clarified butter keeps for weeks or even months in the refrigerator. A pound of butter will yield about 1½ cups clarified butter. Melt the butter in a small heavy saucepan over low heat, without stirring.

Once it has melted, remove the butter from the heat and skim the foam from the surface. Then carefully pour the clear yellow butter into a container, leaving the milk solids on the bottom of the pan (discard the solids). Cover and refrigerate, or freeze for up to several months.

Making Bread Crumbs Fresh bread crumbs should be fluffy and almost coarse, never too dry or too fine. For perfect crumbs, process a 1- to 2-day-old loaf of French bread, crusts removed, in your food processor until you have medium-coarse crumbs.

Shucking Oysters Oyster knives have short sturdy blades with a slightly curved tip. Grip each oyster in a gloved hand or with a kitchen towel and carefully place the tip of the knife firmly in the intersection of the hinge (the little indention where the thicker parts of the shells come together). Once the knife is firmly inserted in the hinge, give a quick but firm twist of your wrist to pry open the shell. Once it's opened, use the side of the oyster knife to pry the shell open a little farther, cut the muscle that attaches the mollusk to the top of the shell, and remove the top shell. Be careful not to pry the oyster apart, leaving it mangled. Slide the knife cleanly under the muscle that attaches the oyster to the bottom shell to release it. For **oysters on the half shell,** leave each oyster in its bottom shell and gently wipe away any bits of shell or debris along the edge. Place the oysters on the half shell on a bed of crushed ice until ready to serve.

Cleaning Soft-shell Crabs Cut away the face of the crab with scissors, cutting about ⅛ inch behind the eyes. Lift up the flaps on either side of the top of the crab and cut away the gills. Pull off the "apron" attached to the tail on the underside of the crab.

Marinating Begin by giving the protein a quick rinse, a pat dry, and some trimming, and then get together the herbs, olive oil, and any other aromatics. We avoid using acidic marinades as they tend to break down a protein's texture. Whether time allows a lengthy marinade (say, overnight) or only 30 minutes, this transition time gives the food a chance to wake up and begin a transformation by marrying flavors. Rather than using stainless steel (never use plastic, which is difficult to clean thoroughly and may retain odors), choose a ceramic or enameled baking dish. I enjoy the sight on my kitchen work counter of a handsome gratin dish with the evening's main course coming to room temperature, scattered about with handfuls of herbs and cloves of crushed garlic that perfume it, and the room.

Braising To ensure a moist braise, cut a piece of **parchment paper** to the size of your braising pan and place it on top of the just barely simmering meat or poultry, then cover the pan tightly with the lid or aluminum foil. The paper helps keep the top of the braise from drying out, so the finished dish remains moist and succulent.

Once your braise is tender, allow the meat to rest in the pan for 10 minutes, then transfer it to a rack set over a platter or baking sheet and cover loosely with foil to keep warm. Strain the braising vegetables and liquid through a fine-mesh strainer into a saucepan and gently push down with the back of a ladle or a wooden spoon to extract all the liquid. (Discard the vegetables—they will have already flavored the broth.) **To skim the braising liquid,** place the pan half on and half off a burner, over medium heat, and bring to a simmer. The fat will accumulate on the cool side, making it easy to skim it off and remove it. Continue simmering and reducing the broth to concentrate the flavor, skimming from time to time until every trace of fat has been removed. When the broth is sufficiently flavorful, usually after reducing by half to three-quarters, we usually finish the sauce by whisking in a couple of tablespoons of cool butter. This gives the sauce a rich silky texture and mellow flavor.

Making Beef Broth and Chicken Broth A few tips to keep in mind when making homemade broth: Bones alone do not make great stock. When making beef stock, fresh meat trimmings add lots of flavor. Lean pieces of shank or shoulder cuts work well. When making chicken stock, all chicken pieces should be trimmed of skin and fat. Proper caramelization of the bones, trimmings, and vegetables concentrates color and flavor. Careful skimming and slow simmering will result in a clear, unclouded broth. Try including some chicken in a beef broth or beef in a chicken broth to add depth of flavor.

Cutting Up a Chicken Rinse and pat the chicken dry. Place the chicken breast side up on a cutting board and pull one leg away and cut through the skin between the body and the thigh. Next bend the leg away from the body until the ball and socket joint is exposed and cut through it; the leg and thigh will come away. Repeat with the other leg and thigh. Separate the leg into two pieces by holding the leg by the ankle joint and slicing through the joint between the thigh and the drumstick. Repeat with the other hindquarter. Remove the wings by pulling the wing away from the body and slicing through the wing joint. Repeat with the other wing. Separate the backbone from the breast by cutting through the rib bones from the tail end all the way up and through the shoulder joint. Reserve the back section and the wings for stock. Place the breast skin side up and, with a strong hand, slice through the center of the breast. Use both hands with one steadying the knife and the other pushing down with the heel of your hand, forcing the knife through the breastbone. Cut the two breasts crosswise to form four pieces. This leaves you with eight pieces. This process also applies to duck and other birds.

Frenching Chicken Breasts Frenched breasts are prepared by cutting off each breast, cutting down through the wing joint and down to the bottom of the ribs so the meaty portion of the wing remains attached to the breast.

Cutting Up a Rabbit Although it may seem intimidating, cutting up a rabbit is really quite easy. First remove the hindquarters, then remove the shoulders. Cut off the "flaps" on either side of the loin. Next remove the loins, which run the length of the backbone: Start at the neck end and cut down along the backbone, slipping your knife under the loin and pulling it away as you go. This creates boneless loins, which cook quickly and are easy to eat. Or, for a more rustic presentation, cut the loin crosswise into 3-inch sections, leaving the bone intact.

Removing Silverskin To remove the silverskin, a tough membrane that looks like a shiny sheet of tendon, from meat, insert the tip of a sharp boning knife or other thin knife just under the taut membrane and create a "tab" at one end that you can hold with your other hand. Angle the knife underneath the silverskin up toward the tough membrane and slide the knife along the length of the meat to remove the membrane. Continue removing the membrane in strips until none remains.

Warming Plates No matter how organized you are, or how simple the menu, by the time you've arranged the food carefully on serving plates, the temperature will have dropped. To avoid the problem, thoroughly warm the plates beforehand by placing them in a 200°F oven for 5 to 10 minutes.

Tools

Cooking should be fun, and I enjoy cooking all the more with certain "tools of the trade." For example, enameled ironware, like Le Creuset gratin dishes, is simply beautiful to me. I love using these for many different purposes—for marinating meats, storing roasted vegetables until ready to serve, and arranging my *mise en place*, as well as for making crusty golden gratins. The following is a list of my personal favorite kitchen tools and equipment.

Casseroles Casseroles are large deep pots, also called Dutch ovens, with tight-fitting lids. I prefer cast-iron pots with an enameled finish—again, Le Creuset is a wonderful choice—but they can be made from tempered glass (Pyrex), stoneware, or earthenware. These latter types are good for the oven but not for use over a direct flame. Flameproof casseroles can be used for sautéing or browning foods on the stovetop before transferring the braise or other dish to a slow oven to finish cooking.

Sauté Pans Sauté pans are heavy pans with sloping shallow sides. I love French black steel for searing meats, fish, and most sautéing. (Previn carries these imported pans; see Sources, page 352.) Once seasoned, these are great for almost everything except reducing high-acid sauces, which will react with the pan and taste metallic. For this, use a nonreactive pan, such as enameled cast iron or stainless steel. For home cooks, 9½- or 10-inch pans are most versatile, but 12-inch pans are great for cooking larger portions of food. I abhor lightweight and most stainless steel pans, as foods tend to scorch easily.

Saucepans and Pots When it comes to **saucepans,** I prefer Sitram, French stainless steel pans with a copper layer sandwiched in the bottom. The pans conduct heat uniformly, without scorching, and they have a handy lip for pouring. They are sturdy with a great overall balance and should last a lifetime. Le Creuset saucepans have both charm and excellent functional qualities—heaviness for distributing heat evenly and a nonreactive enamel coating over the cast iron. Another good choice would be the wonderful all-purpose saucepans manufactured by All-Clad. In addition to making stock, a **tall stockpot** is ideal for blanching large amounts of vegetables and for making soup. Stainless steel stockpots are our first choice, provided they have heavy bottoms. A bonus pan for any kitchen would be a ridged cast-iron **grill pan.**

Gratin Dishes These are typically shallow oval baking dishes made of ceramic or cast iron coated with enamel, such as those by Le Creuset. Copper versions, generally more expensive, may also be found. The ceramic and enameled cast-iron dishes are also ideal vessels in which to marinate foods. Food baked in a gratin dish will have a large surface area that allows it to develop enough crispy crust for everyone to have a portion. And they look good enough to go straight from the oven to the table.

Cooling Racks Wire cooling racks are essential equipment in all our restaurant kitchens because letting practically everything rest on a rack—whether seared or cooked meat, poultry, or fish—makes it better. The rack prevents excess moisture—the juices—from escaping: If these items were placed on a platter or board, the cells touching the surface would open and release their juices. A cooling rack minimizes the surface area contact and allows air to circulate around the food so it doesn't steam in its own juices. Typically we will grill a fillet of grouper, for example, to just a bit underdone and transfer it to a cooling rack to let it rest for a couple of minutes. The residual, or "carryover," heat allows the fish to finish cooking perfectly, and no juices are lost. Set the cooling rack, of whatever size is most practical, over a baking sheet or platter to catch any drips.

Baking Sheets Known professionally as sheet pans, baking sheets are the workhorses of the restaurant kitchen. Available as both half sheet pans and full sheet pans, these are sturdy aluminum pans with a 1-inch rim on all four sides. We roast on them and use them to catch spills in the oven. When baking pastries and cookies, we sometimes choose heavy flat French steel pans without sides. These dark heavy-duty pans conduct heat better and allow a little more even cooking. Otherwise, when baking, we use a Silpat, a silicone pan liner, to line our aluminum sheet pans.

Mixing Bowls I really like using heavy ceramic English mixing bowls, and I have a small, medium, and large set of these. A variety of stainless steel or heatproof glass bowls is also very handy.

Electric Mixers We use both a **heavy-duty stand mixer** and a sturdy electric **hand mixer** for many tasks, from beating egg whites and whipping cream to making compound butters to blending batters to perfection. For a stand mixer, the dependable standby is the KitchenAid 4½- or 5-quart mixer.

Food Processor The food processor is great for myriad tasks, from making fresh bread crumbs and grinding nuts to chopping meat for steak tartare and pureeing vegetables to blending tart doughs. Cuisinart set the standard for home use; Robot Coupe is the professional model for restaurants.

Food Mill This is essentially a sturdy metal strainer fitted with a hand-crank mechanism and interchangeable (fine, medium, and coarse) screens through which cooked foods are passed to achieve a smooth puree. Any fibrous solids, seeds, and so forth are then discarded. This traditional way of pureeing foods results in a finer texture than most other methods, including the food processor and blender.

Knives Always keep your knives sharp. Clean them by hand after each use and wipe them dry. (In the restaurant world, knife etiquette is important business. You never use someone else's knife. Our cooks bring in and take home their own each day.) Make sure to use a wooden or soft composite cutting board for chopping or slicing. Some so-called cutting boards (synthetic) are way too hard and may damage your knives.

The workhorse of any kitchen is the **chef's knife,** with an 8- to 10-inch-long blade for chopping, slicing, mincing, dicing, and so forth. Wüsthof brand has been a favorite of mine, but MCA from Japan and Sabatier from France are other good choices. Originally designed for pastry use, an **offset serrated knife** is really a great multipurpose knife especially useful for slicing tomatoes and citrus fruits. F. Dick and Wüsthof make good ones. A regular **serrated bread knife** is also useful. Keep a 3-inch **paring knife** on hand for everyday tasks. A **boning knife** with a thin flexible blade should be used only for boning. A heavy-duty **meat cleaver** is good for dealing with thick bones, while a **Chinese cleaver** is great for those fearful of nicking their fingers: Its wide blade keeps them at a safe distance. Another knife that is a great addition to any kitchen is a **carving knife** for turkey, beef, and other roasts. Typically these have a thin blade about 10 inches long. A **diamond steel** is important for keeping your knives sharp, but once knives become dull, it won't sharpen them. Have your knives professionally sharpened when necessary.

Oyster knives and **clam knives** are short, sturdy specialty knives. Buy an oyster knife with a tip that is tilted up. Clam knives are a little thinner and sharper.

Shears and Scissors Heavy-duty kitchen shears are fantastic for cutting through poultry bones and the like. A small pair of all-purpose scissors for clipping herbs, cutting parchment paper, etc. is equally essential.

Mandoline An inexpensive plastic vegetable slicer is all you really need—although the expensive classic French mandoline, now made of stainless steel, may be tempting. Both types are super for slicing quantities of vegetables such as radishes, cucumbers, cabbage, etc. Very handy, but mind the fingers and knuckles. Most of them come with hand guards—for a reason.

Microplane Graters These rasp-type graters are a breakthrough. Long and narrow, they work wonders at finely grating all sorts of ingredients including cheese, chocolate, and, perhaps best of all, citrus zest.

Mortar and Pestle The world of cooks is divided between those who think that using a mortar with a pestle is a bit of archaic self-torture, and those who rejoice in that age-old feeling of working with a stone or wooden bowl and gradually transforming ingredients (garlic, basil, spices, etc.) into an essence of flavor. For the latter, the whirling violence of mechanical choppers will never provide the same satisfaction. I prefer Mexican mortars and pestles. They are great big, heavy, greenish black volcanic-rock jobs that are very cheap and, strangely enough, often sold in Asian food stores. I find that marble mortars and pestles have too slick a surface so they are not abrasive enough to be effective.

Whisks At home, I have a very small wooden-handled whisk, the overall length of which is about 10 inches. It is perfect for making vinaigrettes. A large **balloon whisk** is helpful for whisking egg whites and cream. Medium-sized whisks are perfect for making mayonnaise.

Other Favorite Hand Tools Many cooks prefer the new-style ergonomic pivoting **vegetable peeler;** the problem is that the design makes it all too easy to remove too much of the vegetable. Old-fashioned inexpensive peelers really do the job best; my favorite has a Teflon-coated blade. A pair of 8-inch **tongs** is essential. I think of these as an extension of my own hand, using them to turn foods on the grill or in the sauté pan, removing hot food from the pan, and many other tasks. A small French **fish spatula** with a slotted blade is great for lifting delicate items. And a wooden-handled **Chinese mesh skimmer,** or "spider," is very handy for lifting vegetables out of a pot of boiling water and for removing deep-fried foods from the hot oil.

Ladles are another necessity. While they are a little more expensive, I prefer the heavy-duty one-piece designs; they last forever and you can really bear down when pressing an essence through a sieve. A **fine-mesh sieve** is invaluable for straining delicate sauces. We use a stainless steel chinois, or "china cap," a perforated conical strainer, for soups and sauces. Wire-mesh strainers, both coarse and fine, are also important.

Kitchen Twine This is essential for trussing birds and tying bundles of herbs into a bouquet garni.

Thermometers Have an **oven thermometer** on hand to check your oven periodically to see if it needs calibrating. An **instant-read thermometer** is necessary for testing the temperature of roasted meats. A **deep-frying** or **candy thermometer** is handy for those certain occasions. I also keep a thermometer inside my refrigerator to make sure it keeps foods at the proper temperature.

Sources

Aidells Sausage Company
1625 Alvarado Street
San Leandro, CA 94577
1-877-AIDELLS
www.aidells.com
sausages of all kinds

Alecia's Specialty Foods
2332 Montevallo Road SW
Leeds, AL 35094
1-205-699-6777
chutney6000@aol.com
tomato chutney

Browne Trading Company
260 Commercial Street
Portland, ME 04101
1-800-944-7848
www.browne-trading.com
seafood and caviar

Chef's Collaborative
262 Beacon Street
Boston, MA 02116
1-617-236-5200
www.chefscollaborative.org

Coach Farm
105 Mill Hill Road
Pine Plains, NY 12567
1-800-999-4628
www.coachfarm.com
artisanal goat cheeses

Corti Brothers
5810 Folsom Boulevard
Sacramento, CA 95819
1-916-736-3800
*a wide variety of imported and
domestic foods and wines*

CS Steen Syrup Mill
P.O. Box 339
Abbeville, LA 70510
1-800-725-1654
www.steensyrup.com
pure cane syrup

Da Rosario
29-24 40th Avenue
Long Island City, NY 11101
1-800-281-2330
truffles, truffle oil, smoked fish

D'Artagnan
280 Wilson Avenue
Newark, NJ 07105
1-800-327-8246
www.dartagnan.com
*foie gras, game, poultry, duck fat,
duck confit*

Ducktrap River Fish Farm
57 Little River Drive
Belfast, ME 04915
1-800-828-3825; 1-207-338-6280
www.ducktrap.com
smoked fish and seafood

Fresh N Wild
P.O. Box 2981
Vancouver, WA 68668
360-737-3652
wild mushrooms

Gourmand
2869 Towerview Road
Herndon, VA 20171
703-708-0000
www.gourmandinc.com
oils, vinegars, chocolates

Jamison Farm
171 Jamison Lane
Latrobe, PA 15650
1-800-237-5262
www.jamisonfarm.com
naturally raised lamb

J. B. Prince
36 East 3rd Street, 11th Floor
New York, NY 10016
1-800-473-0577
www.jbprince.com
*knives, baking pans, and a wide range
of kitchen equipment*

Lindley Mill
7763 Lindley Mill Road
Graham, NC 27253
1-910-376-6190
stone-ground grits

Manicaretti
5332 College Avenue, Suite 200
Oakland, CA 94618
1-800-799-9830
www.manicaretti.com
Agrumato lemon oil, pastas

Marché aux Délices
P.O. Box 1164
New York, NY 10028
1-888-547-5471
www.auxdelices.com
mushrooms

Niman Ranch
P.O. Box 90460
San Jose, CA 95109
1-510-808-0330
www.nimanranch.com
naturally raised pork and beef

Penzeys Spices
P.O. Box 933
Muskego, WI 53150
1-800-741-7787
www.penzeys.com
spices, dried herbs, dried chiles

Previn
2044 Rittenhouse Square
Philadelphia, PA 19103
1-215-985-1996
www.previninc.com
specialty equipment

Slow Food USA
434 Broadway, 6th Floor
New York, NY 10013
1-212-965-5640
info@slowfoodusa.com
www.slowfoodusa.org

Taste for Seafood
1222 Menlo Drive NW
Atlanta, GA 30318
1-404-352-0829
crawfish

Zabar's
2245 Broadway
New York, NY 10024
1-800-697-6301
www.zabars.com
specialty equipment

Certain cookbooks have been great sources of inspiration to me and remain battered, much-used texts on my bookshelf. Favorites from my mentor Richard Olney include *Simple French Food*, *Ten Vineyard Luncheons*, and the *French Menu Cookbook*. Other books I hold dear are Elizabeth David's *French Provincial Cooking*, *Mediterranean Food*, and *Summer Foods*. Then there is the *Taste of France* by Robert Freson. Of course, there is the encyclopedic Time-Life *Good Cook* series, which I had the good fortune to observe in the making. Other visionary works, in my view, include the Chez Panisse cookbooks by Alice Waters, *Honey from a Weed* by Patience Gray, *The Auberge of the Flowering Hearth* by Roy Andries de Groot, and Curnonsky's *Traditional Recipes of the Provinces of France*. I also admire these exceptional chefs and writers: Daniel Boulud, Paula Wolfert, Deborah Madison, the Roux brothers (Michel and Albert), Jeremiah Tower, James Peterson, Georges Blanc, Edna Lewis, Bill Neal, John Egerton, and John T. Edge.

Since I am passionate about wine, books on oenology are of great interest to me, and I include among my favorites *The Wine Bible* by Karen MacNeil, *The New Sotheby's Wine Encyclopedia*, *Wine Atlas* by Hugh Johnson, *The Great Domaines of Burgundy* by Remington Norman, the *Larousse Encyclopedia of Wine*, and all of Robert Parker's books on Bordeaux.

As those who know me know, I like to surround myself with energetic, creative, brilliant, loving, and thoughtful people—all the better to cover up my weaknesses. Thanks to so many, starting with my wife, Pardis, whose inner beauty is matched by her phenomenal outward beauty and who does more to make our restaurants great than anyone realizes—through her uncommon ability to make every guest feel like the center of attention and her encouragement of our staff to be their very best. I love her dearly and would be lost without her. Thanks to Katherine Cobbs, an angel who arrived from the West just as Pardis and I were about to have simultaneous breakdowns. Her editing and organizing skills, along with her ever-positive attitude, strength, and determination to help me sound out and write the story, are responsible for our meeting our deadlines. Barbara Dawson has walked every step with us from the beginning—crafting the book, writing, and supporting us, while still running the office at Chez Fonfon. John T. Edge came on board and captured with eloquence the southern family we have here in Birmingham. Pat Conroy, whose willingness to write the Foreword, even before the project began, opened the door so the folks in New York would pay attention: My friend, I hope we may savor together many moments at table. Pat's writing has helped all southerners regain confidence in our southern nature. Thanks to Johnny Apple for his article in *The New York Times*, which came at just the right time. His appetite for life inspires us all. John Mariani first wrote about Highlands in 1985, and he has continued to be one of our biggest supporters. Thanks for believing in us.

Patrick Dunne, the gifted writer, designer, and culinary antiques dealer from New Orleans, has been an inspiration and collaborator in helping Pardis and me make our restaurants all the more dazzling.

Christopher Hirsheimer made this project an experience to savor, and her photography is such a natural form of beauty. Her artistry we admire, her friendship we treasure.

Ann Bramson, our editor, pushed, prodded, and berated—challenging us to make the best book possible. Thank you, Ann. Also to Pamela Cannon, who guided us in many ways, Vivian Ghazarian for her brilliant design, Nancy Murray, Amy Corley for believing in us and tirelessly working to promote this book, and all the rest of the staff at Artisan who brilliantly shaped our work into a cohesive text of beauty.

Lisa Queen, our agent at IMG, made all the right connections and gave us the encouragement to believe in ourselves.

Thanks to Jeremiah Tower for the introduction.

Richard Olney and Elizabeth David were the authors who inspired me to see cooking in a whole new way—a sensual and intellectual way—and since first reading their words my appetite has neither slackened nor dwindled.

The following restaurants, organizations, and people have also influenced the way I cook: Ben Barker, Bill Neal, and Hoppin' John; the Chef's Collaborative and the James Beard Foundation; Chez Panisse, Alain Ducasse, Chez Benoit, Harry's Bar, Café Boulud, Jean-Georges, the Connaught, Comme Chez Soi, Guy Savoy, Taillevent, La Gavroche, La Merenda, Le Cagnard, Galatoire's, Tadich Grill, and Swan Oyster Depot. I thank you for your inspiration.

Thanks to Sue Shaffer and Julie Allison for being with me every day and helping with every detail. To Dean Robb for keeping Bottega Café going during my time away. To all of our staff—in particular, Verba Ford, Dolester Miles, James Huckaby, John Rolen, Jeff Mincey, Chris Mancill, Goren "Red Dog" Avery, Wayne Russell, Clarence Young, Ernest Whetstone, Patricia Thompson, and Chris Conner, and the many other wonderful individuals who are, or have been, a part of our Highlands family.

My mother encouraged me to love the act of sharing at table, and my father instilled in me a competitive drive to be the best. I thank you both. My children, Marie and Weston—I love you more than all the stars in the sky. Thanks to their mother, my former wife, Frances Bramlett, whose love of a party and hard work helped to launch these restaurants.

And, finally, I must thank the city of Birmingham and my home state of Alabama for their tremendous support in allowing me to pursue my dream.

Index

A

aïoli, 337
  crawfish, asparagus salad with, 241
almond(s):
  and apple bread pudding, 297
  financier, brown butter, 302
  and lemon butter, panfried soft-
    shell crabs with, 143
  macaroons, 318
  and pear tart, 301
andouille sausage, in Frogmore stew,
  138
appetizers, 75–87
  baked oysters with slab bacon and
    wilted greens, 77
  crab and rice salad, 83
  crab cakes, 82
  fried green tomato and arugula
    salad, 8
  fried quail with cornmeal crust and
    scrambled egg salad, 86
  Highlands baked grits, 20–21
  rabbit loin salad, 87
  ravioli with sweet potatoes, mustard
    greens, and country ham, 92
  seared tuna with celery and butter
    pea salad, 84
  shrimp and crab towers, 79
  spicy baked oysters with
    caramelized onions, 78
  stone crab claws with crudités and
    bagna cauda, 78
  see also hors d'oeuvres
apple(s):
  and almond bread pudding, 297
  charlotte, 296–97
  duxelles, rabbit stuffed with,
    230–31
  pies, fried, 295

artichoke(s):
  baby, in spring vegetable ragout,
    266
  –charred onion relish, grilled
    grouper with, 155
  and Niçoise olive relish, 327
  and Niçoise olive relish, grilled veal
    medallions with, 214
  trimming of, 345
arugula:
  and fried green tomato salad, 8
  and mint, fig and peanut salad
    with, 127
  salad with red onion and
    Parmigiano-Reggiano, 127
asparagus:
  with crawfish meunière, 245
  with farm eggs and ham hock
    vinaigrette, 246
  gratin of, with spring onions and
    mushrooms, 247
  grilled jumbo, with egg and herb
    vinaigrette, 245
  preparing of, 345
  salad with crawfish aïoli, 241
autumn:
  beet salad with spiced pecans,
    pears, and Fourme d'Ambert,
    125
  root vegetable puree, 266
  vegetable ragout, 270
  vegetables, glazed, 255
avocados, smoked trout salad with
  blood oranges, frisée, and, 116

B

bacon:
  and brown butter vinaigrette, soft-
    shell crab with, 142
  lardons, in warm cabbage salad
    with goat cheese and corn bread
    crostini, 126

  slab, baked oysters with wilted
    greens and, 77
  tomato salad with corn bread,
    buttermilk vinaigrette and, 115
baked:
  Highlands grits, 20–21
  oysters, spicy, with caramelized
    onions, 78
  oysters with slab bacon and wilted
    greens, 77
baking sheets, 350
balsamic vinaigrette, 331
Basque-style chicken with peppers,
  176
bass, *see* sea bass; wild striped bass
beans:
  black, in lamb chili with saffron
    rice, 205
  butter, 15
  fava, *see* fava beans
  green, in cured duck salad, 124
  pole, with onions and potatoes, 16
  white, and collard green gratin,
    258
beef:
  broth, 340
  cowboy fillet with sweet potato
    hash browns, 210
  shank and vegetable soup, 103
  sirloin strip with grilled red onions,
    corn bread, and salsa verde, 212
  skirt steak with watermelon and
    red onion relish, 209
beet(s):
  autumn salad with spiced pecans,
    pears, and Fourme d'Ambert,
    125
  baby, in autumn vegetable ragout,
    270
  relish, grilled cobia with, 152
bell peppers, Basque-style chicken
  with, 176
beurre blanc, 338
beverages, alcoholic, *see* spirits

beverages, nonalcoholic:
    Chilton County peach bellinis, 47
    Highlands mint tea, 33
    lemonade for a crowd, 32
    tomato and lime 'tini, 47
black-eyed peas, 15
    in hoppin' John, 9
    in marinated field peas and fresh
        herbs, 253
blue cheese butter, 337
bouquet garni, preparing of, 346
bourbon:
    cabbage, and spoonbread, roast
        venison with, 214–15
    in mint julep, 46
    panna cotta, 280
braised(ing), 348
    rabbit in red wine with wild
        mushrooms, 229
brandy, in Alabama sunset, 46
bread:
    corn, 26
    corn, panzanella, 117
    pudding, savory leek, 265
    sourdough, in cured duck salad, 124
    spoonbread, 20
bread crumbs:
    chicken sauté with lemon, capers,
        and, 173
    making of, 347
    and sauce gribiche, flounder with,
        147
broth:
    beef, 340
    chicken, 339
    lamb jus, 341
    making of, 348
    seafood, 341
brown butter, 338
    almond financier, 302
    and bacon vinaigrette, soft-shell
        crab with, 142
Brussels sprouts, in glazed autumn
    vegetables, 255

butter:
    blue cheese, 337
    clarifying of, 347
butter beans, 15
buttermilk:
    lemon chess tart, 294
    vinaigrette, 331
butternut squash:
    in curried pumpkin soup, 96
    and dried fig risotto, 272
    and dried fig risotto, grilled quail
        with, 186
butter pea(s), 15
    and celery salad, seared tuna with,
        84
    marinated, and fresh herbs, 253

C

cabbage:
    roast venison with spoonbread,
        bourbon, and, 214–15
    salad, warm, with goat cheese and
        corn bread crostini, 126
    in spicy coleslaw, 28
cake(s):
    crab, 82
    pea, 254
    potato, 263
    seven-layer coconut, 311–12
capers, chicken sauté with lemon,
    bread crumbs, and, 173
cappuccino, hazelnut semifreddo, 314
caramel-nut tart, chocolate, 312–13
casseroles, 349
celery and butter pea salad, seared
    tuna with, 84
charred:
    corn relish, 27
    onion–artichoke relish, grilled
        grouper with, 155
cheese:
    blue, butter, 337

cottage, dip, Marie's herbed, and
    crudités, 67
mascarpone, strawberry tart with,
    293
pimiento, Miss Verba's, 32
cheesecake, pumpkin, 307
chicken:
    with autumn vegetables and
        Madeira, 174
    Basque-style, with peppers, 176
    breasts, Frenching of, 349
    breasts with zucchini, field peas,
        and new potatoes, 177
    broth, 339
    cutting up, 348
    roast, with spring vegetables, 179
    sauté, with lemon, capers, and
        bread crumbs, 173
    with watercress sauce, 175
chocolate:
    caramel-nut tart, 312–13
    in cocoa biscotti, 315
    ice cream with Jack Daniel's,
        291
chowder, roasted corn and crawfish,
    97
cilantro, in wild striped bass with
    citrus vinaigrette, 162
citrus suprêmes, preparing, 346
clam(s):
    chowder sauce, flounder with, 105
    in seafood pirlau, 135
cobblers:
    lattice-topped blackberry, 282
    peach and blueberry, 284
cobia:
    grilled, with beet relish, 152
    with Provençal tomato sauce, 158
cocktails, see spirits
cocktail sauce, for Highlands seafood
    platter, 62
cocoa biscotti, 315
coconut crust and pecan streusel,
    sweet potato tart with, 308–9

Cointreau:

    in Pardis's margarita, 44

    in watermelon margaritas, 44

coleslaw, spicy, 28

collard greens and white bean gratin, 258

cookies:

    almond macaroons, 318

    cocoa biscotti, 315

    cornmeal madeleines, 318

    oatmeal, 320

    pecan sandies, 319

    pistachio butter, 319

    shortbread, 320

cooking techniques, 345–49

cooking tools, 349–51

cooling racks, 350

corn:

    charred, relish, 27

    creamed, 22

    and field pea salad, 255

    pudding, 27

    roasted, and crawfish chowder, 97

corn bread, 26

    crostini, warm cabbage salad with goat cheese and, 126

    and figs with molasses vinaigrette, quail stuffed with, 187

    grilled red onions, and salsa verde, sirloin strip with, 212

    panzanella, 117

    tomato salad with bacon, buttermilk vinaigrette, and, 115

cornmeal:

    crust and scrambled egg salad, fried quail with, 86

    madeleines, 318

cottage cheese dip, Marie's herbed, and crudités, 67

cowboy fillet with sweet potato hash browns, 210

crab:

    blue, claws in Highlands seafood platter, 62

blue, in Frogmore stew, 138

cakes, 82

crostini, 62

and rice salad, 83

and shrimp towers, 79

stone, claws with crudités and bagna cauda, 78

and tomato towers, 141

crab, soft-shell:

    with brown butter and bacon vinaigrette, 142

    cleaning of, 348

    panfried, with almonds and lemon butter, 143

cracklin's, 26

crawfish:

    aïoli, asparagus salad with, 241

    meunière, asparagus with, 245

    oyster pan roast with buttery croutons and, 137

    and roasted corn chowder, 97

    in seafood broth, 341

cream(ed), creamy:

    corn, 22

    grits, 22

    lemon-mint, grilled figs with country ham, walnuts, and, 56

crostata, peach, 290

crudités:

    for Marie's herbed cottage cheese dip, 67

    stone crab claws with bagna cauda and, 78

crushed creamer potatoes, 263

D

desserts, 280–320

almond macaroons, 318

apple and almond bread pudding, 297

apple charlotte, 296–97

bourbon panna cotta, 280

brown butter almond financier, 302

chocolate caramel-nut tart, 312–13

cocoa biscotti, 315

cornmeal madeleines, 318

fried apple pies, 295

hazelnut semifreddo cappuccino, 314

Jack Daniel's chocolate ice cream, 291

lattice-topped blackberry cobbler, 282

lemon buttermilk chess tart, 294

oatmeal cookies, 320

peach and blueberry cobbler, 284

peach crostata, 290

peaches in Beaujolais, 285

pear and almond tart, 301

pecan sandies, 319

pistachio butter cookies, 319

pumpkin cheesecake, 307

seven-layer coconut cake, 311–12

shortbread cookies, 320

strawberry ice cream, 291

strawberry milk shake, 292

strawberry tart with mascarpone, 293

sweet potato tart with coconut crust and pecan streusel, 308–9

winter fruits in a spiced syrup, 304

dill, spring lettuces with sweet peas, chives, mint, and, 108

dips, *see* spreads and dips

dough, galette, 342

duck:

    cured, in salad, 124

    two ways, 190–91

E

egg(s):

    farm, with asparagus and ham hock vinaigrette, 246

    and herb vinaigrette, grilled jumbo asparagus with, 245

Published by Artisan

A Division of Workman Publishing

708 Broadway

New York, New York 10003-9555

www.artisanbooks.com

Library of Congress Cataloging-in-Publication Data

Stitt, Frank, 1954

Frank Stitt's Southern table : recipes from Highlands Bar and Grill / by

   Frank Stitt.

     p.   cm.

Includes bibliographical references and index.

ISBN 1-57965-246-8

1. Cookery, American—Southern style. 2. Cookery—Alabama. 3. Highlands Bar and Grill.

I. Title: Southern table. II. Highlands Bar and Grill. III. Title

TX715.2.S68S674 2004

641.5975—dc22   2003063917

Printed in Italy

10 9 8 7 6 5 4 3 2 1

Book design by Vivian Ghazarian

This book was set in Clarendon, Sabon, and Trade Gothic.